P9-DWK-256

TOP CHEF

Library of Congress Cataloging-in-Publication Data available.

ISBN: 978-0-8118-6430-5

Manufactured in China

10 9 8 7 6 5 4 3 2

Chronicle Books LLC
680 Second Street
San Francisco, California 94107

www.chroniclebooks.com

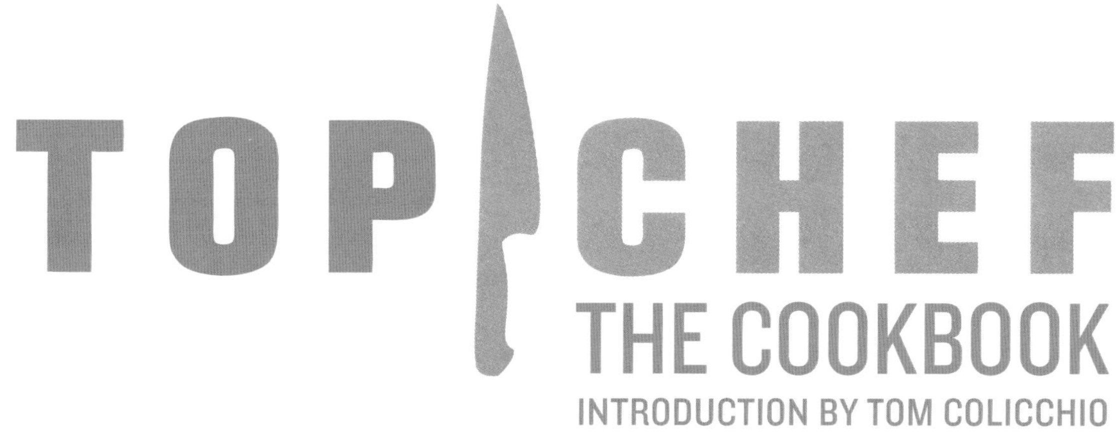

Text by Brett Martin

Food photography by Lisa Hubbard

Recipes edited by Liana Krissoff and Leda Scheintaub

Produced by

Published by

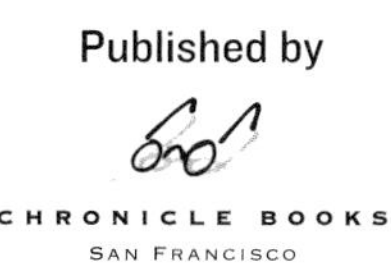

Contents

Introduction

I had a pretty dim view of reality TV—can't stand those shows where people eat bugs or pretend to find true love just to get their fifteen minutes of fame. So when Bravo came to me with *Top Chef,* I dismissed the offer. Twice. The third time around they sent me the entire first two seasons of *Project Runway.* I holed up for a weekend, surprised to find myself first a reluctant convert, then a hard-boiled junkie.

The show was good. There was skill involved, creativity, long hours, hard work. Ideas mattered. Execution was crucial. Small mistakes could derail an entire day of work. It struck a chord with me. Producer Shauna Minoprio, of Magical Elves Productions, called to explain that my role would be something of a hybrid between mentor and judge. My life has always been about stepping into the abyss. I view risk as healthy, crucial even. So I said yes.

I could not have known what I was in for. For starters, there was the shoot itself—long, stretching into the wee hours, at times harrowing. I felt instantly comfortable around the crew, a talented, headset-wearing clutch of young people who resembled carnies. Long after they were done with me, I sensed, they'd be packed and off to the next set of fortune-seekers.

And then there were the chef-testants. The first group was motley and, for the most part, wonderful. I recognized something of myself in each of them, regardless of background and experience. At one point, I too was willing to do whatever it took to get my talent out into the world. Any chef who says he or she hasn't been there is lying.

What we put that first group of chefs, and those from subsequent seasons, through was hard. And while sometimes the Quickfires and Elimination Challenges may have seemed contrived, they were rarely irrelevant. Why? Because just about anyone could be a good cook with unlimited time and resources—two things a "real" chef never has.

Each meal is a rush. Ten minutes from order-in to app, twenty minutes to entrée. Now do it again, two hundred times. Each meal brings blind-siding variables—a diner's allergies, a rush to the theater, a missing delivery. Budgets must be adhered to, equipment breaks down. The trick is to think on your feet, respond calmly and inventively to pressure. The challenges on *Top Chef* give viewers a chance to see the chefs' thought processes as they are forced to ask themselves, "How do I adapt my skills, my training, my personality to the obstacles I've been handed?" This is exactly what real chefs do every day.

We also compete, in our own way. There is always the next hot young thing coming up with great ideas, limitless energy, unbridled enthusiasm. The chef who rests on his laurels and ceases to invent is yesterday's news. The diners who eat in my place are spending their money somewhere else the next night, and you better believe they'll be comparing notes. I think of it this way: my guests wait eight weeks for a table. They may be celebrating a birthday, an important anniversary, or planning to propose. If we ruin their meal, they'll take little consolation in the notion that we usually get it right, that "overall" we are the best at what we do, that this was just an off night. They certainly don't care whether I'm likeable or telegenic.

This is the axiom I carry with me to the Judges' Table: you might be a great contender, but one really bad showing could get you eliminated, just as an off night or a careless effort might remove my restaurant permanently from a diner's list. There's no rest. No excuses. No slacking off.

And I wouldn't have it any other way.

Twenty years ago, a show like *Top Chef* wasn't available to us up-and-comers. All we had was the usual warpath of long hours and low pay. But we also didn't have the phenomena of celebrity chefs to peer up at, to aim for. When I told my father I wanted to cook for a living, I think he pictured me as a fry cook somewhere, cigarette dangling. The idea that one could be famous . . . renowned, sure, but TV-celebrity famous? For cooking? It was preposterous. To this day, I'm still not one hundred percent sure how it happened. But it did, and I was in the right place (and working my ass off) at the right time.

The amazing thing is that, in the space of a few short years, *Top Chef* has become a legitimate stepping stone for young talent, a real proving ground. A way to demonstrate one's craft early on while still immersed in the years of slogging prep-work and crummy hours, that slow but deliberate climb. Some call it a shortcut, but, honestly, it's more of a trial by fire. Making it through takes integrity, vision, and grit, and I applaud all of *Top Chef*'s contestants to date. In that sense—the only one that finally matters—they're all winners in my book.

Cook often, eat well.

—Tom Colicchio
New York City, 2008

Cooking Up Top Chef

"There's a real kinship among chefs, because they live in a kind of netherworld—always working while the rest of the world is celebrating. But there's also a fierce competition."
—DAN CUTFORTH, EXECUTIVE PRODUCER

Maybe, in recent years, you've been at a dinner party and suddenly found yourself picking apart each dish in ruthless detail. Or maybe you've noticed more and more people at the supermarket asking for strange ingredients like rattlesnake and stabilizing gelatins. Perhaps you've caught yourself staring at the office vending machine, wondering how you could work that beef jerky into a dinner menu. Or maybe, the night before you have to cook Thanksgiving dinner, your dreams are haunted by bald men and tall, beautiful Indian women.

If any or all of these things are true, you may be under the spell of *Top Chef.* And you're certainly not alone.

But to tell the story of how *Top Chef* became such a phenomenon, you have to start with the transformation of a cable network.

The Bravo network had previously been the home of commercial-free, sober arts coverage. Under network president Lauren Zalaznick, who took over in 2004, it began to reinvent itself as TV's place for smart, literate, reality programming focusing on culture and the arts. "Fashion, food, beauty, design, and pop culture—those became our mandates," Zalaznick says. Not surprisingly, these were exactly the areas of expertise on display in the network's first major hit: *Queer Eye for the Straight Guy.*

In the realm of fashion, Bravo introduced *Project Runway* and *Make Me a Supermodel*; for beauty, the network generated the hairdressing competition *Shear Genius*, *Blow Out*, and *Work Out*; *Top Design* and *Flipping Out* handled design; and such shows as *The Real Housewives of Orange County* and *Kathy Griffin: My Life on the D-List* have delved deep into pop culture.

So, what about the food mandate? To start answering that question, Bravo's team turned to an experienced partner: Magical Elves Productions. Cofounded by Dan Cutforth, a British expat, and New Yorker Jane Lipsitz, the Elves (as they are known around set) had already coproduced *Project Runway* as well as such reality programs as *Bands on the Run* on VH1 (also for Lauren Zalaznick, which is where she met Jane) and NBC's *Last Comic Standing.* The company's name came from the early days of producing *Bands.* "We were staying up until all hours, sometimes coming up with challenges a few hours before the next day of shooting," Cutforth remembers. "Jane would say, 'Can't we just go to bed?' and I'd say, 'Who's going to do the work? Magical Elves?'"

Neither the Elves nor the Bravo team had much experience with food or cooking. But both had become skilled in a genre of competitive reality programming very different from most of what populated the network and cable airwaves. Instead of taking pleasure in the humiliation of so-called "regular folks" thrown into impossible situations, they were interested in giving extraordinarily talented, artistic people an opportunity to show their stuff. "There had always been a perception of 'reality TV' as somehow tawdry or tabloid," says Frances Berwick, Bravo's executive vice president of programming and production. "What we're trying to do, because our audience is so educated and upscale, is showcase very successful people and their creative energy."

Moreover, shows like *Runway* dealt with the universal and fascinating tension between art and commerce. What happens, these shows asked, when creative people come up against cleverly designed limitations and restrictions? More often than not, the answer was something interesting, entertaining, utterly addictive, and a showcase for real talent.

The *Top Chef* creative team began by meeting with a variety of chefs to get a sense of their lives. "We found out that these people are really passionate about what they do. They're incredibly creative and driven," Cutforth says. "There's a real kinship among chefs, because they live in a kind of netherworld—always working while the rest of the world is celebrating. But there's also a fierce competition."

From the beginning, the creators realized that the new show's success would depend on building credibility within the food world. "If you're going to do a show about food, and obviously the audience can't taste what's on-screen, you need someone trustworthy and credible for the viewer to believe in," says Bravo executive producer Dave Serwatka. To serve all these ends, Tom Colicchio, a chef who commanded vast respect within the restaurant world for his work at New York's Gramercy Tavern and within his own Craft empire, was quickly selected as head judge. The show would also rely on convincing serious chefs from across the country to participate as guest judges. The show further bolstered its kitchen cred by partnering with venerable *Food & Wine* magazine and casting its marketing director, Gail Simmons, as another permanent judge. Finally, they needed a host—first Katie Lee Joel and then Padma Lakshmi—who was knowledgeable about food but able to communicate with an audience of amateurs.

The prospects for an audience that would appreciate such food experience had probably never been better. For twenty years, Americans have been learning more and more about what they eat—where it comes from and how it can be prepared. Food television, once

"The produce guy didn't know what malanga was, and the woman said, 'Don't you watch *Top Chef*?'"

—DAVE SERWATKA, EXECUTIVE PRODUCER

"We try to keep things very simple and approachable: 'Here's an egg. Do something with it.'"

—ANDY COHEN, SVP, BRAVO PROGRAMMING

limited to a few PBS stars and an overhead camera, had exploded. Rare, organic, and exotic ingredients were suddenly available in neighborhood supermarkets. Even casual eaters could tell you the difference between regular and extra-virgin olive oils, discourse on which style of sushi was best, or extol the virtues of foie gras. The United States had become a nation of foodies.

"We take full credit for that," Serwatka deadpans. But he's not wrong that *Top Chef* has pushed the gourmet cause forward. He recalls when his sister heard a woman at the supermarket asking for malanga. "The produce guy didn't know what it was, and the woman said, 'Don't you watch *Top Chef*?'"

Still, the members of the *Top Chef* creative team weren't food experts themselves, and they also knew that the show would need more than just culinary credibility. The challenges would need to be smart but accessible. "We don't talk down to our audience, but we do talk to them," says Andy Cohen, Bravo SVP of programming and production and host of the post-*Top Chef* live webshow. "We try to keep things very simple and approachable: 'Here's an egg. Do something with it.'"

Top Chef's format quickly fell into place. Throughout the process, the name "Top Chef" was intended only as a placeholder; among the discarded candidates were "Too Many Chefs," "Can't Stand the Heat," and Cutforth's favorite, "Grillers in the Mist." Clearly, the correct choice was made.

From the beginning, notes for the show describe a structure of two challenges per episode—one a "Quickfire" off-the-cuff task, which bestows "immunity" on the winner, and the other an "Elimination" Challenge. Some of the challenges would be practical (cater a dinner party, create a burger), while others would have twists (prepare a meal from a vending machine). Still others from the early brainstorms were perhaps best scrapped, such as making the chefs prepare Japanese blowfish, or fugu—deadly if not cut correctly—and then test their skills by eating a piece themselves.

The setting for Season I in San Francisco was chosen in part because, unlike New York and Los Angeles, the city hadn't appeared in an endless succession of previous reality series. The Bay Area is also famous for its serious foodie scene and provided an enviable pool of guest judges.

Nobody seems to remember exactly who came up with the line destined to strike fear in the hearts of contestants: "Please pack your knives and go." One early alternative, perhaps a bit too brutal, was: "Get out of the kitchen."

"The show is built around the idea of knives—the logo, the knife block, and so on," says Cohen. "And it was just an iconic thing, that chefs carry their own knives everywhere," including, as the first batch of contestants was about to learn, out of the kitchen and back home.

Out of the Frying Pan...

In theory, making *Top Chef* seems like a simple enough recipe. Take about a dozen talented, interesting people willing to give up their lives for five or six weeks. Place in one apartment and add a series of cleverly designed tests. Set up cameras and, as Bravo's tagline says, "watch what happens."

Obviously, things are just a bit more complicated. In fact, preparing for and managing each season is a massive undertaking—one that is run day to day by the strangely calm hands of executive producer Shauna Minoprio. Long before the first burner of each season is lit, Minoprio and the rest of the Magical Elves team are hard at work, choosing a city, devising challenges, casting contestants, and scouting locations.

Next comes building the show's primary home, the *Top Chef* kitchen, from scratch. That means bringing in electricity, gas lines, running water, and all the other amenities of a working kitchen, in addition to those of a working television set: a lighting grid, make-up and dressing rooms, space for as many as eight cameras, and so on. In Season 3, casting C.J. Jacobsen also meant painting another few feet up the wall of the set at the last minute, in order to film his 6′8″ frame.

Near the kitchen is always the so-called "Stew Room," the broom closet where chefs wait (and wait and wait and wait) for the judges to make their decisions. While in the Stew Room, the chefs have cameras following their every move. The same is true in the chefs' living space, where they are left little choice but to interact. When chefs enter the competition, they must give up nearly all contact with the outside world. Cell phones, Internet access, music, television, and even most books are prohibited in the house.

There are practical reasons for all these restrictions: the producers don't want the chefs to have access to outside recipes; if chefs discuss current events on camera it will date a show that won't be aired until many months later; if a camera picks up a song playing on the radio, it can't be aired without paying for the rights to do so; and there's always the basic rule that watching people listen to music or read a book just doesn't make for good television. From a dramatic standpoint, all this isolation—plus the chronic lack of sleep—has the added benefit of slowly driving the chefs a little bit crazy.

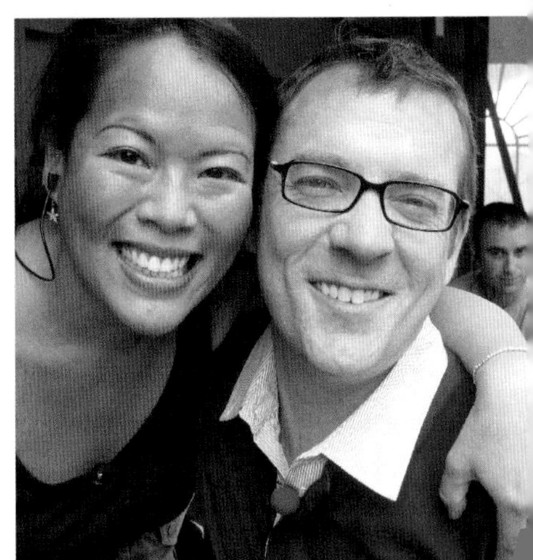

"These are grown adults who have great businesses, run their own kitchens, are really talented, and suddenly have to ask permission to go pee," says Minoprio. "That's pretty hard to take."

The chefs also learn (along with everybody else, including the guest judges) that the default mode for television production is: hurry up and wait. Each episode is usually shot in two days—one for the Quickfire and the next for the Elimination. On the first day, the chefs wake up, rush to get showered and ready, and pile into a van to the kitchen set.

During the challenge, and whenever they're in the house or Stew Room, the chefs are dogged by a swarm of camera crews. Behind the scenes, Minoprio, director of

Previous page, top to bottom: Head Judge Tom Colicchio and the infamous *Top Chef* knife block; Magical Elves executive producers Jane Lipsitz and Dan Cutforth; former contestant and current *Top Chef* culinary producer Lee Anne Wong with Judge Ted Allen. **This page:** The Season 2 cast arrives in the kitchen for what will prove to be an eventful season. **Opposite, clockwise from top left:** Bravo executive producer Dave Serwatka poses with an Asian spread; key ingredients from the *Top Chef* kitchen; Bravo Media president Lauren Zalaznick with Padma Lakshmi; contestants from Season 3 hard at work; executive producer Shauna Minoprio at the Judges' Table.

photography Paul Starkman, and field producers keep track of what's going on and whisper instructions on what to shoot into the cameramen's headsets. Producers constantly scribble interesting quotes or developments in specially designed notebooks that will later be sent to the show's editors. The editors' task will be to distill a forty-four-minute show out of some seventy-plus hours of footage.

Unbeknownst to viewers, every dish on *Top Chef* actually gets made at least twice: once to be tasted and once to be photographed. This technique was learned the hard way during Season I, when dishes were often delivered cold or otherwise degraded after waiting to be photographed. As soon as the buzzer on the challenge is over, the duplicate dishes are whisked away to what is known as the "Food Porn" area, where a man named T-Bone lovingly performs the pans and zooms the audience will later drool over during judging. Needless to say, T-Bone is a good man to make friends with on set, as the food is perfectly edible once it's been shot. He's also the guy with the best inside track on who's doing well on a challenge and who's falling flat.

The Quickfire is usually followed by Padma's announcement of the Elimination Challenge. The production then decamps to go shopping or otherwise start preparing for the challenge. After another night in the fishbowl known as their house, the chefs have an early morning and a long day of high-pressure cooking. Only then does the real ordeal begin: Judges' Table.

WATER

TOP CHEF
PREMIO ITALIAN
Extra Virgin
Olive Oil
TOP CHEF

TOP CHEF

Casting a Hit Show

Opposite: Each season, *Top Chef*'s producers and casting agents meet with hundreds of chefs before settling on the perfect mix of personalities and talents. That makes for some long days, as evidenced by Andy Cohen's profuse doodling. Lucky for us, the scribbles offer a peek at what some beloved and not-so-beloved future characters looked like before becoming chefs.

On Harold Dieterle's casting sheet, Cohen scribbled "big ego." Betty Fraser scored points because she "brought sandwiches." Nobody could claim that Lee Anne Wong didn't warn them about "temper issues in the kitchen."

Of course, every season of *Top Chef* has succeeded based on the talents of the contestants themselves. To cast the first season, the producers started by putting an ad on Craigslist. (Season I contestant Miguel Morales stumbled across it while looking for a date in the personals.) The idea, for that season, was to cast a wide cross-section of people in the food industry—not only restaurant professionals, but home cooks, caterers, nutritionists, etc. It quickly became clear that those other professionals just couldn't keep up with their restaurant brethren. For subsequent seasons, the casting agents focused on those with more experience working on a line. But of course by then they had the luxury of chefs clamoring to be on the show.

For a show focusing on a profession long dominated by straight white men, *Top Chef* has always been intent on showcasing a more diverse set of contestants. But, as on all Bravo shows, whatever their backgrounds or personal lives, contestants for *Top Chef* all have to conform to only one standard: they need real talent, personality, and passion.

"The people who either can't articulate why they want to be on the show, or say that they 'want to be famous,' don't get cast," Cohen says. "The ones who talk about their food and their dreams and how much they love cooking, those are the ones who wind up on the show."

Once an aspiring contestant makes it past the first round of auditions, he or she is flown to Los Angeles for final casting sessions. Secrecy is of the utmost importance to the *Top Chef* producers, so the contestants aren't allowed to tell people where they're going or any details of the show. More important, while in the hotel where the meetings take place, they must not be allowed to meet or interact with other potential chefs. For that reason, they are kept sequestered in their rooms in what is actually a good preview of what they'll endure in the *Top Chef* house, if they make the cut. "It was like the CIA," says Casey Thompson, *not* talking about the Culinary Institute of America. "Whenever they'd take me out of the room everybody would be on their headsets, 'OK. I have Casey walking. Casey walking . . .'"

When a great character walks through the door to casting, the team tends to know it. Stephen Asprinio, for instance, was such a slam dunk that Cohen barely remembers his audition. On the other hand, they know enough not to try to predict how the cast will ultimately interact. Sometimes fate and luck have a role. Says Cutforth, "We've learned that we can never predict what's really going to happen. Better just to put people together and follow along."

TOP CHEF

Stephen Asprinio – 24 – Las Vegas
CIA and Cornell Graduate – Sommelier

Everything about Stephen is eccentric. He went straight to CIA after high school and then went on to Cornell to get his degree to have an edge over everyone else. He is borderline obsessive compulsive and so intelligent that he has trouble looking you in the eye when he talks because he has so many thoughts in his head. He is one of the youngest sommeliers in the country and wants desperately to get back in the kitchen. He said his cooking style is light years ahead of traditional chefs and his background as a Sommelier only makes him a more valuable chef. As he would say, his dishes will be "hot!"

TOP CHEF

Harold Dieterle– 28 – New York City
CIA Graduate – Sous Chef at the Harrison Hotel

Harold is a Sous Chef at The Harrison Restaurant in New York City. Although Harold seems young, he is dead serious about his cooking and the career he has chosen. Because Harold has risen to such a title at such a young age, he is extremely confident about his cooking abilities…sometimes too confident. He states that people often think he is upset all the time because of his serious nature in the kitchen. Out of the kitchen though, he says he is all smiles. Harold will be underestimated from the start but people will soon learn to take him seriously.

TOP CHEF

Le Anne Wong – 28 – New York
French Culinary Institute Graduate and Instructor

This girl says that she is an "iron chef" all the way, and when she first started cooking she used to throw pans at people. Now, she is an executive chef instructor for The French Culinary Institute in NYC and loves what she does - probably because she gets to boss her students around everyday. Even though this girl comes across pretty tough, she still likes to learn. Her passion is pork and says that she can do anything with a pig. Her inspiration is her mom and says that she probably gets her "chops" from her. She wants to be a part of this show because she says that there's nothing like being in the same room with other chefs that have the same sort of love for food as her. However, she says if someone tries to fake their way through their food, she'll be able to tell right away and isn't afraid to confront them about it.

TOP CHEF 2

Betty Fraser – 44 – Los Angeles, CA
Self-Taught – Restauranteur/Caterer

She currently owns and runs GRUB Restaurant and As You Like It Catering. She says that food should be fun and flavorful and you should be able to eat it without being intimidated by it. She can rattle off recipes from the top of her head and is confident that her cooking will be better than someone that has had professional training. This is a very aggressive Type A personality and it'll be interesting to see her interact with other chefs that have the same passion and talents.

TOP CHEF 2

Elia Aboumrad – 23 – Las Vegas, NV
Ecole Lenotre Paris – Asst. Room Chef at The Hotel

Elia is our Spanish firecracker. She learned in some of the toughest kitchens in Europe and even trained under Joel Robuchon! Since moving to the United States, she has struggled in the kitchens because she claims that people here don't have the same work ethic as they do in Europe. Elia doesn't understand complacency and has always been an overachiever, even earning 34 different diplomas in culinary school. Although people will think she is young and naive, she is an incredibly intelligent, creative and innovative young chef.

TOP CHEF 2

Otto Borsich – 46 – Las Vegas, NV
Self Taught – Chef Instructor at Las Vegas CI

After not making it last season, Otto didn't give up and came back once again to convince everyone that he deserves a spot on this show. He has learned to cook in the school of hard knocks, worked up the ranks and now is giving back to students at the Las Vegas Culinary Institute. Otto wants his own vindication and says that at his age it is his time to shine. He is relentless, passionate, definitely a little crazy, and ready to teach the young chefs how it is done!

Top Chef 3
Pitch 8

Hung Huynh - 29 - Las Vegas, NV
Sous Chef - Guy Savoy

29 year old Hung Huynh works as the Executive Sous Chef at one of the most expensive restaurants in Las Vegas, Guy Savoy. He was born in Vietnam, trained in classic French and believes in cooking from the soul. Hung especially loves seafood because he says there are a million varieties and flavors to combine. He is very open about his sexuality, admitting he bats for both teams. Hung speaks four languages and has traveled all over the world learning different types of cuisines. He wasn't impressed with last season's winner and says he can do a hundred times better.

Top Chef 3
Pitch 7

Chris Jacobson - 31 - Venice, CA
Private Chef -

Chris is a unique character, not only is he 6'8" making his kitchen literally look up to him, but this ex-volleyball player has overcome testicular cancer, motivating him to live life to the fullest. Competing to Chris, is second nature and he is ready to throw his competitors under the bus before they have the chance to reciprocate.

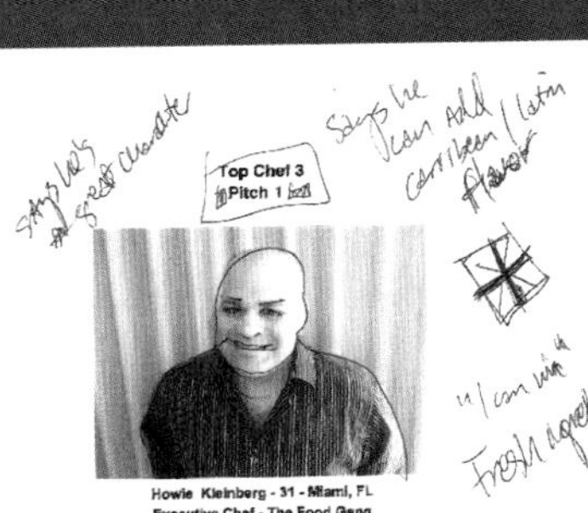

Top Chef 3
Pitch 1

Howie Kleinberg - 31 - Miami, FL
Executive Chef - The Food Gang

Howie is a chef at heart who can't help but let his passion come through in everything he does! Raised by only women due to his father's early death, he has no problem communicating his feelings. A chef for 10 years, Howie says he excels at contemporary American, Asian, and Mediterranean cuisine's. He loves to source the best products and let them speak for themselves. Howie will be a "hurricane" in the kitchen, aggressive in the challenges, and an emotional wreck at the judges table!

The Kitchen and Pantry

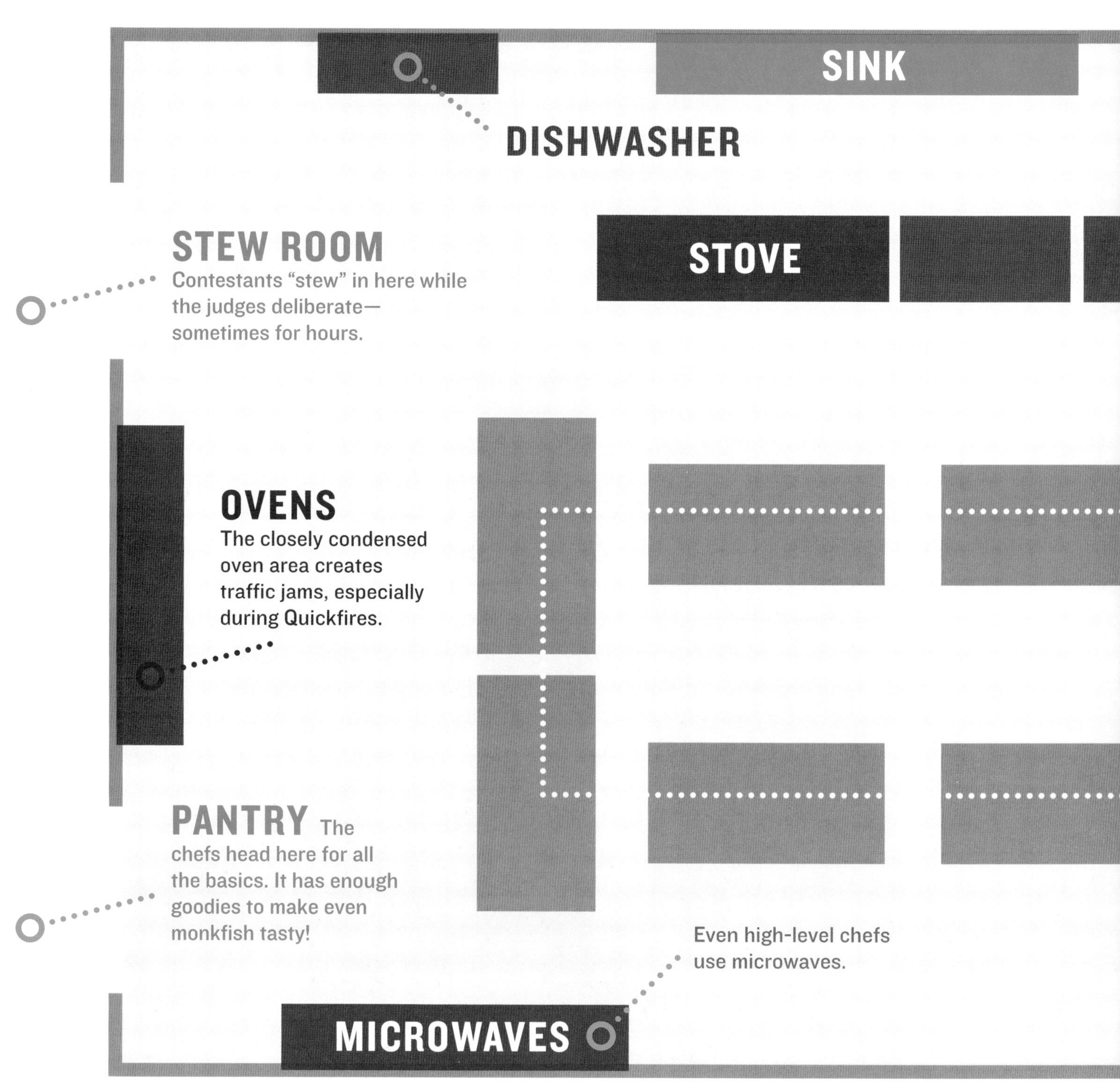

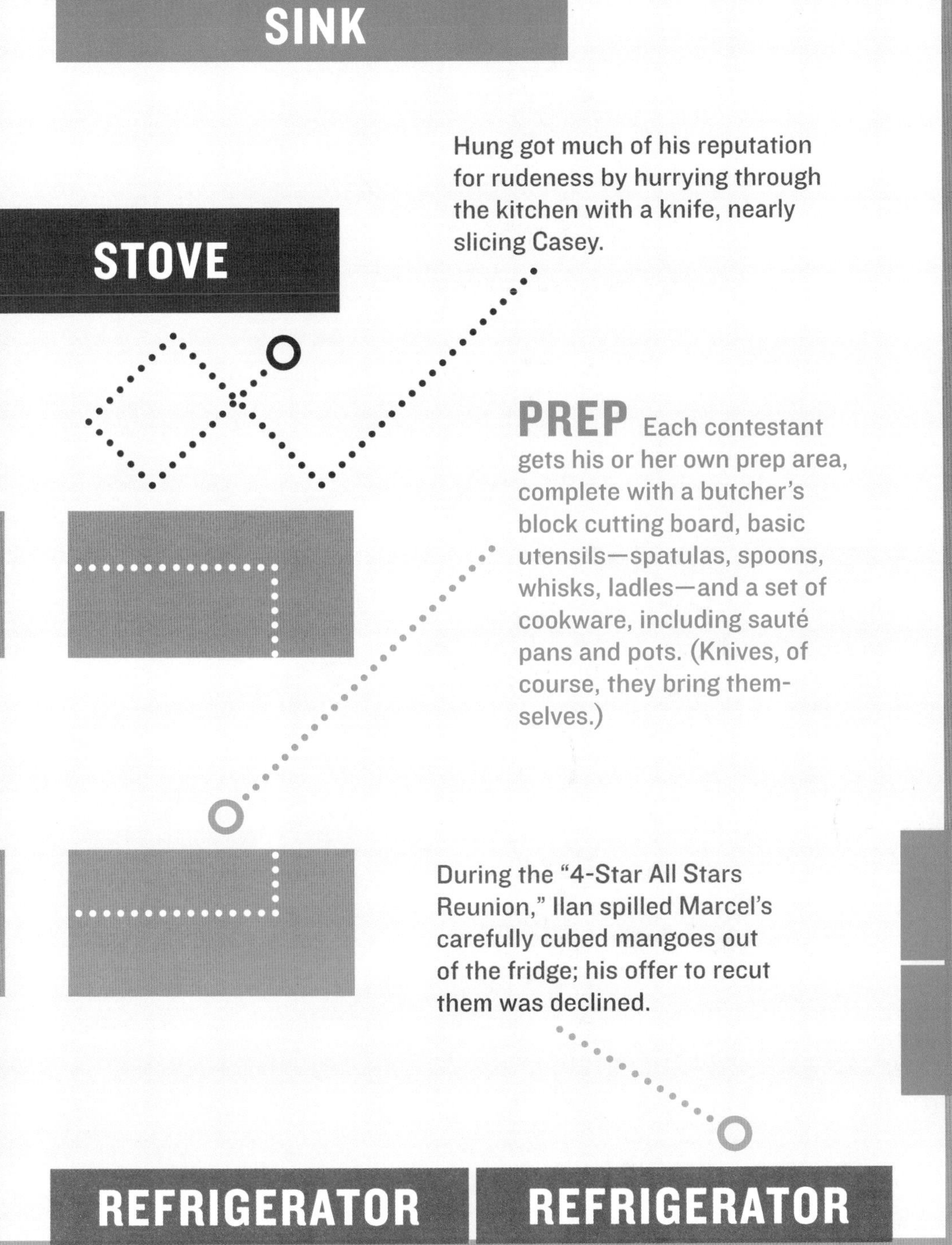

The Floor Plan

For all the exotic locales *Top Chef* visits in the course of a season, no location is more important to the contestants than their home base—the *Top Chef* kitchen and pantry. Around the kitchen are ovens, stoves, broilers, capacious refrigerators, a deep fryer, a set of sinks, and, yes, microwaves. The adjacent pantry is carefully stocked with every imaginable item—always ready for contestants to come running.

The Top Chef Kitchen

Rebuilt in a different city each season, the kitchen must serve double duty as both a television studio and a functional cooking environment.

Even with room for cameras and lights, things can get a little tight in the early episodes of each season. This inevitably leads to rising tension and, occasionally, accusations. Funny how each season's kitchen has featured the same Phantom Oven Turner-Offer.

3000

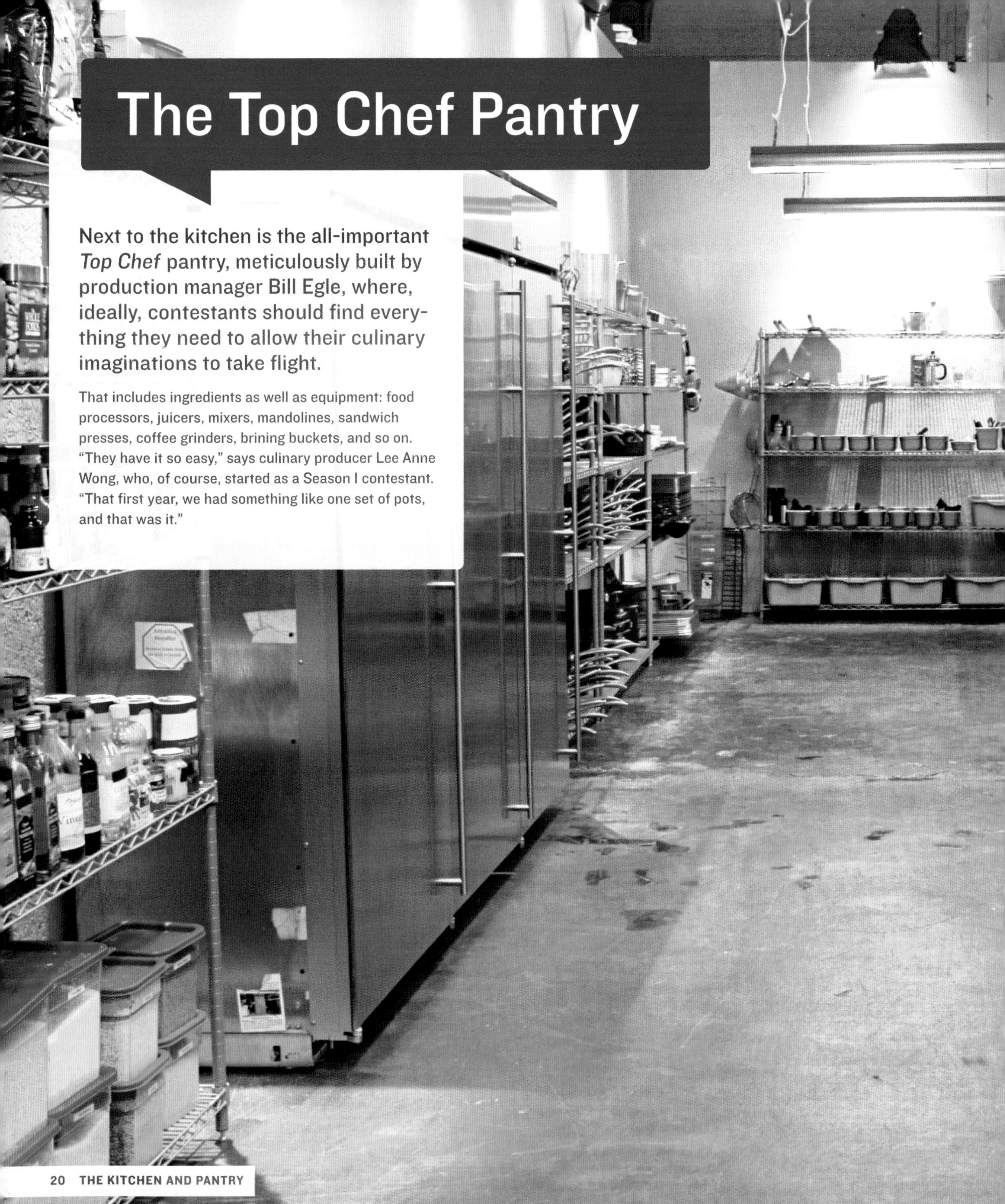

The Top Chef Pantry

Next to the kitchen is the all-important *Top Chef* pantry, meticulously built by production manager Bill Egle, where, ideally, contestants should find everything they need to allow their culinary imaginations to take flight.

That includes ingredients as well as equipment: food processors, juicers, mixers, mandolines, sandwich presses, coffee grinders, brining buckets, and so on. "They have it so easy," says culinary producer Lee Anne Wong, who, of course, started as a Season I contestant. "That first year, we had something like one set of pots, and that was it."

GLAD
ClingWrap

Top Chef Staples

Pantry ingredients change for each challenge and revealing a definitive list might spoil it for future contestants, but you can count on a gourmet's dream selection on the shelves pretty much every week, including the following essentials:

1. **Salt and Pepper.** Obvious but crucial. Since not all salts are created equal, the Pantry features coarse sea salt, fine sea salt, and kosher salt, among others.
2. **Extra-Virgin Olive Oil.** Next to salt and pepper, this is the staple of all staples. No pantry—on TV or otherwise—should be without it.
3. **Stock Pots.** Long-simmered stock is a crucial foundation of nearly all cooking.
4. **Sriracha.** A Southeast Asian hot sauce that works well with almost everything . . . except maybe ice cream.
5. **Tongs.** If a chef's most important tool is her hands, then a good set of tongs is the ultimate hand extender.
6. **Vinegar.** Balsamic, white, white wine, red wine, sherry, and rice wine varieties—just to name a few.
7. **Can Openers.** Their uses are self-explanatory. The mystery is why so many *Top Chef* contestants can't find them when needed. (They're right below the spatulas.)
8. **Chinois.** This ultra-fine sieve—so fine that you need to push things through its mesh—is essential to many refined French classics.
9. **Booze.** From rum to bourbon, the pantry contains a club-worthy bar, good for flavoring or taking the edge off a crazy Quickfire.
10. **Demi-Glace.** A gelatinous super-reduction of veal stock often thought of as a chef's best-kept secret. Adds depth to any soup or sauce.

Other items include:

DRIED FRUITS AND NUTS
- ☐ Hazelnuts
- ☐ Pine nuts
- ☐ Cranberries
- ☐ Mangoes

SWEETENERS
- ☐ Granulated sugar
- ☐ Dark brown sugar
- ☐ Honey
- ☐ Maple syrup

BAKING STAPLES
- ☐ Baking powder
- ☐ All-purpose flour
- ☐ Yeast
- ☐ Vanilla

GRAINS
- ☐ Sushi rice
- ☐ Quinoa
- ☐ Couscous
- ☐ Pasta

SPICES
- ☐ Allspice
- ☐ Ground ginger
- ☐ Black sesame seeds
- ☐ Paprika

LIQUOR
- ☐ Kahlúa®
- ☐ Grand Marnier®
- ☐ Dry vermouth
- ☐ Sherry

DAIRY
- ☐ Whole milk
- ☐ Heavy cream
- ☐ Eggs
- ☐ Butter

OILS, VINEGARS, CONDIMENTS
- ☐ Walnut oil
- ☐ Sesame oil
- ☐ Asian fish sauce
- ☐ Tabasco®

PRODUCE
- ☐ Red onions
- ☐ Leeks
- ☐ Carrots
- ☐ Lemons

FRESH HERBS
- ☐ Basil
- ☐ Chives
- ☐ Cilantro
- ☐ Dill

BAKEWARE
- ☐ Cookie sheet
- ☐ Muffin pan
- ☐ Springform pan
- ☐ Ramekin

COOKWARE
- ☐ Double boiler
- ☐ Dutch oven
- ☐ Saucier pan
- ☐ Sauté pan

ELECTRICS
- ☐ Meat grinder
- ☐ Immersion blender
- ☐ Rice cooker
- ☐ Sandwich press

TOOLS
- ☐ Mandoline
- ☐ Crème brûlée torch
- ☐ Microplane grater
- ☐ Mortar and pestle

TABLEWARE
- ☐ Wine glasses
- ☐ Appetizer plates
- ☐ Soup bowls
- ☐ Chinese spoons

Judges' Table

You wouldn't necessarily guess that Judges' Table would be a difficult segment of *Top Chef* to film. After all, the cooking is all done; the winners and losers are often clear; the set is simple. Nevertheless, everybody involved agrees it's one of the most trying parts of each episode.

The first thing that makes Judges' Table such a pain is logistics. Many of *Top Chef*'s Elimination Challenges take place at remote locations and at dinnertime, which means it is already late in the evening by the time the production packs up to return to the kitchen set. During Season 1, judging took place wherever the challenge did, but since then, everybody has returned to the kitchen. Then, cameras and lights need to be set and reset for each stage of judging—preliminary deliberations, announcing the winner, questioning the bottom three contestants or losing team, deliberating again, and, finally, announcing the loser. With each transition taking at least thirty minutes, it's no wonder that filming Judges' Table usually runs into the wee hours of the morning.

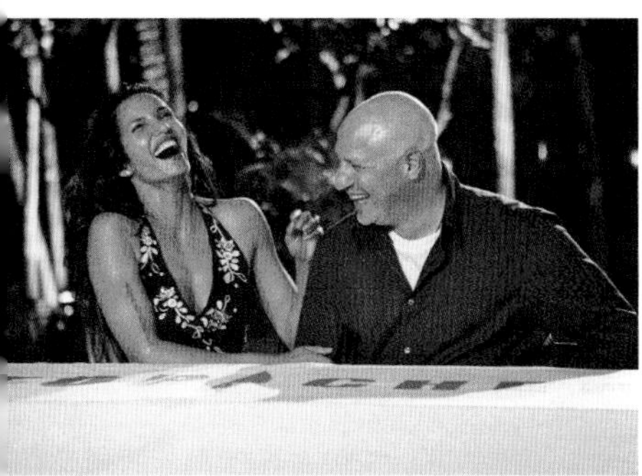

But the biggest reason for the long, drawn-out hours is the seriousness with which the judges take their jobs. Even if the winner seems clear, the judges will methodically work their way through each dish, discussing its merits and faults in remarkable detail. Obviously, the goal is to have plenty of footage to edit into the eventual hour-long episode, but there's also a question of integrity.

"I just feel like we have a responsibility to the contestants," says head judge Tom Colicchio. "They're working their asses off in there. We've got to get it right."

By now, the principal judges—Colicchio, Padma Lakshmi, Gail Simmons, and Ted Allen—know their roles well. "Tom is the moral center of the show. He judges people fairly but strictly, and he brings an enormous understanding of leadership and technique—what it takes to run a restaurant," says Allen. "Padma is the chairman of the board and she brings great knowledge of Asian food. Gail has done everything and, working at a magazine, she has a vast knowledge of what's new and happening. As for me, I hope I bring a certain amount of respect for chefs and a passion for food. And hopefully a little humor, too."

At times, debate gets heated, as in the legendary showdown to determine whether Sam Talbot or Ilan Hall would proceed to the Season 2 finale in Hawaii. Colicchio voted for Ilan; Lakshmi favored Sam. The battle went on until nearly daybreak before the panel finally chose Ilan.

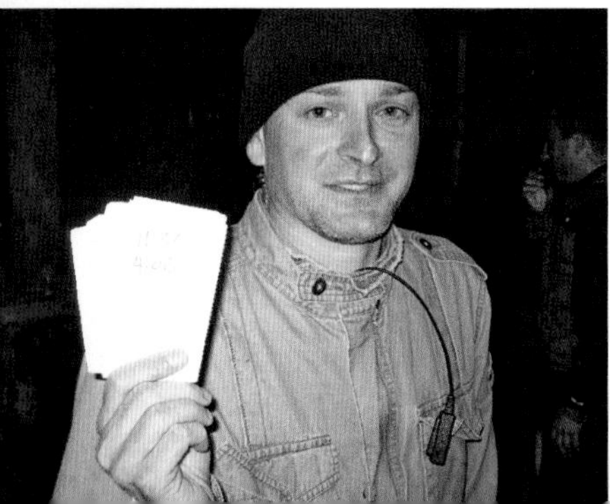

Likewise the debate during the finale of Season 3, which started with a dead heat between Hung Huynh and Dale Levitski for the *Top Chef* title. The judges started deliberating at 11:30 p.m. and talked on camera until 4 a.m. At that point—since the winner would actually be revealed later, during a live broadcast—the producers turned off the cameras and sent the crew home. The judges then debated for another hour and a half, finally coming to a unanimous decision at 5:30 a.m.

"Usually, we wind up talking about the same thing: creativity and ambition versus skill and execution," says Simmons. "We're always looking for the perfect balance."

Above all, Colicchio is intent on reminding the rest of the panel of one of *Top Chef*'s most fundamental rules: judging is based solely on how the contestants did on that day's challenge. What the chef might have done before or what the judges expect him or her to do in the future absolutely cannot be counted.

"Tom compares it to baseball," says Simmons. "If you looked at it on paper, it would seem like the Yankees would win the World Series every year. But you can't decide contests like that."

This principle is often misunderstood by viewers, who express outrage when a strong competitor such as Lee Anne Wong or Tre Wilcox or Sam Talbot is abruptly eliminated after one bad performance. But in the world of *Top Chef,* each dish is *always* judged on its own merit.

Frequent guest judge and chef Anthony Bourdain has the final word: "I'd just like to see one of these producers try to tell Tom Colicchio what to do."

Opposite: Tom and Padma find a light moment in the midst of judging in Hawaii; cameras follow every reaction; supervising producer Andrew Wallace shows off the start and finish times of the marathon Judges' Table in Aspen (in fact, the judges deliberated for another hour and a half once the cameras stopped rolling). **Below:** Guest judge Ming Tsai, Judge Padma Lakshmi, Head Judge Tom Colicchio, and Judge Gail Simmons.

Tom Colicchio

Which *Top Chef* dish do you still dream about?

Tiffani made a raw artichoke dish with braised pork belly that was really delicious. And Hung's duck dish from the Season 3 finale was great.

What was the worst dish you tasted?

Someone in Season 2 gave me a kind of warm clam with coconut milk that was really disgusting.

What would you cook for the finale?

If it was autumn: raw hamachi with lemon and roasted beets. Roasted salsify with poached oysters. A spiced roast lobster with a green-tomato chutney. Squab with honey-glazed onions and endive and a kumquat relish. And then venison with butternut squash tortelloni.

Name five ingredients always in your home pantry.

I don't cook much at home. When I do, I go out and buy ingredients. But there's always a chunk of Parmigiano-Reggiano in the fridge. Cold cuts. Cereal. My wife has all this health stuff. I don't know what the hell is back there.

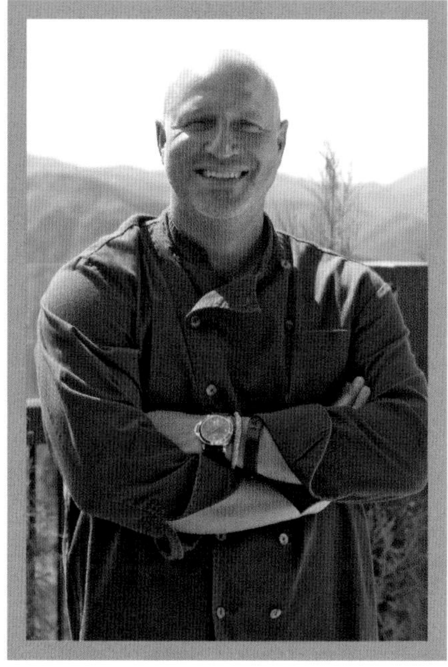

Here's a question: would you want to cook for Tom Colicchio?

On the one hand, it would probably be a terrifying experience. Colicchio knows what he likes and, more important, he knows what he doesn't like. He knows technique and he knows the lack of it. Used a simple sieve when a dish calls for a chinois? You're going to hear about it. Calling a dish *coq au vin* even though you're using a chicken and not a rooster? Consider yourself busted. Few could condemn you for just throwing up your hands, saying to hell with it, and ordering a pizza instead.

Then again, imagine if you actually got it right—the pleasure spreading across Colicchio's face, that stern look turning into a smile, the encouraging pat on the back. Because that's the power that *Top Chef*'s head judge holds: when he is displeased, it can be devastating (and mean the end of the road for the show's contestants). When he's happy, he can make you feel like a member of his exclusive fraternity; he can make a cook feel like a chef.

Such authority and passion is exactly what *Top Chef*'s producers were looking for when they set out to find a head judge. Colicchio earned his place in the food world first as a self-taught line cook at some of New York's best restaurants, then as the chef and co-owner of Manhattan's influential and beloved Gramercy Tavern, and finally at the helm of his Craft restaurant empire. Along the way, he's seen more than his share of bizarre kitchen behavior—the kind that makes anything that takes place on *Top Chef* look like child's play. For instance, there was the female chef who peed her pants during a busy shift and stayed in place, banging out orders, until the rush subsided. "Or there was a chef I knew who worked in only a T-shirt and jockstrap," Colicchio says.

All of which is to say that it was easy for him to see the potential drama of a reality show centered on chefs. Still, he was hesitant when *Top Chef*'s producers approached him. "I didn't want to do a reality show that was about me," he says. "And I'm definitely not an actor. I can't work with a script."

Colicchio takes his role seriously. During his mid-challenge walk-throughs, he carefully straddles the line between mentor and judge. (According to the show's rulebook, he can ask questions but cannot give advice.) At Judges' Table, he strictly enforces the rule that nothing counts except the food on the plate—not personality, past performance, future potential, or any other considerations.

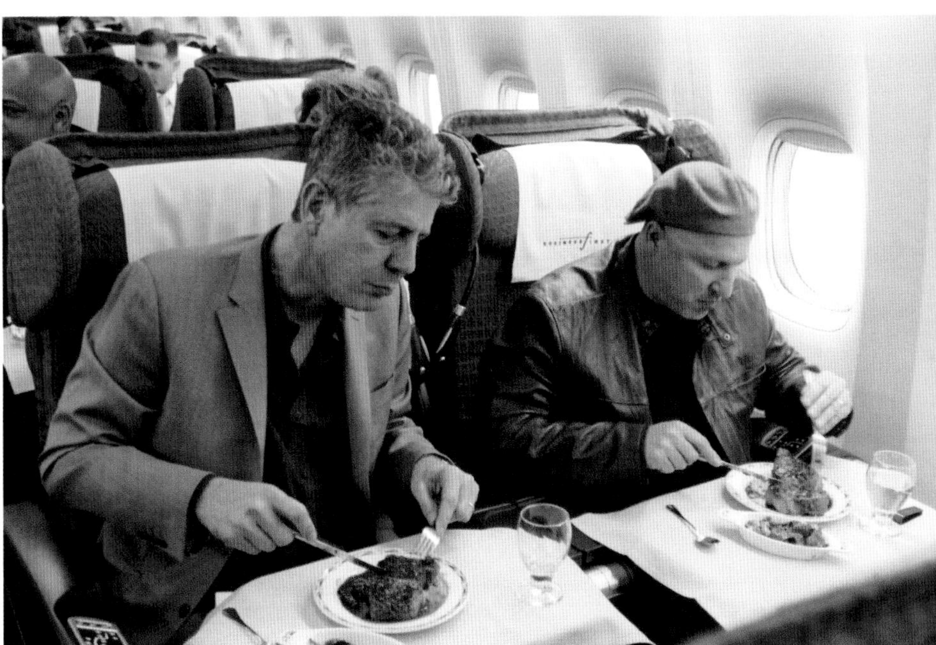

"I think, more than the other judges, I can really identify with the contestants," he says. "I know what they're going through and how they should be judged on their food, not their personalities. I try to treat them the way I would a cook in one of my kitchens."

And, yes, he still has kitchens. That's one side effect of *Top Chef* stardom that Colicchio has found both amusing and alarming. Not long ago, he was walking through Craft in Los Angeles when he was stopped by a woman who was amazed to see him. "She said, 'What are you doing here?' I told her it was my restaurant and she said, 'Oh, you still do that?'"

Colicchio chuckles. "I said, 'Yeah. That's what I do. I'm a chef.'"

Padma Lakshmi

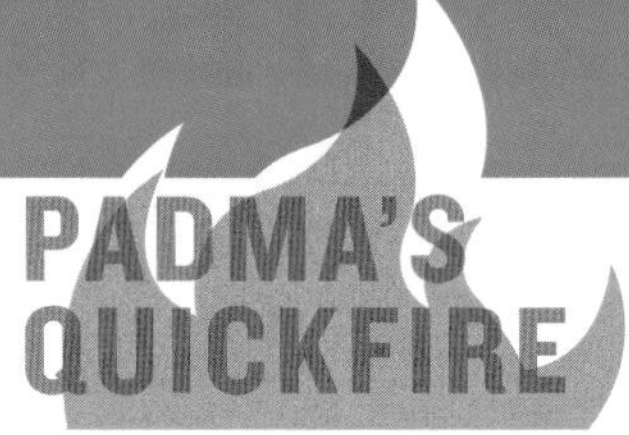

Which *Top Chef* dish do you still dream about?

Ilan's fideos with clams and saffron.

What was the worst dish you tasted?

Hands down, Ilan's chocolate ganache with liver in it. It was really revolting.

When was the most difficult time to say "Pack your knives"?

There have been many. Lia was really hard because I hoped she would go further.

When was the easiest?

You never enjoy it, but there have been one or two people I've had no problem saying it to.

Name five ingredients always in your home pantry.

Coconut milk, shallots, ginger, lemons, and sea salt.

What would you cook for the finale?

I would do four courses, moving from East to West. A first that's light but flavorful, like a South Indian crab cake with tamarind and lime leaves. Then lamb meatballs from the Middle East. The big course would be a brasato al barolo—classic braised beef. I'd finish off with mille-feuilles with a cardamom crème anglaise.

Ask anybody who's had to stand in front of her steely gaze at Judges' Table: Padma Lakshmi may be lovely but she's a no-nonsense kind of gal. That's why, when people ask what is the most important thing about her job as *Top Chef* host and judge, she doesn't start talking about such airy virtues as judgment or taste or empathy.

"My digestive tract," she tells them, going right for the gut. "I'm tasting as many as sixteen dishes a day, each of which has at least ten or twenty ingredients in them. It wreaks a lot of havoc on my tummy."

Not that airy virtues aren't important, too. (At least once the antacids are packed away.) Having grown up in India and the United States, and then traveling the globe as a fashion model, Lakshmi literally brings a world of experience to the Judges' Table. (The cross-cultural perspective is evident in her cookbooks, *Tangy, Tart, Hot & Sweet* and *Easy Exotic.*) She rejects the idea that there's any disconnect between being a model and a lover of food. "First of all, models represent a cross-section of everybody else," she says. "I understand that people say they have trouble trusting a skinny cook. I'm just blessed with a high metabolism. And, you know, I'm working hard at the gym one hour a day." (Before you ask the other question every single person asks, the scar is from a car accident when she was fourteen.)

As host, Lakshmi is the one who develops the strongest bond with *Top Chef*'s contestants. "I get very possessive about them, because I'm right there with them. I'm the only person who tastes every single thing they make," she says. "When I introduce them to a new guest judge—like Eric Ripert or Daniel Boulud—I almost feel like, 'OK, guys, make us proud!'"

Of course, if Lakshmi sometimes plays the encouraging mother to her flock of aspiring chefs, she is also their disciplinarian, the last face that all but the crème de la crème will see before heading off to pack their knives.

Lakshmi is as straightforward about this role as everything else: "I'm the executioner," she says.

TOP CHEF

TOP CHEF

Gail Simmons

GAIL'S QUICKFIRE

Which *Top Chef* dish do you still dream about?

Tiffani and Dave made a Vietnamese-Mexican burrito in the Season I street-cart challenge. Also, Tiffani's artichoke risotto from the finale.

What was the worst dish you tasted?

There was a surf-and-turf dish prepared by Emily at the firehouse challenge during Season 2 that was so salty I could barely eat it.

Ever spit anything out?

I don't think so. There are plenty of things I've wished I hadn't put in my mouth.

Name five ingredients always in your home pantry.

Red wine vinegar, lemons and limes, fresh herbs, strong mustard, a big chunk of Parmigiano-Reggiano.

What would you cook for the finale?

A quail egg, lightly scrambled with herbs and truffles and put back in the shell with butter. A soup. Scallops. A big whole roasted meat—like venison with mushrooms or figs—carved tableside. And a simple, rustic tart.

Balancing the Judges' Table between Tom Colicchio's chefly knowledge and Padma Lakshmi's diner's perspective is Gail Simmons. Gail usually stays out of the kitchen, letting Tom do the walk-throughs and Padma announce the challenges, but her role is crucial.

She's the moderator, the sum-upper, quick to distill the whole table's thoughts into a single, pointed piece of criticism. Sure, these can be hard to swallow sometimes, like when she told Sam his watermelon and cheese dish made her feel sick, but she has the credentials to back them up.

Simmons has experience in nearly every aspect of the culinary world. She's been a culinary student, a cookbook writer, an assistant to the venerable food writer Jeffrey Steingarten, and an apprentice in pro kitchens. Then, of course, there's her role as the special projects editor of *Food & Wine* magazine, which includes being responsible for the *Food & Wine* Magazine Classic in Aspen, the nation's premier food festival. All this, and a wardrobe of satiny tops to boot!

Simmons's wealth of experience has given her not only what fellow judge Ted Allen calls an "encyclopedic knowledge of all things culinary," but also a foot firmly planted on either side of the chef/diner divide. "Oftentimes, I find myself in the middle of Tom and Padma. I understand both their arguments," she says.

Which is not to say that Simmons doesn't have strong opinions of her own. At least one blogger dubbed her "the Lioness," and not just for her appreciation of sinking her teeth into a rare piece of meat. "Gail can come off as much more stern than she is," says Lakshmi. "She's really sweet and cuddly, like a high-school sweetheart." Still, this is undoubtedly a woman who knows what she likes as well as what she doesn't, a list that includes overfussiness in preparation and overcookedness in almost anything. (Future contestants take note: she's not terribly fond of cilantro, veal, or black beans, either.) Most famously, she's particular about how her eggs are cooked, something demonstrated quite clearly during the Season 2 challenge in which the chefs were asked to cook breakfast for a gang of surfers. Ever since, she says, people have tended to think of her as the "crazy egg lady."

"I do love eggs, and I do get upset when they're bad. But I don't get that upset," she laughs. It's worth noting, however, that a similar rant—about a particularly bad brunch

experience that actually ended in egg-related tears—secured Simmons the role of permanent *Top Chef* judge at her audition.

Like Colicchio, when Simmons is hard on a contestant, it seems to come from a place of professional disappointment rather than malice. "I always try to remember how hard it is being in their position," she says. But she does like when things get contentious—whether that means defending Hung's hardball tactics on her blog ("This is a competition," she says) or expressing surprise that more chefs don't talk back at Judges' Table.

"I'm amazed that we say some of the things we say to them and they just answer, 'Yes. You're right. OK.' If I were them, I'd be like, 'How dare you? Shut up!'"

Top Cookbooks

Even a *Top Chef* judge can't eat all the time. Sometimes she'll need to do a little reading between meals. Gail Simmons admits that her collection of cookbooks and books on food verges on the obsessive. Here are some of her favorites—minus, of course, those penned by her fellow judges. (Tom Colicchio's *Think Like a Chef* and *Craft of Cooking*; Padma Lakshmi's *Easy Exotic* and *Tangy, Tart, Hot & Sweet*; and Ted Allen's *The Food You Want to Eat*.)

Timeless Techniques

How to Cook Everything by Mark Bittman

Jacques Pépin's Complete Techniques by Jacques Pépin and Léon Perer

Joy of Cooking by Irma S. Rombauer, Marion Rombauer Becker, and Ethan Becker

Kitchen Sense: More Than 600 Recipes to Make You a Great Home Cook by Mitchell Davis

Larousse Gastronomique: The World's Greatest Culinary Encyclopedia

The Way to Cook by Julia Child

Modern Classics

Bistro Cooking by Patricia Wells

Chez Panisse Vegetables by Alice Waters

I Like You: Hospitality Under the Influence by Amy Sedaris

Roasting: A Simple Art by Barbara Kafka

The Zuni Cafe Cookbook by Judy Rodgers

Regional Favorites

The Barbecue! Bible by Steven Raichlen

Cracking the Coconut: Classic Thai Home Cooking by Su-Mei Yu

Essentials of Classic Italian Cooking by Marcella Hazan

The New Book of Middle Eastern Food by Claudia Roden

Madhur Jaffrey's Quick & Easy Indian Cooking by Madhur Jaffrey

The New American Cheese: Profiles of America's Great Cheesemakers and Recipes for Cooking with Cheese by Laura Werlin

The Lee Bros. Southern Cookbook by Matt Lee and Ted Lee

Ted Allen

Let's say you're planning the perfect dinner party. You want guests who are educated, good-looking, and interesting to talk to. You want to serve good food (otherwise you might just tell one of the cooks to pack their knives and leave). And you want that one guy who makes everybody else laugh, the bon vivant—stylish, witty, informed, and always ready with the quip or bon mot. In the feast that is *Top Chef*, that man is Ted Allen.

For all his sophistication and expansive knowledge of dining and food, Allen is also something of a reassuring, approachable voice for the amateur cooks in the *Top Chef* audience—a persona just as much in evidence when he was the culinary enforcer on *Queer Eye for the Straight Guy*. "When *Queer Eye* was launched, they could have chosen a chef or a sommelier for that role," Allen remembers. "What I try to do is bring a kind of appoachability to the show. I help interpret all these fancy techniques and flavors for regular viewers." It probably doesn't hurt his populist profile that Allen is an oft-declared sucker for bacon, or that his sole professional kitchen experience was as a fry cook at a Ponderosa Steakhouse. (We can only pray that someday the photos emerge.)

"It's very difficult to be a chef, and that's a difficulty I haven't put myself through," Allen says. "So I always try to show the appropriate respect to people who have worked so hard to make it." Of course, Allen is hardly a total amateur, having authored the beautifully named cookbook *The Food You Want to Eat* and been a regular contributor of food writing to such magazines as *Esquire* and *Bon Appétit*. This distinguished background does entitle Allen to a sharp barb or two: he once told Betty Fraser that her dish resembled lawn rakings. And he was hardly able to disguise his disgust at the salmon "catastrophe" that got Tre Wilcox sent home. Such moments are among the few that Allen says he regrets about his time on *Top Chef*.

"I was raised by Southern parents to believe that anybody who puts food in front of you has done you an act of great love," he says. "It's hardly ever appropriate to be flippant or sarcastic about that."

Besides, Allen may be better at a kind of humor that's both slyer and (after years of working with *Queer Eye* costar Carson Kressley) raunchier. "Often I have to kick myself, 'Be a grown-up! Be a grown-up!'" he says. Sometimes the kid wins out: when he wrote his blog entry on Season 3's *Top Chef* winner, he titled it "Well, Hung."

Katie Lee Joel

TED'S QUICKFIRE

Which *Top Chef* dish do you still dream about?

Dale's scallops with purslane and grape sauce.

What was the worst dish you tasted?

In Season 2, each chef was given a color. Betty chose green and turned in some kind of burrito inside of a zucchini inside of a tortilla, with mounds of produce on top. It was an absolute mess.

Ever spit anything out?

No. But there have been a few things I've needed a big slug of water to choke down.

Name five ingredients always in your home pantry.

Cheese—Parmigiano-Reggiano and a wonderful French cheese called Prince de Claverol. A nice free-range chicken. French butter. Rosemary. And Champagne.

What would be the hardest thing about competing?

I would never compete in a TV reality show where I'd have to give up my phone and my iPod. Out of the question.

The Quickfire was done and so was the Elimination Challenge. Somehow the production team had gotten through filming the first episode of a new show called *Top Chef*. The Judges' Table deliberations were complete, the decision unanimous, and now only one thing remained: the first reading of the soon-to-be-legendary line, "Please pack your knives and go." There was only one problem.

"I tried to say the line, but my heart was beating so hard the microphone picked it up," says Katie Lee Joel, the host of Season 1. She laughs. "That actually happened twice. And the guy had to stand there and take it each time."

Part of Joel's nervousness may be attributable to the erratic personality of that first eliminated contestant, Ken Lee. "He had some really outrageous behavior, some of it directed at me," she remembers. But the jitters may also have been a function of the whirlwind that landed the then-twenty-four-year-old in the host's chair. At that point, Joel was a relative TV novice, working mostly on the cooking website she cofounded, oliveandpeach.com. She didn't have an agent at the time of her *Top Chef* audition; her only thought was to make sure "this wasn't one of those shows where they eat bugs or anything." Two days after the audition, she was on a plane to San Francisco.

Luckily she was in good company with fellow judges Colicchio and Simmons, both of whom were also new to reality TV. "It was fun," Joel remembers. "We just all went with it. I remember one time coming back from Napa Valley, we were all dressed up in fancy clothes, and we stopped at an In-N-Out Burger and just pigged out."

Just as luckily, Joel brought a love of food cultivated while growing up in her grandmother's kitchen in West Virginia. That passion made her a sharp and insightful judge and helped her get through the long, sometimes brutal shooting schedule. "It was exhausting," she says. "I starred on a food show and I wound up losing ten pounds."

The hardest part for Joel may have been acting the cold, stern disciplinarian. "I'm a bubbly person. They would tell me, 'Can you not smile so much?'" she says. "Even Ken, when he came up to the table and I knew I was going to eliminate him, I saw something soft in his eyes. I didn't like the guy, but I felt sorry for him."

Meet the Guest Judges

The creators of *Top Chef* always knew that the show would rely heavily on the talents and reputations of its guest judges.

They probably couldn't have dared to hope that the roster of guests would someday comprise a who's who of America's most talented chefs and restaurateurs. It all started with San Francisco's Hubert Keller, who was brave enough to allow sixteen contestants (and an entire camera crew) into his Fleur de Lys kitchen during a dinner rush and set the tone for the show when he uttered, "Nobody sticks their finger in the sauce!"

Since then, some of the country's most famous chefs have shared their expertise, from Eric Ripert on one coast to Suzanne Goin on the other. The roster of non-cooking food pros has been equally impressive, from *Food & Wine* magazine editor-in-chief Dana Cowin to legendary restaurateur Sirio Maccioni. Why would all of them be willing to endure the rigors of shooting reality TV? "There are lots of good reasons," says another guest judge, Rocco DiSpirito. "It's really fun. And just sitting next to Tom Colicchio kind of elevates you in the public eye."

Sometimes the compliment goes the other way, as when the deans of the French Culinary Institute—including gastronomic giant André Soltner—agreed to host and judge a Season 3 challenge. "When I was coming up, André Soltner was God," Colicchio says. "When it came time to introduce him as a judge, I actually had to stop and collect myself. I couldn't get the words out. It was just thrilling."

Miami

Michelle Bernstein
Michy's
Season 2, Episodes 5 and 13;
Season 3, Episode 14

Norman Van Aken
Norman's
Season 3, Episode 2

Barton G. Weiss
Barton G. The Restaurant
Season 3, Episode 4

Michael Schwartz
Michael's Genuine Food and Drink
Season 3, Episode 10

Massachusetts

Ming Tsai
Blue Ginger—Wellesley, MA
Season 2, Episode 2

Todd English
Olives—Charlestown, MA
Season 3, Episode 14

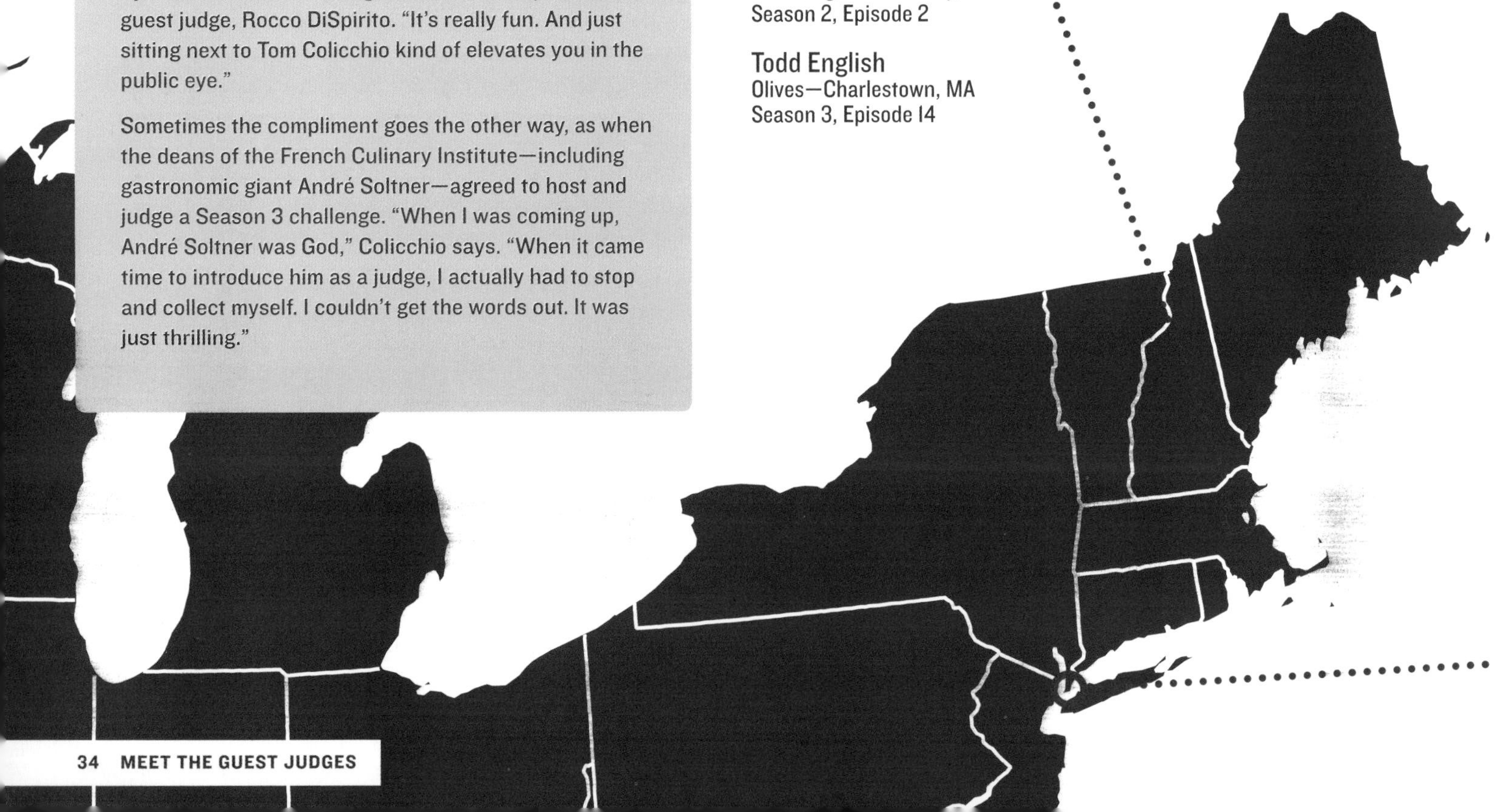

New York

Jeffrey Chodorow
China Grill
Season 1, Episode 7

James McDevitt
Budo
Season 1, Episode 9

Drew Nieporent
Nobu
Season 1, Episode 12

Anthony Bourdain
Brasserie Les Halles
Season 2, Episode 6;
Season 3, Episodes 1 and 11

Eric Ripert
Le Bernardin
Season 2, Episode 11;
Season 3, Episode 13

Wylie Dufresne
WD~50
Season 2, Episode 13

Alfred Portale
Gotham Bar and Grill
Season 3, Episode 3

Daniel Boulud
Daniel
Season 3, Episode 8

Geoffrey Zakarian
Town
Season 3, Episode 9

Sirio Maccioni
Le Cirque
Season 3, Episode 12

André Soltner
French Culinary Institute
Season 3, Episode 12

Napa Valley

Greg Cole
Celadon
Season 1, Episode 9

Lissa Doumani
Terra
Season 1, Episode 9

Philippe Jeanty
Bistro Jeanty
Season 1, Episode 9

Douglas Keane
Cyrus
Season 1, Episode 9

Keith Luce
Press Restaurant
Season 1, Episode 9

Cindy Pawlcyn
Mustards Grill
Season 1, Episode 9

Victor Scargle
Julia's Kitchen at COPIA
Season 1, Episode 9

Honolulu

Alan Wong
The Pineapple Room
Season 2, Episode 12

Roy Yamaguchi
Roy's
Season 2, Episode 13

San Francisco

Hubert Keller
Fleur de Lys
Season 1, Episodes 1 and 11;
Season 2, Episode 13

Elizabeth Falkner
Citizen Cake
Season 1, Episode 2

Laurent Manrique
Aqua
Season 1, Episode 3

Jefferson Hill
The Rotunda at
Neiman Marcus
Season 1, Episode 4

Mike Yakura
Sutra and Aura
Season 1, Episode 5;
Season 2, Episode 10

Hiro Sone
Ame
Season 1, Episode 9

Los Angeles

Hiroshi Shima
Sushi Roku
Season 2, Episode 2

Suzanne Goin
Lucques and AOC
Season 2, Episode 4

Raphael Lunetta
JiRaffe
Season 2, Episode 7

Lee Hefter
Spago
Season 2, Episode 8

Govind Armstrong
Table 8 and L'Scorpion
Season 3, Episode 7

Additional Judges

Chef John Ash
Wedding planner Marcy Blum
Actress Lorraine Bracco, owner of Bracco Wines
Chef Stephen Bulgarelli
Chef Jimmy Canora
Chef and restaurateur Scott Conant
Actress Jennifer Coolidge
Dana Cowin, editor-in-chief of *Food & Wine* magazine
Deans of the French Culinary Institute
Chef and restaurateur Rocco DiSpirito
Chef Maria Frumkin
Chef Tom Humphries
Chef Robert Ivan
Actress Debi Mazar
Chef James McDevitt
Chef and restaurateur Michael Mina
John Shafer, owner of Shafer Vineyards
Mixologist Jamie Walker
Mixologist Kristin Woodward

Breakfast

47

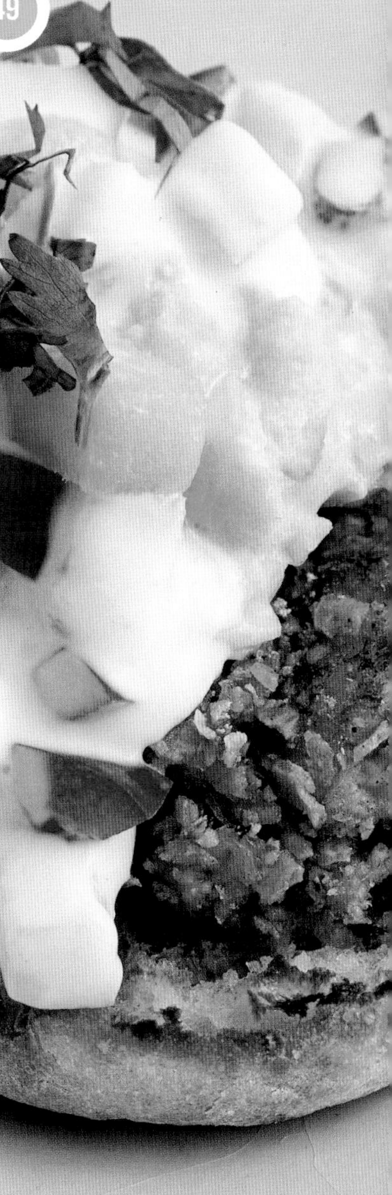
49

Breakfast, Lunch, and Dinner Waffle
with Ham, Cheese, and Fried Egg

CHEF: Elia
SEASON 2, EPISODE 7
ELIMINATION CHALLENGE: Prepare breakfast on the beach for surfers.

- 1/3 cup refried beans (homemade or canned), warmed
- 1 tablespoon olive oil
- Salt and freshly ground black pepper
- 1 tablespoon plus 2 teaspoons unsalted butter
- 1 large egg
- 1 frozen waffle
- Maple syrup for drizzling
- 2 thin slices Muenster cheese
- 2 thin slices coppa ham
- 1 tablespoon chopped fresh flat-leaf parsley

20 minutes
Serves 1
Winner

1. Preheat the broiler.
2. In a small bowl, combine the refried beans with the olive oil, adding a little water to thin to spreadable consistency if needed. Mix well and season with salt and pepper to taste.
3. In a small skillet, melt 1 tablespoon of the butter over medium heat. Crack the egg into the skillet and fry to desired firmness. Remove from the skillet and set aside.
4. While you're frying the egg, toast the waffle to desired doneness. Spread with the remaining 2 teaspoons butter and top with the refried bean mixture, spreading to cover the edges of the waffle so it doesn't burn.
5. Drizzle with maple syrup and top with the cheese.
6. Put the waffle on a baking sheet and broil until the cheese melts, 2 to 3 minutes, watching carefully so it does not burn.
7. Remove from the oven, top with the ham and fried egg, and sprinkle with the parsley. Season with salt and pepper to taste and serve immediately.

SURFER, GUEST JUDGE "AWESOME. IT FILLED YOU UP AND DIDN'T HAVE YOU FEELING ALL FULL LIKE YOU'RE GOING TO SINK WHEN YOU GO IN THE WATER."

Crêpes
Filled with Almond Whipped Cream and Strawberries

CHEF: C.J.
SEASON 3, EPISODE 11
QUICKFIRE CHALLENGE: Make Padma breakfast.

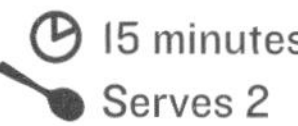

15 minutes
Serves 2

HOW TO:
Save Some for Later

This crêpe recipe makes enough batter for 8 to 10 crêpes. Stack the leftover crêpes, wrap them tightly in plastic, and refrigerate or freeze them. They can be thawed and reheated quickly in a dry skillet.

Crêpes:
2 large eggs
1 ½ cups milk, or more if needed
Pinch of salt
1 ½ cups unbleached all-purpose flour
4 tablespoons unsalted butter, melted, plus some for the pan

Almond Whipped Cream and Strawberries:
1 cup heavy cream
1 teaspoon almond extract
¼ cup confectioners' sugar
1 pint strawberries

For the Crêpes:

1. In a blender, combine the eggs, milk, and salt; blend until smooth.
2. Sprinkle in the flour and blend until smooth. Add the butter and blend again. Add a bit more milk if necessary to make a thin, smooth batter.
3. Heat a 9-inch sauté pan or crêpe pan over medium-high heat. Brush lightly with butter, then pour in ¼ to ½ cup of the batter, tilting the pan to distribute it thinly over the bottom. Cook for about 1 minute, until just browned on the bottom, then use your fingers to flip the crêpe over; cook for 10 seconds on the other side, then transfer to a plate. Repeat with the remaining batter, stacking the crêpes on the plate as they are cooked.

For the Almond Whipped Cream and Strawberries:

1. In a chilled bowl with chilled beaters, whip the cream, almond extract, and confectioners' sugar until soft peaks form. Set aside.
2. Hull and thinly slice the strawberries. Set aside.

To Serve:

1. Place 2 crêpes on each of 2 serving plates and top with some of the strawberries and whipped cream; fold into a triangle and top with the remaining strawberries and whipped cream.
2. Serve immediately.

C.J. "WOMEN LOVE CRÊPES. IF THERE WAS ANOTHER SPICE GIRL, SHE'D BE CRÊPE SPICE."

Steak and Eggs
with Papaya, Banana, and Grand Marnier® Shake

CHEF: Hung
SEASON 3, EPISODE 11
QUICKFIRE CHALLENGE: Make Padma breakfast.

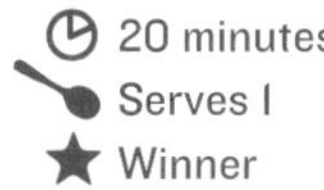

20 minutes
Serves 1
Winner

Shake:
2 cups peeled, seeded, and diced papaya
1 banana, sliced
1 cup milk
1 cup crushed ice
¼ cup Grand Marnier®
2 tablespoons fresh lemon juice (optional)
Honey

Steak and Eggs:
One 8-ounce New York strip steak
Salt and freshly ground black pepper
2 tablespoons vegetable oil
2 large eggs
1 small onion, cut into ¼-inch slices
1 cup sliced button mushrooms

For the Shake:

In a blender, combine the papaya, banana, milk, ice, liqueur, and lemon juice, if using. Blend until smooth, add honey to taste, and blend to combine. Pour into a tall, chilled glass.

For the Steak and Eggs:

1. Season the steak with salt and pepper on both sides. Heat the oil in a medium sauté pan or skillet over high heat. Add the steak and cook for 3 to 4 minutes on each side for medium-rare, or to desired doneness. Add the eggs and cook to the desired firmness. Remove to a serving plate and set aside to rest.
2. Return the pan to the heat and add the onion and mushrooms; cook, stirring, until just softened and browned, about 5 minutes. Season with salt and pepper to taste. Spoon the onion and mushrooms onto the plate next to the steak and eggs, and serve immediately.

PADMA LAKSHMI, JUDGE "I'M REALLY NOT A FAN OF STEAK AND EGGS, BUT THIS WAS REALLY VERY GOOD."

Eggs in a Hole

CHEF: Sara M.
SEASON 3, EPISODE 11
QUICKFIRE CHALLENGE: Make Padma breakfast.

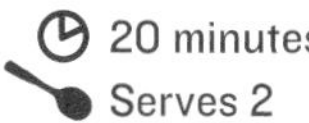
20 minutes
Serves 2

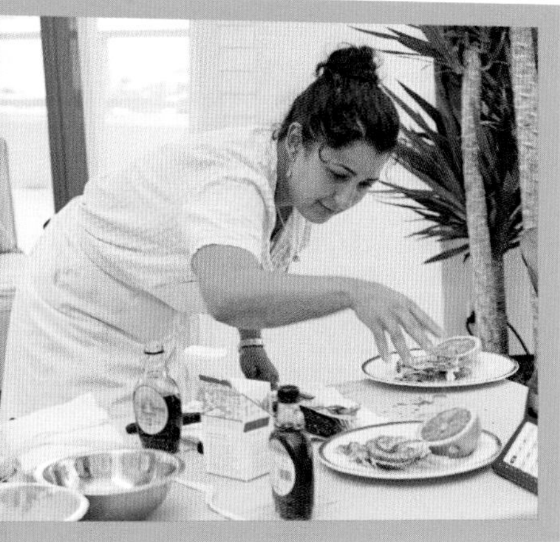

"Eggs in a Hole is definitely a classic. I love to eat them, and I guess Padma does, too, because mine were ugly as hell and she still chose me for the top three!"
SARA M.

1 grapefruit
4 large eggs
½ cup milk
2 tablespoons sugar
½ teaspoon salt
½ teaspoon ground cinnamon
4 slices multigrain bread
4 tablespoons unsalted butter
4 thin slices prosciutto (about 2 ½ ounces)
Maple syrup for serving

1. Using a sharp knife, peel the grapefruit, removing all the white membrane. Carefully cut down along the side of one section to the center of the grapefruit, then turn the knife and lift the section out. Remove the remaining sections from the membranes, separating them. Set aside.
2. In a wide, shallow dish, whisk together 2 of the eggs, the milk, sugar, salt, and cinnamon.
3. Using a 2 ½-inch round biscuit cutter, cut a hole in the center of each of 2 slices of bread. Put all 4 slices of bread in the egg mixture and let them soak for 1 minute on each side.
4. In a sauté pan or skillet large enough to fit the bread slices in one layer, melt the butter over medium-high heat. When the foam subsides, carefully transfer the bread slices to the pan. Crack 1 egg into each hole in the bread slices. Cook until the bread is well browned on the bottom, about 3 minutes. Gently turn the slices over and cook until the second side is well browned, about 2 minutes.
5. Place 1 of the holeless bread slices on each of the serving plates. Lay 2 slices of the prosciutto over each and top with the bread slices with egg. Drizzle with maple syrup and serve immediately, with the grapefruit sections alongside.

Fruit Kabobs
with Honeyed Red and Blue Yogurt

CHEF: Lisa
SEASON 1, EPISODE 3
ELIMINATION CHALLENGE: Serve a monkfish lunch to a group of children.

20 minutes
Serves 12 to 15

WHAT ARE . . .
Kabobs

Marinate chunks of just about any food, thread them onto a skewer, grill or broil them, and you can call it a kabob—or a "kebab," or a "shish kebab." Usually featuring cubes of meat or fish, and perhaps vegetables or tofu, the pure simplicity of food-on-a-stick seems to call out for dipping sauces—hence the curried mayonnaise accompanying the very classically seasoned grilled lamb kabobs on page 117. Here the idea of the kabob is pared down to its essence: chunks of fruit, skewers, sauce.

½ seedless watermelon
1 cantaloupe or honeydew melon, halved, seeds removed
1 pineapple, peeled, cored, and cut into triangles
2 cups plain yogurt
2 tablespoons good-quality honey
½ teaspoon vanilla extract
Seeds scraped from ½ vanilla bean (optional)
Red and blue food coloring

1. Using a medium-size melon baller, scoop the watermelon and cantaloupe into balls. Thread 1 piece each of watermelon, cantaloupe, and pineapple onto each of 12 to 15 bamboo skewers.
2. In a medium bowl, combine the yogurt, honey, vanilla extract, and vanilla bean seeds, if using. Put half of the yogurt into a separate small bowl; color one half of the yogurt with red food coloring, the other with blue.
3. Pour the yogurt into two squeeze bottles. Into small serving cups, squirt red yogurt and swirl with blue yogurt. Serve with the fruit skewers.

TOM "DO KIDS LIKE YOGURT?" **LISA** "THEY LIKE BLUE YOGURT." **KID** "WE'RE, LIKE, CRAZY ABOUT THAT YOGURT."

Spanish Tortilla
with Chipotle Aioli

CHEF: Ilan
SEASON 2, EPISODE 7
ELIMINATION CHALLENGE: Prepare breakfast on the beach for surfers.

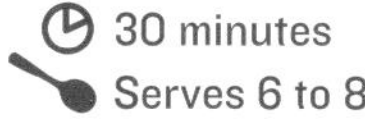

30 minutes
Serves 6 to 8

Chipotle Aioli:

- ½ cup mayonnaise
- 2 tablespoons sun-dried tomato cheese spread (store-bought)
- 1 canned chipotle chile in adobo sauce, minced
- 1 garlic clove, minced
- Salt and freshly ground black pepper

Spanish Tortilla:

- 12 large eggs
- Salt and freshly ground black pepper
- One 7.5-ounce bag original flavor Terra Chips, crumbled
- 4 rye crisp crackers, crumbled, plus several more whole crackers for serving
- 4 scallions, white and light green parts only, thinly sliced, plus more for garnish
- 2 tablespoons unsalted butter

For the Chipotle Aioli:

In a small bowl, combine the mayonnaise, cheese spread, chipotle, garlic, and salt and pepper to taste. Whisk until smooth. Set aside while you make the tortilla.

For the Spanish Tortilla:

1. In a large bowl, whisk the eggs vigorously and season with salt and pepper. Gently fold in the crumbled Terra Chips, crumbled rye crisp crackers, and scallions.
2. In a large nonstick skillet, melt the butter over medium heat. Add the egg mixture to the pan, reduce the heat to medium-low, and cook until it begins to firm and is lightly browned on the bottom, 5 to 7 minutes. Loosen the sides of the tortilla with a spatula.
3. Remove the pan from the heat and cover with a large heat-proof plate. (Get someone to hold the plate for you if you can.) Carefully invert the tortilla onto the plate, then gently slide it back into the pan with the browned side on top. Cook until fully set and the bottom is lightly browned, about 5 minutes. Remove from the heat, shake the tortilla loose from the pan, and slide onto a clean plate. Cut into wedges.

To Serve:

Spread some of the aioli onto rye crisp crackers and top with tortilla wedges. Spoon some aioli on top and garnish with sliced scallions. Serve immediately.

GAIL SIMMONS, JUDGE "THERE WAS SOMETHING ABOUT ILAN'S DISH THAT I REALLY, REALLY ENJOYED, EVEN THOUGH THE EGGS WERE A LITTLE OVERDONE."

Black Forest Ham and Egg Bundle
with Corn and Leek Ragout on Rustic Toast

CHEF: Betty
SEASON 2, EPISODE 7
ELIMINATION CHALLENGE: Prepare breakfast on the beach for surfers.

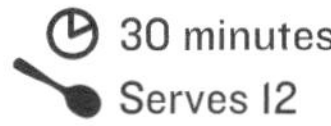

30 minutes
Serves 12

- 2 tablespoons thinly sliced fresh basil
- 1 tablespoon olive oil
- Salt and freshly ground black pepper
- 5 tablespoons unsalted butter, or more if needed
- 1 leek, white and light green part, washed and sliced ⅛ inch thick; dark green part cut into long strips for tying up bundle
- 10 cremini mushrooms, quartered
- ⅓ cup fresh corn kernels
- 6 orange tomatoes, cut into 4 slices each, ends reserved for another use
- 12 large eggs
- ½ cup grated Monterey Jack cheese
- 12 thin slices Black Forest ham
- Basil oil
- 3 tablespoons chopped chives for garnish
- 12 slices rustic toast

1. In a small bowl, combine the basil, oil, and a pinch each of salt and pepper. Stir to combine. Set aside.
2. In a large skillet, melt 2 tablespoons of the butter over medium heat. Add the sliced leek, mushrooms, and corn. Cook for about 8 minutes, until tender. Using a slotted spoon, transfer the mixture from the skillet to a medium bowl. Cover to keep warm.
3. In a small saucepan of boiling water, cook the strips of leek for about 2 minutes, until soft. Drain and set aside.
4. Season the tomatoes with salt and pepper to taste. Add to the skillet, adding more butter if necessary to keep them from sticking. Cook over medium heat, turning once, until the tomatoes just begin to soften, about 1 to 2 minutes. Remove from the heat and set aside.
5. In a large bowl, whisk the eggs vigorously until smooth. Season with salt and pepper; stir well to combine.
6. In another large skillet, melt the remaining 3 tablespoons of butter over medium-low heat. Add the eggs and cook for 6 to 8 minutes, stirring frequently, until cooked to desired firmness. Sprinkle the cheese over the eggs and stir to combine.
7. Lay the ham slices on a work surface in a single layer, with a long strip of leek underneath each. The ends of the leeks should extend beyond the edges of the ham. Divide the egg mixture among the ham slices. Spoon the mushroom mixture over the eggs. Drizzle with basil oil and sprinkle with chives. Roll each slice of ham around the filling and tie the roll with the leek strips. Place 1 slice of toast on each serving plate. Top with the tomato slices and a ham and egg bundle. Serve immediately.

WHAT IS . . .
Black Forest Ham?

In the E.U., where "Black Forest ham" is by law written on only the true article, this question has an easy answer: a boneless ham, made in the Black Forest region of southwestern Germany, that has been dry-cured in a mixture of salt, juniper berries, and other spices and cold-smoked over pine or fir branches. Real Black Forest ham is rich, smoky, and firm-textured, and does not resemble the typical U.S. deli ham in the least.

In the States, just about anything can be called Black Forest ham. For this recipe, a deli-style Black Forest ham will do fine (though most are brine-cured and a bit on the sweet side), but if you want to make this dish a little fancier, try a real Black Forest ham imported from Germany. To be even more extravagant, use dry-cured and smoked Westphalian ham or thinly sliced baked country-style Southern ham, which is also dry-cured and smoked.

Crabcakes Benedict
with Mango Cream Sauce

CHEF: Mia
SEASON 2, EPISODE 7
ELIMINATION CHALLENGE: Prepare breakfast on the beach for surfers.

Mango Cream Sauce:

- 4 tablespoons unsalted butter
- 2 tablespoons unbleached all-purpose flour
- 1 cup heavy cream, warmed to room temperature
- 1 large mango, peeled, pitted, and diced
- ¼ cup finely chopped red bell pepper
- ¼ cup minced fresh cilantro
- Salt and freshly ground black pepper

Crabcakes Benedict:

- 12 large eggs
- 12 crabcakes (homemade or store-bought)
- One 9-ounce bag corn tortilla chips, finely crushed
- Olive oil
- Salt and freshly ground black pepper
- 6 English muffins
- 2 tablespoons unsalted butter
- Chopped fresh flat-leaf parsley for garnish

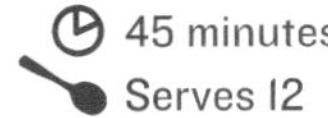
45 minutes
Serves 12

For the Mango Cream Sauce:

1. In a medium saucepan, melt the butter over medium heat. Add the flour and whisk vigorously until the mixture is smooth and fragrant but does not change color. Add the cream and whisk until the mixture is well combined.
2. Reserve ½ cup of the mango. Add the red pepper, cilantro, remaining mango, and salt and pepper to taste. Bring to a simmer, then reduce the heat to low and simmer for 8 to 10 minutes, stirring frequently, until the mixture is thick but smooth and the ingredients are cooked through. You may need to whisk the mixture from time to time to keep it from separating. Remove from the heat, cover, and set aside until ready to serve. Gently reheat just before serving if necessary.

For the Crabcakes Benedict:

1. In a small bowl, whisk 2 of the eggs with 2 teaspoons water. Using a pastry brush, brush both sides of each crabcake with the egg wash. Dip each crabcake in the corn chips, coating both sides. Set the crabcakes aside on large plates.
2. In a large skillet, heat 1 inch of oil over medium heat. Add the crabcakes, in batches if necessary, cooking until golden brown on each side, about 5 minutes per side, adding more oil to the pan for a second batch if necessary. As the crabcakes are ready, transfer them to a tray and cover with aluminum foil to keep warm.
3. In a large bowl, whisk the remaining 10 eggs to combine and season with salt and pepper to taste.
4. Split the English muffins in half and toast them.
5. While the English muffins are in the toaster, wipe out the skillet, add the butter, and melt over medium-low heat. Add the eggs and cook to desired firmness, stirring frequently. Add more salt and pepper to taste if needed. Cover with foil to keep warm if necessary.

To Serve:

Put 1 English muffin half on each plate. Top each English muffin with a crabcake. Spoon some of the scrambled eggs over each crabcake. Top with the mango sauce and garnish with the reserved mango and the parsley. Serve immediately.

"All the surfers needed to see on my sign was 'crabcakes' and I had a line of people. I couldn't serve them fast enough."
MIA

Season I: Elimination Bracket

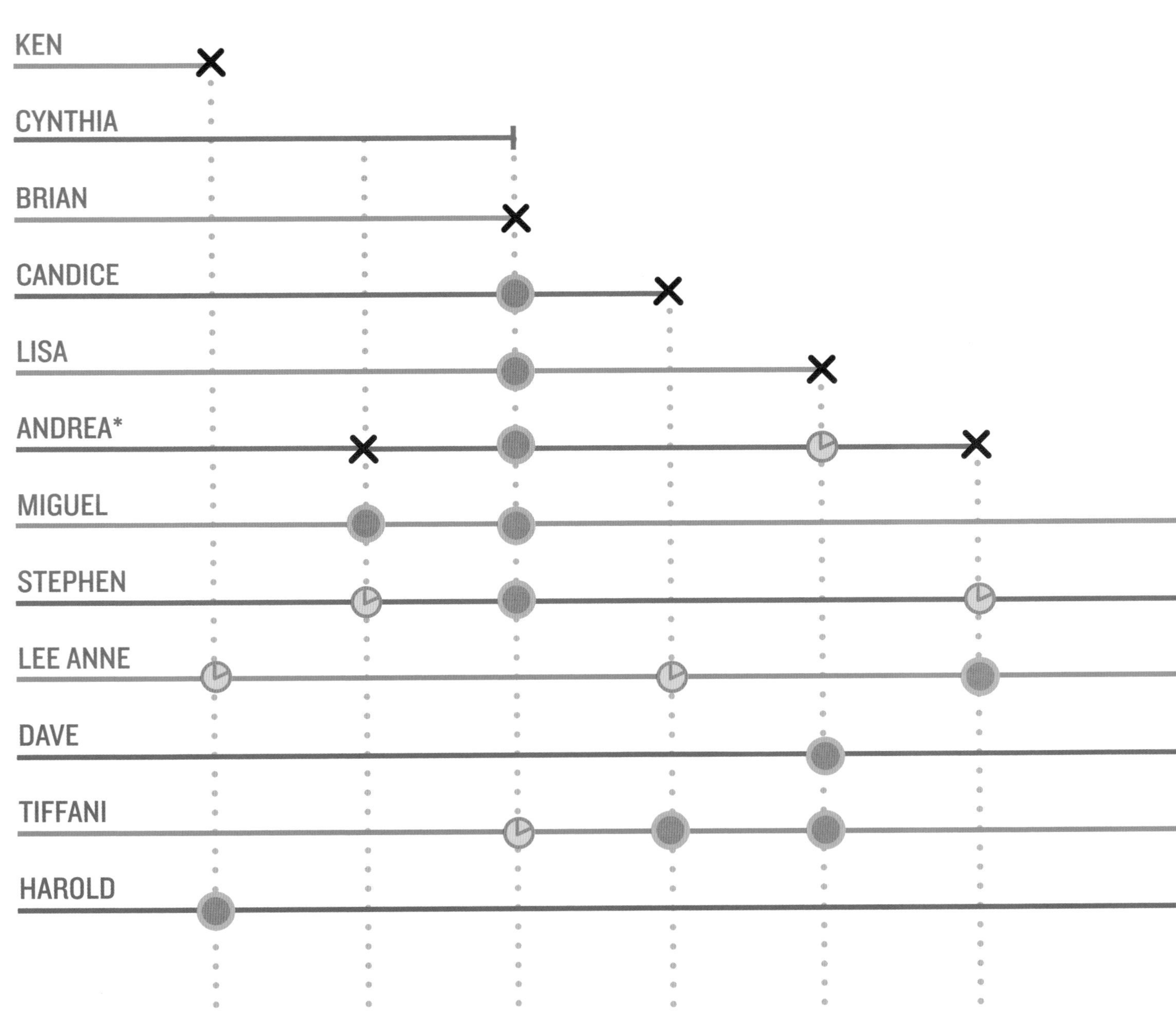

Winner of title "Top Chef"

Winner of Elimination Challenge

Winner of Quickfire

Winner of both Quickfire and Elimination Challenges

Contestant Eliminated

Withdrew from Competition

* Andrea was first eliminated in the second episode, but then returned when Cynthia bowed out to take care of her sick father.

* Top Chef Reunion Show (No one was eliminated)

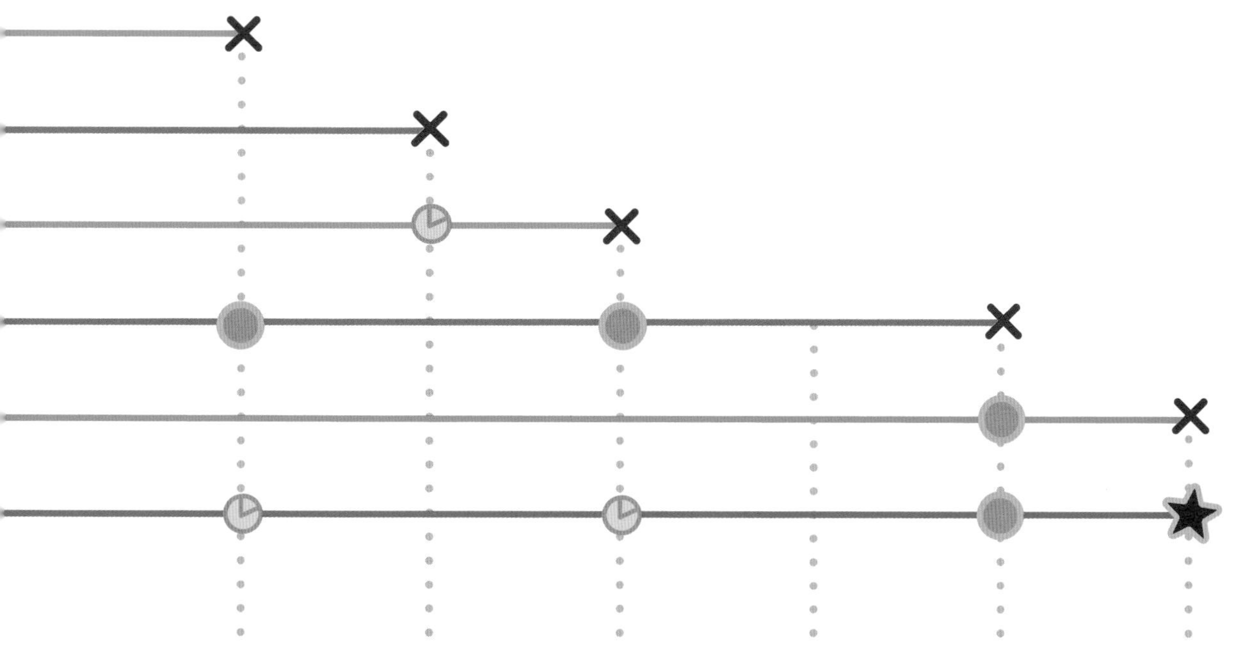

Season I: Episode Guide

Episode

 Winner of Title "Top Chef"

 Winner of Elimination Challenge

 Winner of Quickfire

 Guest Judge

 Contestant Eliminated

Season I
Fire Up the Grill

If there was any doubt that watching people cook would be interesting, it was gone by the end of episode I of *Top Chef*, when a madman named Ken was eliminated.

The first cast of chefs was notable for its diversity of backgrounds; in addition to professional chefs, it featured self-taught cooks, nutrition experts, and culinary students, among others. It quickly became clear that the pros were rising to the top, including two fierce ladies (Lee Anne and Tiffani), a "chef's chef" (Harold), and a couple of characters you had to see to believe (Stephen and Dave). The final showdown, in which Harold claimed the title, was the perfect confluence of social and stovetop skills.

Who Deserves to Be Here?

 Survive the line at Hubert Keller's Fleur de Lys restaurant.

 Prepare a signature dish to be served to the other contestants.

It's straight into the fire as the cast joins the line at Chef Hubert Keller's Fleur de Lys. Cool under pressure, Lee Anne impresses Keller while Ken shocks him speechless. ("Nobody sticks their finger in the sauce!") Ken's flavorless halibut doesn't live up to his swagger, and he is the first to pack his knives.

 Chef Hubert Keller

 Lee Anne

Ken

 Harold

Food of Love

 Prepare a fruit plate.

 Make a sexy dessert for a fetish party at a San Francisco sex boutique.

After some pretty tame fruit plates, the contestants cook up sexy desserts for Madame S. Andrea's Earth Mother sensibilities leave party guest RuPaul yawning, while Miguel dons a red wig, shows a little cleavage, and makes the Madame swoon.

 Chef Elizabeth Falkner and Madame S.

 Stephen

 Andrea

 Miguel

3

Nasty Delights

 Prepare octopus for Chef Laurent Manrique.

 Working in two teams, serve a monkfish lunch to a group of children.

The chefs take the ugliest foods the judges can find and make them look (and taste) good enough to eat. Impressing Chef Laurent Manrique proves to be a cakewalk compared with getting a gym full of ten-year-olds to eat monkfish. Andrea returns when Cynthia bows out to care for her sick father.

 Chef Laurent Manrique

 Tiffani

 Cynthia (withdrew) and Brian

 Andrea, Candice, Lisa, Miguel, and Stephen

Food on the Fly

 Create a dish using $20 worth of ingredients from a gas station.

 Create a gourmet entrée that can be reheated in a microwave.

In this episode, the chefs have to think highbrow using the humblest of ingredients—gas-station munchies and a microwave. Stephen is in his element and gives the mothers judging the microwave cook-off an earful of "education." Tiffani speaks their language, and wins with her simple sea bass.

 Chef Jefferson Hill

 Lee Anne

Candice

 Tiffani

Blind Confusion

 Identify strange foods by taste.

 Fuse two of San Francisco's culinary cultures in a new kind of street food.

After an impossible Quickfire quiz, Miguel and Dave blow off steam by going head to head in a snack food taste test. Tiffani wins her second Elimination Challenge with Dave, while Lisa drops the ball (and the jicama) and gets the boot.

 Chef Mike Yakura

 Andrea

 Lisa

 Dave and Tiffani

6 Guess Who's Coming to Dinner

 Create an appetizer using the limited ingredients Ted Allen preselects.

 Create a seven-course dinner party for Ted Allen. Each chef works on another chef's recipe.

As if a seven-course dinner party for food guru Ted Allen isn't daunting enough, Tom tells the chefs they'll be swapping dishes with one another. Miguel cracks under the pressure (that's salt, not sugar!) and Andrea serves her last dud of a dish.

 Ted Allen  Stephen

 Andrea  Lee Anne

7 Restaurant Wars

 Build a sandwich for Tom's 'wichcraft restaurants.

 Divide into two teams and turn an empty space into a restaurant in 24 hours.

Dave's low-key comfort food trounces Stephen's classy ode to Spanish wine. Under their restaurant's homey exterior, though, Dave and Tiffani butt heads—and the phrase "I'm not your bitch, bitch" is immortalized.

 Restaurateur Jeffrey Chodorow  Harold

Miguel  Dave

8 Wedding Bell Blues

 Design and pitch a wedding-reception menu.

 Cater a wedding reception for 100 guests using the menu chosen in the Quickfire Challenge.

Grooms-to-be Scott and Scott choose Lee Anne's Asian fusion menu, and the chefs have one night to cook a reception for one hundred. A Betty Crocker cake and cold salmon disappoint, and the team boots Stephen for playing Top Sommelier. Again.

 Wedding planner Marcy Blum  Lee Anne

 Stephen  No one

9 Napa's Finest

 Re-create a classic junk food into a gourmet dish.

 Prepare a dish with expensive black truffles to be paired with a super-rare wine.

The chefs start at the bottom of the culinary spectrum, reinventing corn dogs and nachos, then go straight to the top. With thousand-dollar-a-pound truffles and a wine Stephen would kill for, they make a meal for Napa's pickiest gourmands.

 Northern California chefs  Harold

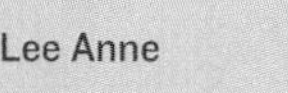 Lee Anne  Dave

10 Top Chef Reunion Show

The cast gets together to relive the past nine episodes, heating up the *Top Chef* reunion stage. Stephen shows his softer side and apologizes to Candice for their epic argument over cookie cutters. Dave, with help from some of his castmates, bickers with Tiffani for most of the show. Brian ogles over Candice, and Harold proclaims he is, above all else, "a cook." With equal parts laughter and tears, the first Top Chef Reunion Special comes to an end. "It is what it is," as they say.

11 Vegas Finale: Part 1

 Prepare hotel room-service meals in thirty minutes for different customers.

The final three arrive in Vegas and run room service for a night. Harold stuns the "high rollers" with his simple soup and has poker players going all-in for his prepackaged chicken wings. Dave can't take the stress and comes out empty-handed.

 Chef Hubert Keller  Harold and Tiffani

 Dave

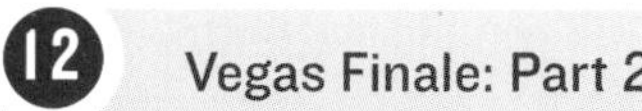

12 Vegas Finale: Part 2

 Prepare a five-course meal to be served to a table of luminaries from the culinary world.

Tiffani pulls out all the stops and cooks double the dishes, while Harold plays it cool (with the help of a few under-the-table cocktails). The judges go for quality over quantity, and Harold's beef and quail make him the first Top Chef.

 Actress Lorraine Bracco and Drew Nieporent  Harold

Tiffani

"So long as I'm not going to another gas station or cooking for five-year-olds, I'm fine."
HAROLD

TOP STATS

Age
30

Hometown
New York, NY

Favorite summer beverage
Gin and tonic

Philosophy
"I'm a cook. That's what I do: I cook."

Currently
Owner of Perilla in New York City

Featured recipes
Duo of Beef, p. 98
Strip Steaks, p. 108
Quail, p. 142
Red Snapper, p. 160
Ceviche, p. 175
Fig Tart, p. 233

Harold Dieterle

SEASON I
WINNER
WINS: 3 ELIMINATION CHALLENGES, 2 QUICKFIRES

Way back in the first challenge of the first episode of the first season of *Top Chef*, a tall, handsome contestant with a Long Island accent was quickly eliminated from the cooking line by guest judge Hubert Keller. This did not sit well with Harold Dieterle: he went on to win that episode's Elimination Challenge and never looked back.

Stoic, reserved, and inevitably described as a "chef's chef," Harold was hardly the flashiest of the bunch, but his professionalism couldn't completely mask his sharp wit or competitive fire. Making no enemies proved to be a good strategy, helping him secure the cooperation of his former opponents in the Las Vegas finale and ultimately securing his win. And *Top Chef*'s first Top Chef also became *Top Chef*'s first public success story when Harold's New York restaurant, Perilla, opened in 2007 and received a star from the *New York Times*.

What does it mean to be a "chef's chef"?
I think it's a compliment. It means not trying to reinvent the wheel with my cooking—keeping everything simple, clean. It means I like to spend time in the kitchen. I like to cook. The kitchen is kind of my sanctuary.

Watching the show, it sometimes seemed like you were . . .
Not enjoying myself? A lot of the time I wasn't. I mean, it wasn't what I expected. I really thought I'd be cooking all the time. Instead, there was all this time with cameras in your face, doing interviews, people asking, "How did this feel?" It's almost like you're seeing a shrink.

Why did you decide to try out?
First of all, I always enjoy doing cook-offs and competitions. That was a driving factor. And I knew I wanted to open a restaurant. You look at guys like Tom Colicchio and you realize that, aside from being really, really talented chefs, they also get press. They get noticed.

What was the hardest adjustment about being on the show?
I hadn't had a roommate since culinary school. I was in a room with Miguel and Brian, and later Miguel and Stephen. Both painful snorers. Plus, they keep you in such a bubble. After a couple of days, I was ready to go home. You need to be mentally fortified to get through it. It's like going to war.

When did you realize that the show was going to be a little more than just cooking?
It had to be Miguel coming down the stairs with his S&M wig on and nothing else but tighty-whities. It was so offensive. It was one of the funniest things I've ever seen.

KATIE LEE JOEL, SEASON I HOST "I KNEW THAT HAROLD WOULD WIN FROM THE VERY FIRST NIGHT. HIS FIRST DISH WAS FAR ABOVE EVERYONE'S, AND I JUST SAID, 'THIS GUY'S GOT IT.'"

THE REAL RESTAURANT WARS

One of the most anticipated episodes of every *Top Chef* season is "Restaurant Wars," in which the contestants are divided into two teams and judged on their hastily assembled mock restaurants. If there's anybody in a position to judge how close Restaurant Wars is to the actual process, it's Harold Dieterle.

High off his big win, he opened his own restaurant, Perilla, garnering the praise of New York diners, including *New York Times* food critic Frank Bruni. So, was Restaurant Wars good practice for the real deal? "Not at all," laughs Dieterle. "They've done well by incorporating things like décor and service, but there's just nothing like opening a restaurant."

As many have learned before him, cooking is all but the smallest part of starting up a food business. Much more time is spent in such glamorous pursuits as wrestling with employee tax codes, hiring dishwashers, and waiting on permits.

True to form, Dieterle prefers cooking in the kitchen to schmoozing in the dining room. Still, he's learned to open up some. "These days, people want to meet the guy who makes their food," he says. "At first I was a little apprehensive, but I think I'm adjusting."

"I am a nice person, but I don't feel like that's what I came here to prove. I came here to prove that I can cook."
TIFFANI

TOP STATS

Age
30

Born in
Germany

Hometown
Boston, MA

Currently
Opening her first restaurant in San Francisco, CA

Philosophy
"I like simple, I like clean, I like elegant."

Featured recipes
Cubanos, p. 106
Pasta and Octopus, p. 177
Sea Bass, p. 178

Tiffani Faison

SEASON I
ELIMINATED: EPISODE I2, "VEGAS FINALE: PART 2"
WINS: 3 ELIMINATION CHALLENGES, I QUICKFIRE

All no-nonsense skills and grim determination, Tiffani showed up for Season I with one thing in mind: winning.

With Stephen in the kitchen, she may have been a dark horse to play the antagonist, but it quickly became clear that she was a supremely talented competitor. Tiffani says that watching her performance on TV led her to examine large aspects of her behavior; she regrouped by working the line at a friend's seafood restaurant on Nantucket. Never lost in all the fussing and fighting was what a good cook she was. From all the challenges she won, to the close second-place finish, to her restaurant soon to open in San Francisco, Tiffani is a culinary force to be reckoned with. And she ultimately gained some measure of vindication as the hands-down champion of the *Top Chef Holiday Special*.

What was it like as the show started to become more popular?
Before the show aired, I actually stopped cooking and was waiting tables in Las Vegas. Then the episodes started and, week by week, it was like a monster taking over: week one, nobody recognized me. Week two, a few. By the end I was having a hard time making money because everybody wanted to talk instead of letting me serve food.

Were you surprised to find yourself as the villain of Season I?
It was hard for me because I had found an industry where, for the first time in my life, I felt so completely accepted. In the cooking world, being aggressive and strong and competitive are supposed to be desirable traits. I'd never had to apologize for that before.

You definitely took the heat off Stephen.
I was Stephen's get-out-of-jail-free card.

Why do you think you clashed with Dave so much?
I don't know. I thought he would be my homie because we're both gay. I really didn't know he disliked me so much until I watched the show. But we got together at the reunion and talked. You get to the point where you realize how ridiculous it is to hold on to all the bull@#$!. We're actually friends now.

Did you learn anything from your experience?
I really think that everyone, at some point, should watch themselves on TV. The easy thing to say is, "Oh, it was just the editing. They made me look that way." But you're responsible for how you act. Even if it's taken out of context.

What did you see that you didn't like?
I had an attitude about some things that was totally unnecessary. It's been a real struggle since the show, figuring out how to keep those parts of me that make me successful at what I do while adding a little more softness and openness. How do you open up to people while still keeping your edge?

KATIE LEE JOEL, SEASON I HOST "THE CULINARY WORLD DOESN'T REALLY CELEBRATE WOMEN YET, AND THAT HARDENS MANY PEOPLE IN THIS INDUSTRY. TIFFANI WATCHES OUT FOR HERSELF, AND THERE'S NOTHING WRONG WITH THAT. IT OBVIOUSLY TOOK HER A LONG WAY."

"I am just such a freak about food, and I love sharing."
DAVE

TOP STATS

Age
43

Hometown
Long Beach, CA

Former Job
Owner of a technical recruiting firm

Currently
Executive chef of Crave on 42nd in New York City and working to open his restaurant in Los Angeles

Philosophy
"Simple foods, but with flavor. I just like to make real food for real people."

Featured recipes
Panini, p. 95
Cubanos, p. 106
Mac and Cheese, p. 185
Lasagna, p. 196

Dave Martin

SEASON I
ELIMINATED: EPISODE II, "VEGAS FINALE: PART I"
WINS: 3 ELIMINATION CHALLENGES, 0 QUICKFIRES

It's probably fair to say that Dave was *Top Chef*'s first big surprise. Nobody would have predicted that the emotional, easily flustered chef with the bleached blond hair was going to make it to the final three.

On top of everything else, he was a late convert to professional cooking, having worked for years in Southern California's tech industry. But, with big flavors and homey ingredients, make it he did, setting off sparks and plenty of tears (mostly his own) along the way. The battle between Dave and Tiffani became the first great feud in the show's history, culminating in Dave showing up hungover, and possibly still drunk, to help out his nemesis in the finale. It's his priceless put-down, though, that will live on as the first and best catchphrase in the show's history: "I'm not your bitch, bitch."

Have you watched any of the subsequent seasons of *Top Chef*?

Not much. I'm busy. The last thing I want to do is watch a show I was on. But I'm really glad I was in Season I. There was a lot of disorganization, but it was original; it was fresh and fun. Nobody knew what to expect. Now they come in with a game plan, thinking they're going to become famous.

That's not what you thought?

I knew it was a good way to get exposed. But just because you're on a show doesn't mean you're going to be successful. You have to do the legwork. It's not magic. Harold has a restaurant, but you have to understand how hard he worked to put that in place.

How did the feud with Tiffani start?

She just bugged me. She was always telling me what to do. It gets annoying. I was sick and tired of it. But I think Tiffani has changed since the show. She had a lot of pent-up aggression and angst then. When we were down in Miami for the reunion, we had a totally different relationship. I think she's happier.

Were you aware of how famous the "bitch" line would be when you said it?

It just popped out. You can ask any of my friends: whatever I say is live and real.

Were you surprised by anything when you watched yourself?

There were some tics I wasn't aware I had. But that was just stress. Nervousness. As for the crying, I'm a really passionate person. And after a couple of weeks of everybody yelling, your nerves are shot.

Do you think there was a Dave in Season 2 or 3?

No! Are you kidding? Another Dave? There's no such thing!

TOM COLICCHIO, JUDGE "YOU ASK SOMEONE TO DO HIS SIGNATURE DISH, AND HE DOES ENCHILADAS? I WAS SHOCKED HE MADE IT AS FAR AS HE DID BASED ON WHAT HE MADE EARLY ON. THAT SAID, HE'S NOT A BAD COOK, AND HE HAS ENOUGH PASSION FOR TEN CHEFS. YOU'VE GOT TO ADMIRE THAT."

DAVE-ISMS!

To Tiffani: "You know, you're not saving a life, so it doesn't work for me."

About the sex shop challenge: "I went too literally with the bondage."

Looking for Stephen: "*Donde* Top Sommelier?"

Speculating on the finale: "I thought we were going to take a 20-mule team out to the Grand Canyon and get a Bunsen burner and a bow and arrow, and whatever you can catch you cook. And it's gotta be gourmet and it better look good."

About cooking with Tiffani: "I'm helping someone that I have little or no respect for. I'm drinking. It's the only way I can make it."

To Tiffani: "I'm not your bitch, bitch."

“It was nice for me to be able to educate my peers within this competition.”
STEPHEN

TOP STATS

Age
26

Hometown
Denver, CO

Currently
Opening Forté di Asprinio in Palm Beach and working as estate sommelier for the Livernano winery

Favorite style of wine
Champagne

Chef he most admires
Jean-Georges Vongerichten

Philosophy
“It's not about just the food or just the wine; it's about the experience.”

Featured recipes
Baby Manila Clams, p. 78
Corn Sopes, p. 103
Colorado Lamb, p. 110

Stephen Asprinio

SEASON I
ELIMINATED: EPISODE 8, "WEDDING BELL BLUES"
WINS: I ELIMINATION CHALLENGE, 2 QUICKFIRES

With his megamoussed hair and his tendency to address the rest of the world as though it was one big kindergarten class, Stephen Asprinio seemed almost immediately to get under his Season I competitors' skin.

But it was always clear that he knew his stuff—not only about his specialty, wine, but about food, too. And though he had bad moments, like his fight with Candice Kumai, he showed a surprisingly human side by helping Harold Dieterle with a dessert—and even delivered a heartfelt apology to Candice on the reunion show. Still, it's hard to get over those overly wide, under-the-chef's-jacket ties.

Was it difficult watching yourself on the show?
I was ashamed, in some ways, about how I came off—very abrasive, very intense in the wrong ways, like I was better than everybody else. At the same time, I know it was for the right reasons. For me it was about not accepting mediocrity, about not settling. It was about taking risks.

It was obvious that you were passionate.
It's true. I wanted to project that I really care, you know? I give a damn. I do wish they had shown a little more of my human side. At the end of the day, no matter what had happened, we would all get together and have a drink and start laughing. They didn't show me smiling too much. They let me smirk, but they didn't let me smile.

Yet Tiffani turned out to be the season's big villain.
We always knew she would be incredibly competitive. She was there to win. I was there more for the experience, not just for the $100,000. So I wasn't going to compromise any of my values. I have no interest now in being a chef.

You don't?
I'm a restaurateur now. I *hire* chefs. I'm looking for empire status; I want to be one of the most influential hospitality professionals in the U.S.

GAIL SIMMONS, JUDGE "I HATED STEPHEN THAT FIRST SEASON. HE WOULD STAND IN FRONT OF US WITH THAT SMIRK ON HIS FACE, LIKE HE KNEW EVERYTHING. I'VE SINCE FOUND OUT THAT HE'S REALLY A SWEET GUY. BUT BACK THEN, I WANTED TO JUST SLAP HIM."

POP THE CHAMPAGNE!

Whatever else you may have thought about Stephen, the man has chops when it comes to wine. His most impressive stunt involved running a dull champagne sabre down the length of a bottle of bubbly and popping the cork in a shower of foam. The trick, he admits now, looks more difficult than it is. In fact, anyone who doesn't mind spilling some suds can pull it off.

1. Carefully remove the wire cage around the cork.

2. Locate the seam of glass that runs from the top to the bottom of the bottle. This is where the two halves of the bottle are joined.

3. Take your sabre (in a pinch, a butter knife will do) and run it up the length of the seam, hitting the lip of the bottle's spout. The pressure of the bubbles within, combined with this sharp knock to the bottle's weakest point, will cause the top to fly off.

4. Spike up your hair like Archie and wear huge-knotted ties (optional).

Lee Anne Wong

SEASON I
ELIMINATED: EPISODE 9, "NAPA'S FINEST"
WINS: I ELIMINATION CHALLENGE, 3 QUICKFIRES

Of all the people behind the scenes of *Top Chef*—from executive producers to production assistants—none understands the show in quite the same way as Lee Anne Wong.

That's because before she was culinary producer—in charge of stocking the *Top Chef* pantry, buying equipment, budgeting time and money for challenges, and many other food-related tasks—Lee Anne was one of the strongest Season I competitors. She made it to fourth place, and her elimination kicked off one of the first grassroots campaigns of outrage: "There were 'Bring Back Lee Anne Wong' websites," she says. Also memorable was the tension between Lee Anne and Tiffani, made worse by the fact that, by the end, the two remaining female chefs had to share a room. Nowadays, says Bravo's Dave Serwatka, Lee Anne is one of the most valuable members of the *Top Chef* team. The only problem as far as Lee Anne is concerned is that she's not allowed to come back for reunion specials like the "4-Star All Stars Reunion." "I'm very competitive, and now I see them coming back and cooking for charity," she says. "I'm like, 'I want to play, too!'"

Do you get a kick out of watching the new contestants, now that you're on the other side of the camera?

I think it's funny because, the first few weeks, they don't know what's going on. And then they're just worn down. In order to make it through this competition, you need to have talent, you need to have an ego, and you definitely need to have a sense of humor.

Did you have a hard time living in the house?

It's a little bit crazy. You're living in a bubble. The only people you can talk to for thirty days are the other chefs, and you're trying to beat them for money. But I really loved and adored most of my fellow contestants.

When you say "most," you know the next question.

Tiffani and I buried the hatchet a long time ago. She's one of the most talented chefs I've ever seen. Girlfriend can cook. But at the time, we were sharing a room, and there was just so much negative energy coming from her. I couldn't even speak to her. And then when I lost to her I was really depressed for a while.

Did being on the show teach you anything?

In terms of cooking, I've learned to simplify enormously. What got me kicked off was trying to do too much with a lamb dish. That would never happen now. And it's helped me threefold in terms of handling challenges in my real job. Like, now I'll be in the weeds at work, with so much to do, and I break it down like I'm on the show: "You can do this in thirty minutes and then this in one hour."

Is there anything you regret?

Yeah. I regret putting so much stuff in my lamb dish! And I regret not being on a season where they send four people to the finale. Instead of being "in the final four," I was just "number four."

KATIE LEE JOEL, SEASON I HOST "IF I HAD HAD MY PICK, IT WOULD HAVE BEEN LEE ANNE AND HAROLD IN THE FINAL TWO."

"I love competing, and I'm sad to see any one of us go, but honestly I hope it's not me."
LEE ANNE

TOP STATS

Age
30

Hometown
New York, NY

Currently
Executive chef of event operations at the French Culinary Institute; culinary producer for *Top Chef*

Philosophy
"Food is sexy."

Featured recipes
Deep-Fried Oysters, p. 84
Corn Sopes, p. 103
Curry Chicken, p. 147

For more from Lee Anne, check out her blog, "The Wong Way to Cook," at BravoTV.com.

Miguel Morales

SEASON I
ELIMINATED: EPISODE 7, "RESTAURANT WARS"
WINS: 2 ELIMINATION CHALLENGES, 0 QUICKFIRES

Imagine this. It's spring 2006. You're at home in your living room, flipping through cable channels, and you decide to check out the new food show Bravo's been promoting.

Best Chef, or something like that. It started last week. So, you flip over and what do you see? A twenty-eight-year-old, Russian–Puerto Rican Jew, on the hefty side, wearing a beret, a red wig, and no shirt, feeding dessert to a dominatrix. Welcome to *Top Chef*! From his heavy New York accent and his eminently quotable put-downs to his tendency to pass gas, revealed on the first reunion special, there will never be another contestant quite like Miguel. Nor will there ever be a more perfect nickname: all hail Chunk le Funk!

How has it felt watching *Top Chef* grow into a phenomenon?
I think all of us from the first season feel like we were the best. We were there making history. It's been fun watching other people go through it. If you put a camera in front of someone, whether a professional or an amateur, everything changes. Not many people can pick up the ball and run with that. It's easy to sit at home and say, "Oh, yeah. I can do that!" It's a lot harder with thirty cameras in front of your face.

Where did the snake line come from?
Honestly, I didn't even remember that happening. I just remember being very upset at that moment and thinking, Man this is really getting to me. At a certain point, you get exhausted. And you're in a fishbowl. I remember going to sleep and seeing the camera guy there, and then waking up and seeing another camera guy in the same place. It's like, Whoa!

Are you a natural performer?
I guess you could say that. If you interviewed anybody I worked with, they'd tell you it was the Miguel show, 24/7. I really wanted to show that chefs don't always have to be standing there yelling and screaming. There are lots of ways to succeed. First and foremost, I'm a chef, but I'm also a personality.

How did you come up with your "sexy" outfit?
People thought it was a costume that Bravo gave me. When I was packing to go on the show, I saw a hat that my cousin, who works for the fire department, had given me. I thought, This might be good to spunk up the house someday. So I threw it in my bag. Then I realized it matched the inside of my coat. Everybody was trying to convince me to go nude. I actually came downstairs in my tighty-whitey briefs once, but by the time they got the camera, I was already back in my clothes.

If you don't mind my asking, what was with all the farting?
Oh, that's just lactose intolerance.

You're just a gassy guy?
I pass gas. Like every other human. And I like dairy and sweets. So, there you go.

"Chunk le Funk is ready for the challenge, baby."
MIGUEL

TOP STATS

Age
28

Hometown
New York, NY

Currently
Cooking at The Mandarin Oriental in New York City

Heard about *Top Chef*
While browsing Craigslist to "meet young ladies."

Philosophy
"Kitchen life is exhausting. You have to be partially sane and insane at the same time."

Featured recipes
Falafel, p. 190
Total Orgasm, p. 238

Ken Lee

"You either like me or you don't like me. I don't give a @#$."

BIO BITE

Packed his knives

Episode 1, "Who Deserves to Be Here?"

Calling Ken the show's first villain might be putting it too lightly—this guy was **just plain kooky.** From shouting in his sleep to screaming in the kitchen, Ken freaked out pretty much everyone. Without the cooking chops to back up his bluster, he quickly became the first *Top Chef* casualty.

Andrea Beaman

"My food will help move you. You'll have a nice B.M."

BIO BITE

Packed her knives

Episode 2, "Food of Love"; Episode 6, "Guess Who's Coming to Dinner"

Andrea is the only *Top Chef* contestant with the distinction of being eliminated twice. The judges might have been a little bored with her veggie-centric offerings, but **the fans loved her.**

Featured recipe

Quinoa Pilaf, p. 198

Brian Hill

"I cook for celebrities—people that can afford me, if you will."

BIO BITE

Packed his knives

Episode 3, "Nasty Delights"

Brian, personal chef to the rich and famous, started out as a foil to Ken—a calm, soothing voice of reason. It was quite a surprise, then, when he began **lusting after Candice** and when, with what seemed like good intentions, he decided that kids would love mushy, maple syrup–coated baby carrots. Even monkfish sounds better than that.

Featured recipe

Apple Crisp, p. 236

Cynthia Sestito

"My head hasn't been here. It was probably the first time in my life that I didn't want to deal with food."

BIO BITE

Packed her knives

Episode 3, "Nasty Delights"

Older and wiser than her rambunctious co-contestants, Cynthia seemed **perfectly at home in the kitchen**, casually chatting with Chef Laurent Manrique while others cowered in awe. To everyone's disappointment, though, her time on the show was cut short by a family illness.

Candice Kumai

"I am trying to steer out of the modeling world and go into the culinary world."

BIO BITE

Packed her knives

Episode 4, "Food on the Fly"

Candice, a young, charming culinary student and model, seemed a little out of her element in such a high-level, cutthroat contest. Still, she held her own in a classic fight with Stephen, bringing the bigheaded "educator" down to size with **seven perfect words**: "You're a tool and a douche bag."

Lisa Parks

"I'm a go-getter. I'm very aggressive when I go after something."

BIO BITE

Packed her knives

Episode 5, "Blind Confusion"

Lisa is a lawyer and a mother as well as a cook, and it was that combination of **logic, leadership, and culinary chops** that helped her shine in challenges like serving lunch to a gym full of kids. Handing out street food on a Mission District corner was a different story, though. Next time, keep track of the jicama!

Featured recipe

Fruit Kabobs, p. 44

Quickfire Madness

Everybody loves a nice, solid main course—a classic roast, say, or chicken stew. But who doesn't really look forward with more anticipation to an exciting appetizer? Something flashy, surprising, and experimental?

In the *Top Chef* universe, the Elimination Challenges are a little like those main courses, and the appetizers are the Quickfires—those twisted, sometimes cruel little tests that demand brilliance and creativity at breathtaking speed. Here are some of our favorites.

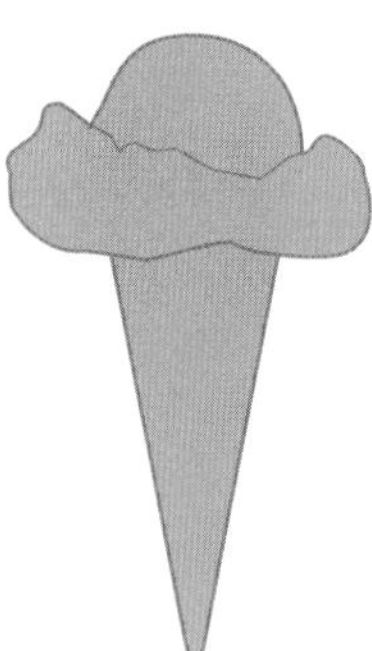

Season 2, Episode 3

Create an original ice cream flavor.

HIGHLIGHT: Cliff's Marshmallow and Cookie Ice Cream (see page 234).

LOWLIGHT: Casey's spicy sriracha ice cream. "It was just wrong," says guest judge Govind Armstrong.

Season 3, Episode 10

Create a dish using only $10 worth of products from an assigned supermarket aisle.

HIGHLIGHT: Hung's whacked-out Technicolor magic cereal village.

LOWLIGHT: Howie commits the one unspeakable *Top Chef* crime: he turns in nothing at all.

Season 1, Episode 1

Work the line at chef Hubert Keller's Fleur de Lys restaurant for 30 minutes.

HIGHLIGHT: Lee Anne leaps to the lead by showing off her line skills while crazy Ken begins his quick disintegration by sticking a finger in his sauce.

LOWLIGHT: An inauspicious debut for eventual champion Harold, who is quickly booted.

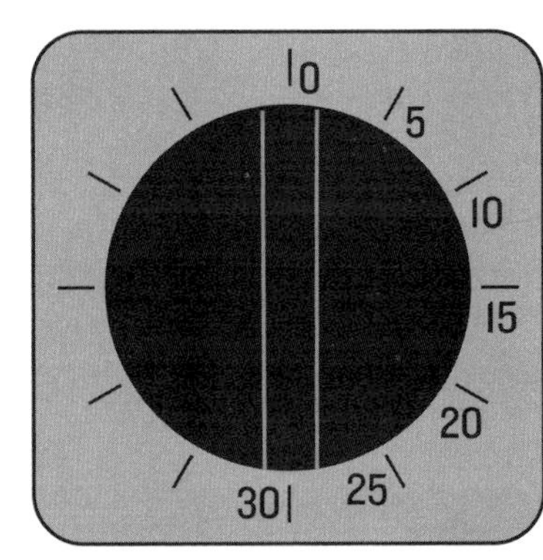

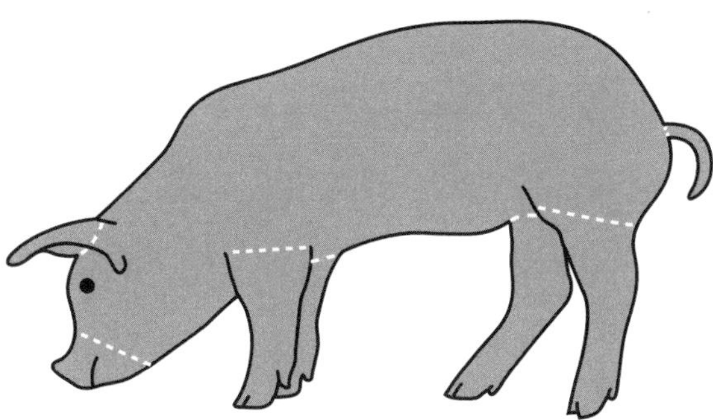

Season 2, Episode 5

Create a dish using offal, the leftover parts of animals.

HIGHLIGHT: Sam's Sweetbread and Scallion Beignets, flavored with Chinese five-spice, and a sweet soy broth. (See page 96.) Guest judge Michelle Bernstein admits she still dreams of this dish.

LOWLIGHT: Elia's unrinsed kidneys. Says Bernstein: "They tasted like pee."

Season 3, Episode 6

Culinary Bee

HIGHLIGHT: Joey, flustered by Padma "looking all sexy today," fails to identify taro root.

LOWLIGHT: Hung, feeling cocky, identifies celery seed as anise seed before even tasting it.

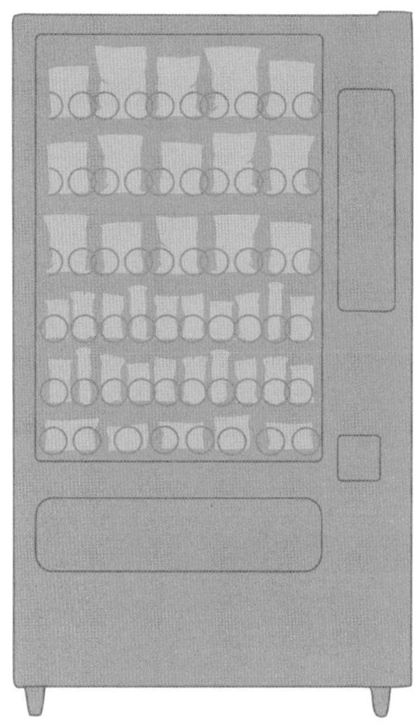

Season 2, Episode 4

Using $10 of ingredients from a vending machine, create an *amuse-bouche*.

HIGHLIGHT: Carlos somehow pulls off a Sunflower Seed and Carrot Loaf with Cilantro, Sesame Oil, and Squirt®. (See page 191.)

LOWLIGHT: A bent Cheeto® sticking out of a piece of chocolate gives us a glimpse into the dark recesses of Michael's mind.

Appetizers and Small Plates

78

83

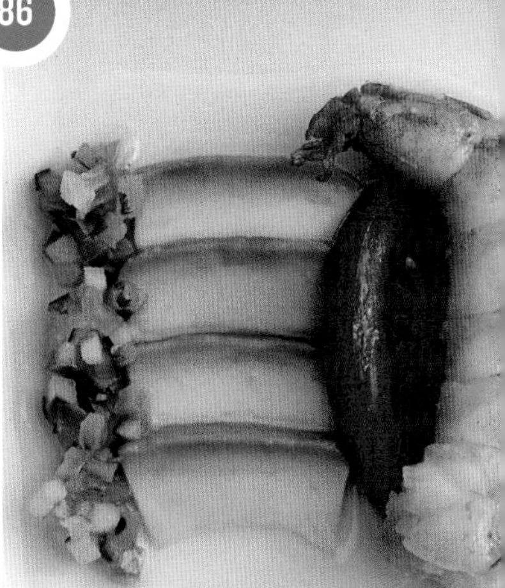
86

Beef Carpaccio
with Watercress, Fried Capers, and Shiitake Broth

CHEF: Casey
SEASON 3, EPISODE 10
ELIMINATION CHALLENGE: Cater an ultraexclusive party thrown by Pure nightclub.

Shiitake Broth:
1 teaspoon olive oil
1 shallot, chopped
1 garlic clove, chopped
Clean trimmings from 2 pounds shiitake mushrooms (about 5 ounces)
1 ½ cups low-sodium chicken stock
Salt

Mayonnaise:
1 large egg
1 teaspoon fresh lemon juice
Grated zest of ½ lemon
1 cup olive oil
Salt

Parsley Sauce:
1 teaspoon soy sauce, or more to taste
1 cup packed fresh flat-leaf parsley leaves
1 cup packed fresh spinach leaves
¼ cup olive oil

To Serve:
1 pound beef sirloin steak with some marbling
1 cup watercress leaves
2 tablespoons capers, fried
Coarse sea salt
1 small package crisp flatbread chips

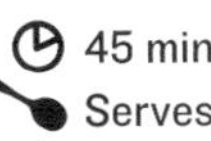

45 minutes
Serves 15 to 20
Winner

For the Shiitake Broth:

In a small saucepan, heat the oil over medium heat. Add the shallot, garlic, and mushroom trimmings; sauté for about 3 minutes, until just beginning to soften. Add the stock and bring to a boil. Reduce the heat and simmer for 20 minutes. Season with salt to taste.

For the Mayonnaise:

Put the egg and the lemon juice and zest in a blender and blend on high speed until combined. With the motor running, add the oil in a thin stream through the hole in the lid. Season with salt to taste.

For the Parsley Sauce:

Put all the ingredients in a mini food processor and process to combine, stopping the motor and scraping down the sides once or twice. Add more soy sauce if necessary.

To Serve:

1. Using a very sharp knife, slice the beef paper-thin. Lay each slice flat and put 1 watercress leaf in the center. Top with a small dollop of the mayonnaise and roll the beef into a cone shape.
2. Spoon some broth into 15 to 20 Chinese soupspoons. Place the rolled beef in the broth, spoon a bit of the parsley sauce over the beef, and garnish with capers. Sprinkle lightly with sea salt. Serve immediately with flatbread chips.

HOW TO:
Fry a Caper

To fry capers, rinse them well and pat dry with paper towels. In a small saucepan, heat about 1 inch of vegetable oil to 375°F, then add the capers. Fry for about 15 seconds, until crisp and browned. Remove with a slotted spoon and transfer to paper towels to drain.

Seared Scallops
with Purslane and Marinated Grapes

CHEF: Dale
SEASON 3, EPISODE 14
ELIMINATION CHALLENGE: Cook the best meal of your life.

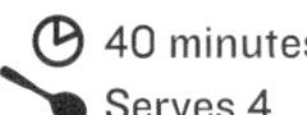

40 minutes
Serves 4

⅓ cup extra-virgin olive oil
1 tablespoon minced fresh tarragon
2 tablespoons rice vinegar
1 ½ teaspoons grated lemon zest
Salt and freshly ground black pepper
½ cup halved white grapes
1 small fennel bulb, trimmed
4 U/10 dry-pack sea scallops
3 tablespoons olive oil
½ cup purslane, thick stems removed
About 2 tablespoons freeze-dried sweet corn
Fresh tarragon sprigs for garnish

1. In a medium bowl, combine the ⅓ cup extra-virgin olive oil, minced tarragon, vinegar, and lemon zest. Season generously with salt and pepper to taste and add the grapes, tossing to coat them with the marinade. Set aside.
2. Cut the fennel in half lengthwise and remove the tough inner core. Thinly shave the fennel using a mandoline or a very sharp knife. Set aside.
3. Remove the small side muscle from each scallop. Rinse the scallops under cold water and pat dry. Lightly season on both sides with salt and pepper.
4. In a medium sauté pan or skillet, heat the oil over high heat. Add the scallops and cook without turning for about 3 minutes, until crisp and well browned on the bottom. Using a thin metal spatula, turn the scallops over and cook for 2 to 3 minutes on the second side, until browned on the bottom but still slightly translucent in the center. Transfer to a plate.
5. Using a slotted spoon, remove the grapes from the marinade and toss them with the fennel and purslane; spoon some of the marinade over the salad and toss to coat. Taste and add more of the marinade or salt and pepper as necessary. Divide the salad among 4 serving plates. Place 1 scallop on top of each salad and garnish with the corn and tarragon sprigs. Serve immediately.

WHAT ARE . . .
Sea Scallops?

Sea scallops are much larger than the more common bay scallops—"U/10" means that there are fewer than 10 scallops per pound.

ROCCO DISPIRITO, CHEF AND RESTAURATEUR, GUEST JUDGE "DALE'S DISH WAS FRIGGIN' AMAZING."

Tuna Tartare

with Niçoise Olives, White Asparagus, and Egg Vinaigrette

CHEF: Hung
SEASON 3, EPISODE 8
ELIMINATION CHALLENGE: Turn an empty space into a restaurant in 24 hours.

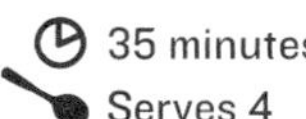

35 minutes
Serves 4

Tuna:
8 ounces top-quality tuna steak, diced
1 tablespoon chopped fresh chives
Large pinch of paprika
Salt and freshly ground black pepper

Egg Vinaigrette:
1 large hard-boiled egg, finely chopped
2 tablespoons mayonnaise
1 ½ tablespoons sherry vinegar
½ teaspoon sugar
½ teaspoon salt

White Asparagus:
½ bunch white asparagus, tips only
1 small shallot, minced
1 tablespoon sherry vinegar
Salt and freshly ground black pepper
3 tablespoons extra-virgin olive oil

To Serve:
6 black Niçoise olives, pitted and finely chopped
Large pinch of paprika
4 slices toasted brioche

For the Tuna:

In a medium bowl, toss together the tuna, chives, paprika, and salt and pepper to taste.

For the Egg Vinaigrette:

In a small bowl, combine all the ingredients.

For the White Asparagus:

1. In a small saucepan of boiling water, blanch the asparagus for 30 seconds to 1 minute, until just tender. Drain and transfer to a bowl of ice water to cool. Drain.
2. In a small bowl, whisk together the shallot, vinegar, and salt and pepper to taste. Add the oil in a thin stream and whisk to combine.
3. Add the asparagus and toss to coat with the dressing.

To Serve:

On each of 4 serving plates, make a small pile of the olives. Top with the tuna mixture and spoon some of the egg vinaigrette next to the tuna. Place a few asparagus tips on the plate. Sprinkle each serving with a bit of paprika and set a slice of toasted brioche on each plate. Serve immediately.

"This was very, very delicate and subtle. A smart thing to do if you have Daniel Boulud sitting in your restaurant."
TED ALLEN, JUDGE

DANIEL BOULUD, CHEF AND RESTAURATEUR, GUEST JUDGE "I THINK IT'S A REAL BISTRO DISH, A BEAUTIFUL PLATE."

Watermelon and Tomato Trio

Watermelon Steak, Tomato Salad, and Watermelon Refresher

CHEF: Marcel
SEASON 2, EPISODE 7
QUICKFIRE CHALLENGE: Create an uncooked entrée out of farmers' market produce.

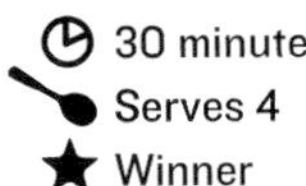

30 minutes
Serves 4
Winner

"If you buy the right ingredients, you don't really need to cook them; they taste really good as they are."
MARCEL

1 small seedless watermelon
Salt
1 large heirloom tomato
1 pint cherry tomatoes
Pinch of sugar, or more to taste
2 tablespoons extra-virgin olive oil
Freshly ground black pepper
1 tablespoon champagne vinegar, or more to taste
2 large sprigs opal basil, cut into chiffonade, plus small sprigs for garnish
Nasturtium leaves for garnish
Bee pollen for garnish
Fleur de sel

1. Using a sharp knife, cut the ends off the watermelon and stand it upright. Cut all of the rind off the watermelon, leaving the flesh in one piece. Cut crosswise into four 1½-inch-thick rounds. Using a biscuit cutter or another 1½- to 2-inch-diameter round cutter, cut a "steak" from the center of each slice. Season the steaks with salt and put one on each of 4 serving plates; set aside in the refrigerator to chill.
2. Cut the ends off the large tomato and save. Cut the tomato into 4 slices. Place 1 tomato round on top of each watermelon steak.
3. In a blender, puree 2 cups of the remaining watermelon flesh with the heirloom tomato trimmings and ¾ cup of the cherry tomatoes. Season to taste with salt and sugar, then pour the liquid through a fine-mesh sieve into a 2-cup measure.
4. Return half of the liquid to the blender and add the oil and salt and pepper to taste. (Put the other half in the refrigerator to chill.) Blend to combine, then add the vinegar and blend again. Taste the dressing and add more salt or vinegar as necessary.
5. Cut the remaining cherry tomatoes in half and put them in a medium bowl with the chiffonade of basil and enough of the dressing to coat the tomatoes. Toss together well, then divide the cherry tomato salad among the 4 serving plates. Garnish with nasturtium leaves, opal basil sprigs, and bee pollen. Sprinkle with fleur de sel.
6. Pour the reserved watermelon-tomato puree into 4 small glasses or cups and serve alongside the watermelon steaks and salad.

Ham and Cheese Mini Quiches
with Pesto

CHEF: Frank
SEASON 2, EPISODE 4
QUICKFIRE CHALLENGE: Create an amuse-bouche using ingredients from a vending machine.

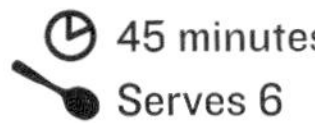

45 minutes
Serves 6

Ham and Cheese Quiche:
Unsalted butter for the muffin tin
Six 1 ½-inch toast rounds or crostini
2 large eggs
2 tablespoons heavy cream
Salt and freshly ground black pepper
2 slices ham, diced
2 slices Swiss cheese, diced

Pesto:
1 large garlic clove
¼ cup pine nuts
⅓ cup coarsely grated Parmesan cheese
Salt and freshly ground black pepper
1 ½ cups loosely packed fresh basil
⅓ cup extra-virgin olive oil

For the Ham and Cheese Quiche:

1. Preheat the oven to 350°F. Butter a 6-hole muffin tin and place the toast rounds in the muffin holes.
2. In a large bowl, whisk together the eggs and cream. Season with salt and pepper to taste and add the ham and cheese. Divide the batter among the muffin holes and bake until the quiches are just set in the middle, 12 to 15 minutes. Loosen the sides of the quiches with a butter knife, then invert the pan to release the quiches.

For the Pesto:

With a food processor running, drop the garlic through the feed tube to mince. Stop the motor and add the pine nuts, cheese, salt and pepper to taste, and basil. Process until finely chopped, then, with the motor running, slowly add the oil in a thin stream through the hole in the lid, processing until incorporated. Transfer to a bowl.

To Serve:

Place the quiches on serving plates and top with the pesto. Serve immediately.

HOW TO:
Make the Perfect Quiche

Though this recipe is easy to pull off, some attempts at making quiche can result in an overdone or soggy mess (just ask Frank). Follow these rules and you'll enjoy your quiche just as the French have for the past 500 years.

1. Fully prebake your crust—make sure it's crisp so your final product stays crisp.

2. Do not overcook—overcooking will turn your eggs into rubber, so watch your quiche carefully. When it's done, the center should still be a bit liquidy. The eggs will continue to set as they cool.

3. Cool properly—always cool on a wire rack to help prevent condensation from gathering around the bottom, avoiding the dreaded soggy quiche.

4. Don't skimp on ingredients—quiche is supposed to be rich and creamy. Make it with whole milk and cream.

Braised Pork Shoulder
with Tomato Marmalade

CHEFS: Sam, Ilan, Marcel, Betty (Orange Team)
SEASON 2, EPISODE 8
ELIMINATION CHALLENGE: Cater a holiday party for *Los Angeles* magazine.

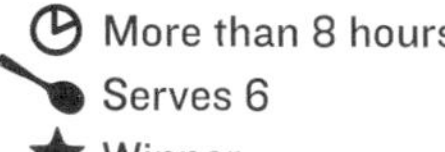

More than 8 hours
Serves 6
Winner

Pork:
One 3- to 5-pound pork shoulder roast
Salt and freshly ground black pepper
3 tablespoons olive oil
1 carrot, peeled and diced
2 celery ribs, diced
1 onion, diced
4 garlic cloves, minced
1 tablespoon Chinese five-spice powder
½ cup fresh orange juice
1 cup red wine vinegar
1 cup demi-glace or beef stock

Tomato Marmalade:
1 pint cherry tomatoes, halved
½ cup sugar
⅓ cup sherry vinegar
2 garlic cloves, finely chopped
2 tablespoons chopped fresh basil
1 scallion, thinly sliced
1 teaspoon capers, drained
1 teaspoon red pepper flakes

To Serve:
24 three-inch round slices bread; or 12 small dinner rolls, split in half

For the Pork:

1. Preheat the oven to 200°F. Generously season the pork with salt and pepper.
2. In a large, nonreactive, ovenproof pot with a tight-fitting lid, heat the oil over high heat. Add the pork and cook until well browned on all sides, about 10 minutes total.
3. Remove the pork from the pot and set aside. Add the carrot, celery, onion, garlic, and five-spice powder to the pot. Stir well to combine and cook over medium heat until the vegetables have softened and are beginning to brown, about 8 minutes.
4. In a medium bowl, combine the orange juice, vinegar, and demi-glace.
5. Place the pork on top of the vegetables and pour the orange juice mixture on top. Cover the pot and put it in the oven.
6. Cook for 8 to 10 hours, until the pork is falling apart and very tender. Remove from the oven. Using tongs, remove the pork from the cooking juices and let cool until warm. Shred the meat using your fingers or a fork. Spoon some of the cooking juices over the meat and season with salt and pepper to taste.

For the Tomato Marmalade:

1. In a medium saucepan, combine the tomatoes and sugar. Place over medium heat and cook, stirring frequently, until the sugar is dissolved.
2. Add the vinegar, garlic, basil, scallion, capers, and red pepper flakes. Bring to a brisk simmer and cook, stirring frequently, for about 20 minutes, until the marmalade is syrupy and thick. Season with salt and pepper to taste and remove from the heat.

To Serve:

1. Put the bread rounds on a baking sheet and toast them under the broiler or grill them lightly.
2. Pile the pork onto the toasts. Top each with a bit of the marmalade and serve.

WHAT IS . . .
Braising

Slow cooking with a little liquid in a covered pot, braising can bring out the tenderness in the toughest cuts of meat. Steady heat breaks down connective tissue while the meat and bone release their deepest, richest flavors. The key points are to brown the meat before braising and then keep a lid on tight to seal in the cooking liquid.

Poached Baby Manila Clams
over Grilled Sea Beans

CHEF: Stephen
SEASON 1, EPISODE 6
QUICKFIRE CHALLENGE: Create an appetizer using limited ingredients Ted Allen preselects.

30 minutes
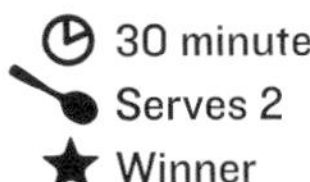
Serves 2
Winner

WHAT ARE . . .
Maroon Carrots and Marcona Almonds?

Maroon carrots are a sweet variety with a maroon or purple skin and orange flesh. Your local farmers' market or specialty grocer is your best bet for finding them.

Marcona almonds (pronounced "mar-SO-nah") come from Spain and are rounder, softer, and sweeter than typical almonds. You'll find these at a specialty grocer as well.

Juice of 1 maroon carrot
1 teaspoon fresh ginger juice
6 sea beans
6 baby Manila clams, scrubbed
1 teaspoon ground Marcona almonds
2 pinches of chili powder
2 pinches of sea salt
6 fresh cilantro leaves

1. In a small saucepan, combine the carrot juice with the ginger juice and place over medium-high heat. Cook, stirring, until reduced to a syrup, about 2 minutes. Watch carefully, as reducing a small quantity goes very quickly. Pour into a small bowl and set aside.
2. To grill the sea beans, heat a lightly greased grill pan over medium heat until hot. Add the beans and cook until lightly browned, 2 to 3 minutes. Remove from the heat and set aside.
3. Place a small amount of water in a medium saucepan and bring to a boil. Add the clams, reduce the heat to a simmer, cover, and cook until the clams open, about 2 minutes. Discard any unopened clams.
4. Drain the clams, remove them from their shells, and pat dry with paper towels.
5. Sauce the plates decoratively with the carrot reduction. Arrange the clams over the sea beans on the plates and dust each plate with the ground almonds, chili powder, and salt. Top with the cilantro leaves and serve immediately.

STEPHEN "MY STYLE OF CUISINE IS KIND OF OUTSIDE THE BOUNDARIES, TAKING DIFFERENT FLAVOR COMBINATIONS THAT TRADITIONALLY AREN'T USED."

Baked Escargot in Their Shells

CHEF: Ilan
SEASON 2, EPISODE 1
ELIMINATION CHALLENGE: Prepare a dish using all the ingredients in a closed crate.

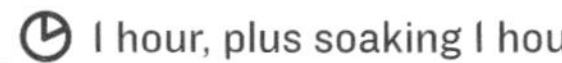

1 hour, plus soaking 1 hour
Serves 4
Winner

"It was tight, clean, and Ilan should be damn proud of it."
CLIFF

12 snails in their shells
2 tablespoons unsalted butter
1 shallot, finely chopped
6 garlic cloves, finely chopped
2 canned artichoke hearts, drained and finely chopped
¼ cup finely chopped cocktail peanuts
Salt and freshly ground black pepper
¾ cup milk
4 slices American cheese, finely chopped
1 russet potato, peeled and cut into large chunks

1. Soak the snails in enough water to cover for 1 hour, stirring occasionally and changing the water every 15 minutes. Drain.
2. Put the snails in a medium saucepan and pour in fresh water to cover. Place over medium-high heat and bring to a boil. Reduce the heat and simmer for 5 minutes, or until you can pull a snail from its shell by pricking it with a pin. Drain, cool slightly, then remove all the snails from their shells and reserve the shells. Finely chop the snails.
3. Preheat the oven to 400°F.
4. Heat 1 tablespoon of the butter in a large skillet over medium heat. Add the shallot, 5 of the garlic cloves, the artichokes, and snails and sauté until softened, about 5 minutes. Add the peanuts and cook until golden, about 5 minutes more. Season with salt and pepper to taste.
5. Put the milk in a small saucepan over medium heat, add the remaining garlic clove, and season with salt. Bring just to a boil, then add half of the cheese. Whisk until the cheese is melted, then remove from the heat.
6. Meanwhile, place the potato in a medium pot filled with water and add salt. Place over medium-high heat, bring to a boil, then lower the heat and simmer for about 15 minutes, or until tender when pierced with a fork. Drain and place in a large bowl. Mash the potato and, as it starts to get nice and fluffy, fold in the sautéed snail mixture along with about ¼ cup of the milk-cheese mixture, enough to make the potatoes creamy.
7. Stuff the potato-snail mixture into the snail shells (you can scoop any remaining filling alongside) and bake for 15 minutes, or until bubbly.
8. While the snails are in the oven, return the saucepan with the milk and cheese to low heat. Add the remaining 1 tablespoon butter and the remaining cheese, whisking until the cheese melts.
9. Pour the cheese sauce on top of the snails and serve piping hot.

TOM COLICCHIO, HEAD JUDGE "HE MADE THE INGREDIENTS BETTER BY PUTTING THEM TOGETHER."

Morcilla and Squid Lau Lau

CHEF: Ilan
SEASON 2, EPISODE 12
ELIMINATION CHALLENGE: Rethink two classic Hawaiian dishes.

- 2 tablespoons salt, plus more to taste
- 4 taro leaves
- 1 tablespoon extra-virgin olive oil
- 1 onion, diced
- 2 dried morcilla sausages, cut into ¼-inch cubes
- ½ teaspoon smoked Spanish paprika, or more to taste
- Freshly ground black pepper
- 1 large banana leaf
- 2 large squid, bodies only, cleaned and cut into ¼-inch rings

2 hours, 30 minutes
Serves 4
Winner

1. Fill a large pot with water and 2 tablespoons salt. Add the taro leaves. Bring to a boil and cook for 2 hours. Drain well. Set aside and let the leaves cool to room temperature. Taro leaves must be cooked for at least 2 hours, to cook out toxins that may cause an allergic reaction in the throat.
2. In a large skillet, heat the oil over medium-high heat. Add the onion and cook until soft, about 5 minutes. Add the sausage and reduce the heat to low. Cook until the sausage is beginning to soften, about 15 minutes. Add the smoked paprika and stir to combine. Season with salt, pepper, and more smoked paprika to taste—the mixture should be very highly seasoned, as it will mellow as it's grilled.
3. Preheat a charcoal grill and set the grate about 8 inches above the coals.
4. On a work surface, spread out the banana leaf and cut it into 4 pieces, each about 6 by 10 inches. Divide the onion and sausage mixture among the banana leaves. Top with the squid rings. Top each portion with a cooked taro leaf. Wrap each bundle: fold the long sides over the filling, then fold the ends up. Secure with toothpicks or tie the bundles with string like a package.
5. When the flames have died down and the coals are white, put the bundles on the grill, sausage side down. Cover the grill and cook for 5 minutes. Remove from the grill and serve immediately, letting your guests unwrap the bundles at the table.

WHAT ARE . . .

Lau Lau and Morcilla?

Lau lau (pronounced "LAOW-LAOW") is a Hawaiian dish typically consisting of pork and fish wrapped in banana leaves and steamed or grilled.

Morcilla (pronounced "more-SEE-yah") is a Spanish blood sausage, usually made with pork and rice. You can use fresh morcilla if dried is unavailable.

TOM COLICCHIO, HEAD JUDGE "IF THE SPANISH HAD ARRIVED 300 YEARS AGO TO THIS ISLAND AND BROUGHT THEIR CUISINE, THIS WOULD HAVE BEEN A PERFECT MARRIAGE OF THE TWO CULTURES. I REALLY, REALLY ENJOYED THAT DISH."

Hamachi Poke
with Pineapple Poi and Taro Chips

CHEF: Marcel
SEASON 2, EPISODE 12
QUICKFIRE CHALLENGE: Rethink two classic Hawaiian dishes.

50 minutes, plus marinating 1 hour
Serves 6
Winner

Hamachi Poke:

- 2 tablespoons extra-virgin olive oil
- 2 tablespoons sake
- 2 tablespoons mirin
- 3 tablespoons fresh lemon juice
- 1 teaspoon grated fresh ginger
- 1 tablespoon finely chopped Maui or other white onion
- Sea salt (preferably Hawaiian)
- Freshly ground black pepper
- 1 pound sashimi-grade hamachi (yellowtail), skin and excess fat removed and cut into ½-inch cubes (to yield about 2 cups)
- ¼ cup chopped sea beans

Pineapple Poi:

- 2 teaspoons xanthan gum
- 4 cups fresh pineapple chunks

Taro Chips:

- 1 small taro root
- Vegetable oil for frying
- Salt

For the Hamachi Poke:

1. In a medium nonreactive bowl, combine the oil, sake, mirin, lemon juice, ginger, and onion. Whisk together. Season with salt and pepper to taste (keeping in mind that the sea beans will be salty).
2. Add the hamachi and sea beans. Gently toss with a rubber spatula to completely coat the fish and sea beans with the marinade. Cover and refrigerate for at least 1 hour for the flavors to combine while you make the pineapple poi and taro chips.

For the Pineapple Poi:

1. Place ¼ cup water in a blender, followed by the xanthan gum. Add the pineapple chunks and blend on high speed until the pineapple is pureed and the mixture is smooth with a slightly sticky consistency.
2. Transfer to a container, cover, and refrigerate until ready to use.

For the Taro Chips:

1. Peel the taro root and slice very thinly with a sharp knife or mandoline. Place the slices in a large bowl of cold water to keep them from discoloring.
2. In a large heavy pot, heat about 3 inches of oil to 350°F.
3. Drain the taro slices and pat dry completely. Add the slices to the hot oil in batches, being careful not to overcrowd the pot. Fry until crisp and lightly golden, about 2 minutes. Remove with a slotted spoon and transfer to paper towels to drain. Sprinkle with salt. Cool completely before serving.

To Serve:

Place large spoonfuls of the pineapple poi on serving dishes. Using a slotted spoon, ladle the hamachi poke over the pineapple and sprinkle with sea salt. Place a couple of taro chips alongside.

WHAT ARE . . . Poke and Poi?

Poke (pronounced "PO-keh") is a Hawaiian fish salad, usually raw, served as an appetizer.

Poi (pronounced "POY") is traditionally made of taro root cooked and pounded to a sticky paste. Here the "poi" is made with pineapple, with xanthan gum giving it its sticky quality, and the taro is made into a chip served alongside.

Deep-Fried Oysters
with Lemon Cream

CHEF: Lee Anne
SEASON 1, EPISODE 6
QUICKFIRE CHALLENGE: Create an appetizer using the limited ingredients Ted Allen preselects.

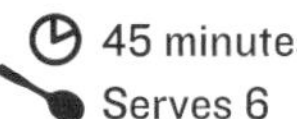

45 minutes
Serves 6

"It's a classic, but you've given it a nice twist. Are you trying to seduce me?"

TED ALLEN, GUEST JUDGE

18 fresh oysters
2 cups heavy cream
1 ½ teaspoons lemon juice, or to taste
1 ½ teaspoons grated lemon zest
1 tablespoon grated Parmesan cheese
Salt and freshly ground white pepper
4 slices bacon
1 plum tomato, peeled, cored, and finely diced
½ shallot, finely minced
3 tablespoons diced sea beans
2 teaspoons finely minced fresh flat-leaf parsley
1 teaspoon extra-virgin olive oil
Vegetable oil for frying
¾ cup all-purpose flour
1 cup club soda
Coarse salt for serving

1. Shuck the oysters, removing them completely from their shells into a bowl, along with their juices. Reserve the bottom halves of the oyster shells and rinse under hot water to clean. Dry the shells and set aside. Strain the oyster liquid through a fine-mesh sieve and set aside. Refrigerate the oysters, covered, until ready to fry.
2. In a small saucepan, heat the cream over medium heat and bring to a simmer. Reduce the heat to medium-low and simmer until the cream is reduced by about two-thirds, about 1 hour. Remove from the heat, strain if a skin forms on the surface of the cream, and return to the pan. Add the lemon juice, lemon zest, and cheese. Season with salt and white pepper to taste. Cover and set aside until ready to serve. Gently reheat before serving if needed.
3. Put the bacon in a medium skillet over medium heat. Cook until crisp on both sides, about 5 minutes. Transfer to paper towels to drain and cool slightly, then crumble the bacon. Set aside until ready to serve.
4. In a small bowl, combine the tomato, shallot, sea beans, and parsley. Add the extra-virgin oil and stir to coat.
5. In a medium, heavy pot, heat 2 to 3 inches of vegetable oil over medium-high heat to 375°F. Put the flour in a medium bowl and whisk in just enough club soda to make a fairly smooth paste (a few lumps are OK), then add the remaining club soda.
6. One at a time, dip the oysters into the batter, letting excess drip off. Then, working in small batches, gently place the oysters in the oil. Fry until the oysters are puffed and golden brown, about 30 seconds. Remove with a slotted spoon and transfer to paper towels to drain. Sprinkle with salt.
7. To serve, form 3 small mounds of coarse salt on each of 6 serving plates to make little platforms for the oysters. Moisten with a little water and place the reserved oyster shells on the mounds. Place a fried oyster in each shell and spoon a teaspoon of the warm lemon cream over each one. Top with the tomato mixture and sprinkle with the crumbled bacon. Serve immediately.

Hama Hama Oysters with Mango
and Split Prawns, Hamachi, and Daikon

CHEF: Cliff
SEASON 2, EPISODE 2
QUICKFIRE CHALLENGE: Create a sushi dish for master sushi chef Hiroshi Shima.

Hama Hama Oysters with Mango:
4 hama hama oysters
½ teaspoon soy sauce
½ teaspoon mirin
1 teaspoon fresh lime juice
1 tablespoon diced mango
½ teaspoon minced jalapeño chile
1 teaspoon minced shiso leaves

Split Prawns, Hamachi, and Daikon:
1 teaspoon soy sauce
1 teaspoon mirin
½ teaspoon sugar
¼ teaspoon fresh ginger juice
1 teaspoon fresh lime juice
¼ cup very thinly sliced daikon radish
2 prawns (jumbo shrimp), peeled, deveined, and butterflied
Salt
3 ounces sashimi-grade hamachi, thinly sliced

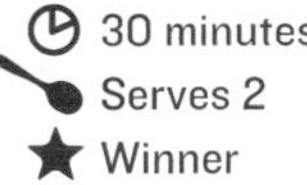
30 minutes
Serves 2
Winner

For the Hama Hama Oysters with Mango:

1. Shuck the oysters into a bowl and discard the top shells. Scrub the bottom shells and set aside on 2 plates. (See page 84, step 1.)
2. In a small bowl, combine the soy sauce, mirin, lime juice, mango, jalapeño, and shiso leaves. Put the oysters with their juice in the mixture. Set aside for 5 minutes to marinate.
3. Spoon the oysters with their marinade onto the reserved shells.

For the Split Prawns, Hamachi, and Daikon:

1. In a small bowl, combine the soy sauce, mirin, sugar, ginger juice, and lime juice. Whisk to dissolve the sugar. Add the daikon and set aside for 5 minutes to marinate, then drain and squeeze out excess liquid.
2. Fill a medium bowl with ice water and bring a small saucepan of water to a boil. Sprinkle the prawns with salt, add salt to the water, and poach the prawns for 2 to 5 minutes, or until just cooked through. Drain, then transfer to the ice-water bath, drain again, and pat dry.
3. Divide the hamachi between 2 serving plates, top with the daikon, and place a prawn on top. Serve alongside the oysters.

Note:

Hama hama oysters are a firm and mild variety found in Washington State; if you can't find them, any type of oyster can be substituted.

HOW TO:
Choose an Oyster

Because oysters thrive in a variety of temperatures, they are found on both coasts: Atlantic oysters from Maine to Florida, and Pacific oysters from Washington to California. A third type, Olympia, are found in Washington's Puget Sound. The flat, or Belon, oyster, native to Europe, is now farmed in the United States.

So how do you choose? If you live on a coast, choose an oyster native to your region. Also consider that the taste of oysters is determined by where and how they grow. Atlantic oysters tend to be briny and light with a firm flesh. Pacific oysters are creamier and smoother in flavor. The Olympia oyster, a tiny one, is often salty with a metallic taste. The flat oyster, prized for its outstanding flavor, can be quite pricey. Do a little taste-testing and you'll come to recognize your favorites.

HIROSHI SHIMA, SUSHI CHEF, GUEST JUDGE "EVEN WITH THE MANGO, THE OYSTERS STILL HAD THE FLAVOR OF THE OCEAN."

Olive Oil–Poached Shrimp

with Avocado and Cucumber, Lime, and Grilled Pepper Salad

CHEF: Lia
SEASON 3, EPISODE 4
ELIMINATION CHALLENGE: In teams of three, create a trio of one ingredient.

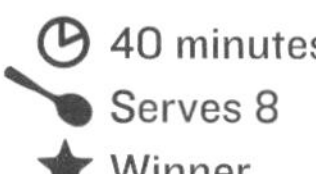

40 minutes
Serves 8
Winner

"You don't get shrimp poached in olive oil every day. I think this was a nice way to handle it."
TED ALLEN, JUDGE

2 tablespoons coriander seeds, crushed
1 tablespoon red pepper flakes
One 750-ml bottle olive oil
1 lime
½ cup sugar
1½ teaspoons cornstarch
Salt
⅓ English cucumber
1 large poblano chile
2 tablespoons minced fresh cilantro
Zest and juice of 1 Meyer lemon
Juice of ½ navel orange
1 tablespoon sherry vinegar
1 vine-ripened tomato
8 large shrimp, peeled and deveined
2 Hass avocados

1. In a medium saucepan over medium-high heat, toast the coriander seeds and red pepper flakes until fragrant, about 1 minute. Add the oil. Heat until just hot to the touch, then remove from the heat and let steep for 10 minutes. Strain through a sieve lined with cheesecloth and transfer to a medium saucepan.
2. Using a vegetable peeler, remove the zest of the lime, then trim off any white pith. (Reserve the lime.) Cut the zest into very fine dice, put it in a small saucepan, and cover with cold water. Bring to a boil, then immediately drain in a sieve. Return the zest to the pan, cover with cold water again, bring to a boil, then drain. In the saucepan, combine the sugar and ½ cup water. Add the zest and bring to a boil over high heat. Remove from the heat and let the syrup cool.
3. Pour the syrup through a sieve set over a clean saucepan; set the candied zest aside in a small bowl. Combine the cornstarch and 1½ teaspoons water. Stir the cornstarch slurry into the syrup and add 1 teaspoon salt. Bring to a boil and cook until thickened, about 3 minutes. Let cool.
4. Cut the cucumber in half and scrape out the seeds. Cut the cucumber, peel included, into very fine dice and put in the bowl with the candied zest.
5. Roast the chile directly over a gas flame, turning with tongs until all sides are lightly charred. Place the chile in a heat-proof bowl, cover with plastic wrap, and set aside for 20 minutes. Remove the blackened skin, seeds, and stems. Cut the bright green parts into very fine dice, to make 2 tablespoons. Add to the cucumber mixture, along with the juice of half the reserved lime (reserve the remaining lime for another use), ½ teaspoon of the infused oil, the cilantro, and salt to taste. Set the salad aside.
6. In a small bowl, combine the lemon zest and juice, orange juice, vinegar, and salt to taste. Slice the tomato into 8 thin wedges and add to the marinade. Set aside.
7. Warm the remaining infused oil over low heat. Sprinkle the shrimp with salt and add them to the oil—it should not be hot enough to sputter. Cook for 4 to 6 minutes, turning once, until firm. Transfer the shrimp to paper towels to drain.
8. Peel and thinly slice the avocados. Lightly brush some of the lime syrup onto each of 8 serving plates. Place a shrimp on one side of the brushstroke. Place avocado slices next to the shrimp. Put 1 wedge of marinated tomato between the shrimp and avocado. Using a slotted spoon to drain excess liquid from the cucumber salad, place a small line of the salad next to the avocado. Serve immediately.

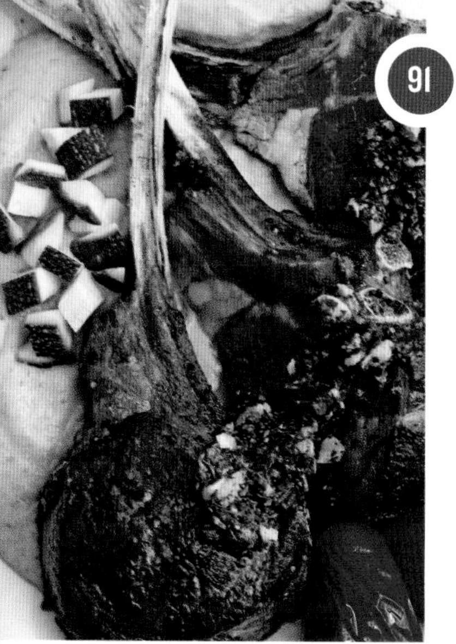

Entrées: Meat

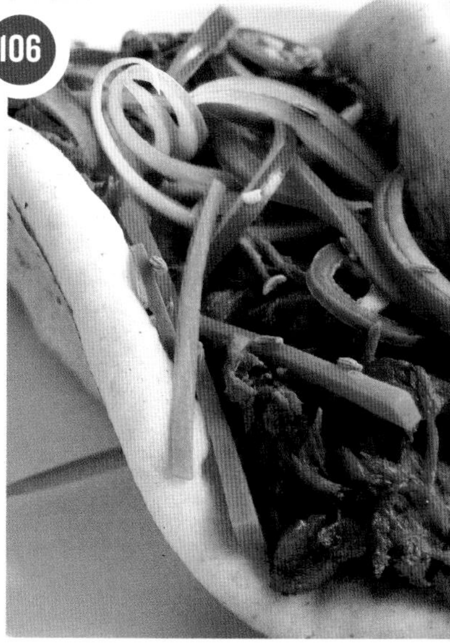
106

114

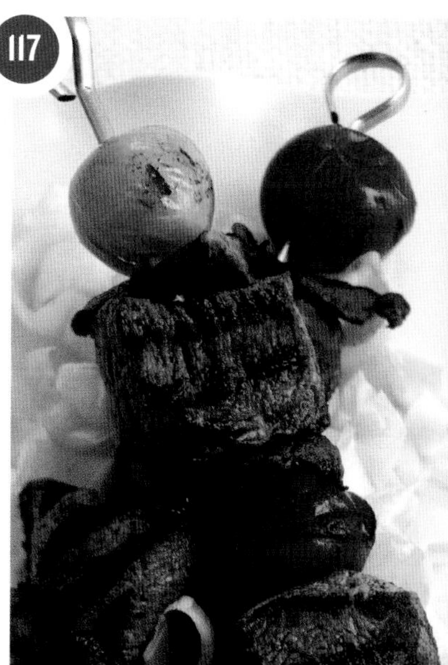
117

Colorado Rack of Lamb
with Ratatouille and Sauce Vert

CHEF: Dale
SEASON 3, EPISODE 14
ELIMINATION CHALLENGE: Cook the best meal of your life.

- 2 small bunches fresh flat-leaf parsley, stemmed
- 10 fresh thyme sprigs
- 18 garlic cloves
- 1 tablespoon whole peppercorns, crushed
- One 1 ½-pound Colorado rack of lamb (with 6 to 8 bones), chine bone removed, frenched
- 20 cured white anchovy fillets, or 10 to 15 regular anchovy fillets
- ½ cup extra-virgin olive oil
- Juice and grated zest of 1 lemon
- Salt and freshly ground black pepper
- 6 tablespoons olive oil
- 1 eggplant, peeled and cut into 1-inch cubes
- 1 onion, chopped
- About 3 ½ pounds duck fat (enough to submerge the rack of lamb)
- 1 pint cherry tomatoes
- 2 fresh basil sprigs
- 1 zucchini, very finely diced

More than 3 hours, plus marinating overnight

Serves 2 to 4

TIMESAVER!

Make the sauce and start marinating the lamb a day in advance. The eggplant puree can also be made the day before and reheated just before serving.

1. Finely chop 1 bunch of the parsley, the thyme, and 10 cloves of the garlic and combine with the crushed peppercorns. Coat the lamb with the herb mixture, cover, and let sit in the refrigerator overnight.
2. Finely chop the remaining 1 bunch parsley and 6 cloves of the garlic and put them in a small bowl. Mince the anchovies, mashing them to a paste, and add them to the bowl, along with the ½ cup extra-virgin olive oil, the lemon juice and zest, and salt and pepper to taste. Cover and let sit in the refrigerator overnight. The next day, bring the anchovy sauce to room temperature, taste, and add more salt and pepper as necessary.
3. In a large sauté pan or skillet, heat 2 tablespoons oil over medium heat. Add the eggplant and onion and cook, stirring frequently, until very soft, about 20 minutes. In a food processor, puree the eggplant and onion, then season with salt and pepper to taste and set aside.
4. Put the duck fat in a pot large enough to contain the whole rack laid on its side. Melt the fat over low heat. Season with salt to taste. Scrape the herbs off the lamb and into the fat. Add half of the anchovy sauce. Increase the heat and bring to a soft boil.
5. Meanwhile, in a large sauté pan or skillet, heat 2 tablespoons oil over high heat. Add the lamb and sear until well browned on both sides, 6 to 8 minutes total.
6. Remove the duck fat from the heat and immediately submerge the lamb in the fat. Let the lamb sit in the fat for 30 minutes for rare, 45 minutes for medium-rare.
7. While the lamb is submerged in the fat, warm 2 tablespoons oil in a small sauté pan or skillet over medium-low heat. Add the tomatoes, basil, and the remaining 2 cloves garlic and cook for 10 to 12 minutes, until tomatoes are soft but still hold their shape.
8. When the lamb is done, use tongs to lift it out of the fat and let it drain slightly on a baking sheet lined with paper towels.
9. Divide the eggplant puree among 2 to 4 serving plates. Top each serving with a few tomatoes and a small pile of the raw zucchini. Slice the lamb between the bones and place 2 or 3 chops over the zucchini on each plate. Spoon some of the remaining sauce over the chops and serve immediately.

Roasted Lamb Medallions
with Maitake Mushrooms, Braised Pistachios, and Blackberry

CHEF: Stephanie
SEASON 4, EPISODE 14
ELIMINATION CHALLENGE: Create a classic four-course tasting menu.

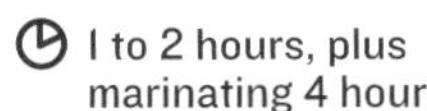
1 to 2 hours, plus marinating 4 hours

Serves 4
★ Winner

WHAT ARE . . .
Maitake Mushrooms

Maitake mushrooms—also known as hen of the woods—are found all over the United States growing at the base of deciduous trees, but they can be difficult to find in stores. Check specialty food stores and farmers' markets, or substitute other mushrooms such as stemmed shiitakes, chanterelles, morels, roughly chopped portobello, or a combination (these mushrooms need cook only 5 to 6 minutes in the sauté pan).

2 racks of lamb (about 1¾ pounds each)
¼ cup yellow miso paste
1 teaspoon dried thyme
½ onion, diced
3 garlic cloves, chopped
½ cup red wine
2 cups low-sodium chicken stock
1 pint blackberries
1 cup white balsamic vinegar
¼ cup sugar
½ cup shelled pistachios
1 small shallot, minced (2 tablespoons)
⅓ cup manzanilla olives, minced (2 tablespoons)
2 teaspoons extra-virgin olive oil
½ tablespoon unsalted butter
1 pound maitake mushrooms, cleaned well and broken into bite-size chunks

1. With a sharp knife, cut the loin meat from the bones of each rack, leaving it in one piece and reserving the bones of one of the racks. Remove any excess fat and trim the silverskin from the loins. Rub with the miso and sprinkle with the thyme. Cover and let marinate in the refrigerator for at least 4 hours and up to overnight.
2. Cut between the rib bones to separate them. Heat a large saucepan over high heat, add the bones, and cook until well browned on all sides, about 8 minutes. Remove the bones to a plate and drain all but 1 tablespoon of the fat from the pan. Add the onion and garlic and sauté over medium-high heat until browned, about 5 minutes. Add the wine and stir to scrape up any browned bits. Simmer until reduced by half, about 5 minutes. Add 1½ cups of the stock, half of the blackberries, and the lamb bones. Bring to a boil, then lower the heat and simmer until thick, about 40 minutes. Pour through a fine-mesh sieve into a small saucepan and cover to keep warm.
3. Put the remaining ½ pint blackberries, the vinegar, and sugar in a small nonreactive saucepan. Bring to a boil, stirring, then simmer until the sauce is thick and syrupy, about 15 minutes. Pour through a fine-mesh sieve into a small bowl and set aside.
4. Put the pistachios and the remaining ½ cup stock in a small saucepan, season with salt and pepper to taste, and simmer until soft, 8 to 10 minutes. Set aside.
5. In a small bowl, combine the shallot, olives, and 1 teaspoon of the oil. Set aside.
6. Preheat the oven to 450°F. Scrape the miso paste off the lamb loins. In a heavy skillet over high heat, cook the lamb until well browned on all sides, about 6 minutes. Transfer to a roasting pan and roast until the internal temperature registers 120 to 130°F for rare to medium-rare, about 6 minutes. Remove to a cutting board and let rest for 10 minutes. Cut into ½-inch-thick slices.
7. While the lamb is resting, in a medium sauté pan, heat the remaining 1 teaspoon oil and the butter over medium-high heat. Add the mushrooms, season with salt and pepper to taste, and sauté until browned in spots and soft, about 10 minutes.
8. Divide the mushrooms among 4 serving plates. Arrange the lamb slices on top and spoon some of the lamb sauce over them. Top with a small spoonful of the olive mixture, scatter some pistachios around the plate, and drizzle with the blackberry-vinegar syrup. Serve immediately.

Bacon-Wrapped Shrimp
with Cheese Grits and Chipotle-Tomato Butter Sauce

CHEF: Tre
SEASON 3, EPISODE 7
ELIMINATION CHALLENGE: Create a snack for late-night Miami partiers.

1 hour, 15 minutes
Serves 6
Winner

Chipotle-Tomato Butter Sauce:
- 1 tablespoon grapeseed oil
- ½ onion, chopped
- 3 garlic cloves, chopped
- 4 plum tomatoes, chopped
- 3 canned chipotle chiles in adobo sauce
- 1 teaspoon whole black peppercorns
- 1 ½ cups low-sodium chicken stock
- 4 tablespoons unsalted butter
- ½ bunch fresh cilantro
- Juice of ½ lemon
- Salt

Grits:
- 2 cups low-sodium chicken stock
- ⅔ cup milk
- 4 tablespoons unsalted butter
- 2 cups instant grits
- 1 cup grilled corn kernels
- ½ cup diced poblano chiles
- ½ cup grated aged white Cheddar cheese
- 2 tablespoons chopped fresh cilantro
- Salt and cracked black pepper

Shrimp:
- 9 thin slices bacon
- 18 large black tiger shrimp, peeled and deveined
- 2 teaspoons cracked black pepper
- 2 tablespoons grapeseed oil

For the Chipotle-Tomato Butter Sauce:

1. In a medium saucepan, heat the oil over medium heat. Add the onion and garlic and sauté until just starting to soften, about 4 minutes. Add the tomatoes, chipotles, and peppercorns. Cook, stirring, for 3 minutes.
2. Add the stock and bring to a brisk simmer. Cook for 5 minutes, then transfer to a blender and blend until smooth. Return the liquid to the saucepan and place over low heat. Whisk in 1 tablespoon of the butter at a time. Add the cilantro and lemon juice. Remove from the heat and let steep for 5 minutes. Season with salt to taste. Pour through a fine-mesh sieve set over a clean saucepan and cover to keep warm.

For the Grits:

In a large saucepan, combine the stock and milk. Bring to a simmer and add the butter. When the butter has melted, gradually whisk in the grits. When the grits begin to thicken, lower the heat. Fold in the corn, chiles, cheese, cilantro, and salt and pepper to taste. Cook, stirring gently, until the cheese is melted and the grits are thick. If the grits are too thick, add a bit of water or more stock. Cover and keep warm.

For the Shrimp:

1. Cut the bacon slices in half crosswise. Wrap each shrimp with ½ slice of bacon. Sprinkle with cracked black pepper.
2. Divide the oil between 2 medium sauté pans or skillets and heat over medium heat. Add the shrimp and cook until the shrimp is opaque and the bacon is crisp, turning frequently, 5 to 8 minutes.
3. Spoon a small mound of grits onto the center of each plate. Drizzle some of the sauce around the grits. Place 3 shrimp around the grits. Serve immediately.

"Tre took a real classic comforty food like cheese grits and executed it beautifully. To top it all off, two words: Bay Con. I thought that dish was exquisite."

TED ALLEN, JUDGE

Salami and Gouda Panini
on a Sun-Dried Tomato Roll

CHEF: Dave
SEASON 1, EPISODE 11
ELIMINATION CHALLENGE: Prepare room-service meals in thirty minutes or less.

- 2 tablespoons orange-blossom honey
- 1 teaspoon dry mustard
- 2 small sun-dried tomato rolls (or ciabatta-type rolls), split in half
- 8 thin slices Genoa salami
- 8 thin slices sharp Gouda
- 4 strips jarred roasted red bell pepper
- 2 tablespoons unsalted butter, melted

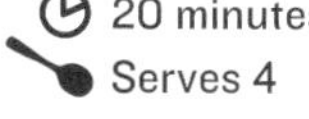
20 minutes
Serves 4

1. Heat a panini press according to the manufacturer's directions until hot. (Alternatively, heat a ridged grill pan over medium heat.)
2. In a small bowl, whisk together the honey and mustard and spread it over 2 of the bread halves. Top with 4 slices of salami, 4 slices of cheese, and 2 red pepper strips each and top with the other half of the roll.
3. Brush the butter on the outside of the sandwiches, top and bottom.
4. Put the sandwiches on the press, then pull down the top and cook until browned and crisp, 4 to 6 minutes. If you're using a grill pan, place a heavy pan on top of the sandwiches and cook, pressing down on the pan and turning the sandwiches once.
5. Cut the sandwiches in half and serve immediately.

WHAT ARE . . .
Salumi and Salami?

Not too long ago, it was simple: you'd order a pepperoni pizza or a salami on rye. These days you may find yourself choosing from an array of boutique cured meats that requires a debriefing from your waiter. The first thing to know is that salumi is not a misspelling of salami, but a general term referring to cured meats, usually pork or beef. Salami is a specific type of salumi. Many salamis are named for their region of origin, such as Genoa or Milano.

Sweetbread and Scallion Beignets
with Chinese Five-Spice, in Soy Broth

CHEF: Sam
SEASON 2, EPISODE 5
QUICKFIRE CHALLENGE: Create a dish using offal, the leftover parts of animals.

45 minutes, plus brining 1 ½ hours
Serves 4 to 6
★ Winner

HOW TO:
Brine Sweetbreads

Some chefs soak sweetbreads in cold water with a little lemon juice and then blanch them before getting to the heart of the recipe. Here, a simple brine will draw out any excess blood, firm up the sweetbreads a bit, and impart flavor all at once. No blanching is necessary.

- 3 cups milk
- ½ cup kosher salt
- ¼ cup sugar

Combine all the ingredients in a large bowl and stir to dissolve the salt and sugar (this could take a few minutes). Add sweetbreads and refrigerate for 1 ½ hours.

Batter:
- 3 cups all-purpose flour
- 1 tablespoon baking powder
- 1 tablespoon baking soda
- 1 tablespoon Chinese five-spice powder
- ½ teaspoon ground cinnamon
- 3 large eggs
- 1 cup milk
- 1 bunch scallions, cut into ¼-inch slices
- Salt and freshly ground black pepper

Melted Onions:
- 1 tablespoon unsalted butter
- 1 red onion, thinly sliced
- ½ yellow onion, thinly sliced
- 1 carrot, diced
- ½ cup white wine
- ½ cup low-sodium chicken stock
- ¼ cup pitted kalamata olives
- Salt and freshly ground black pepper

Soy Broth:
- ½ cup soy sauce
- ½ cup Worcestershire sauce
- 1 tablespoon lavender seeds
- 1 cinnamon stick
- 1 cup veal demi-glace

To Serve:
- Vegetable oil for frying
- 1 ¼ pounds veal sweetbreads, brined for 1 ½ hours
- 1 tablespoon capers, drained
- ½ cup basil leaves, cut into chiffonade
- ¼ cup chopped chives

For the Batter:

In a large bowl, combine the flour, baking powder, baking soda, five-spice powder, and cinnamon. Stir in the eggs, milk, 1 cup water, and the scallions. Add a pinch each of salt and pepper. Set aside in the refrigerator.

For the Melted Onions:

In a medium sauté pan or skillet, melt the butter over medium heat. Add the onions and carrot. Sauté until almost soft, about 4 minutes. Add the wine, stock, and olives. Cook until the vegetables are soft, 5 to 7 minutes. Add salt and pepper. Set aside.

For the Soy Broth:

In a small saucepan, combine all the ingredients with 2 ½ cups water. Simmer over low heat until fragrant and slightly reduced, about 20 minutes. Cover and remove from the heat; let steep for 10 minutes. Pour through a fine-mesh sieve into a saucepan and cover to keep warm.

To Fry and Serve:

1. In a large, heavy pot, heat 2 to 3 inches of oil to 350°F.
2. Drain the sweetbreads and cut them into ½-inch pieces. Working in batches, dip the pieces in the batter, then carefully lower them into the hot oil. Cook, turning, until nicely browned, 5 to 8 minutes. Transfer to paper towels to drain.
3. Dip the capers in the batter, drop them into the oil, and fry for 30 seconds. Drain.
4. Divide the onions among shallow dishes and place the sweetbread beignets on top. Ladle the broth into the bowls and sprinkle with the basil, chives, and capers. Serve.

Braised Pork Shoulder
in Sour Orange Mojo with Yucca and Pickled Onions

CHEF: Howie
SEASON 3, EPISODE 5
ELIMINATION CHALLENGE: Prepare a Latin lunch for the cast of a telenovela.

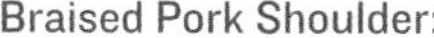

Braised Pork Shoulder:

- One 6-pound boneless pork shoulder, trimmed and cut in half if necessary
- Salt and freshly ground black pepper
- 2 tablespoons extra-virgin olive oil
- 15 garlic cloves, thinly sliced
- 4 cups low-sodium chicken stock
- 4 cups fresh orange juice
- ¾ cup fresh lime juice, or more to taste
- ¾ cup distilled white vinegar
- ½ cup soy sauce, or more to taste
- 1 ½ cups lightly packed light brown sugar, or more to taste
- One 2-inch piece ginger, sliced
- 2 cinnamon sticks
- 2 pieces star anise
- Fresh cilantro for garnish

Yucca:

- 3 pounds yucca
- About 2 quarts low-sodium chicken stock
- ¼ cup distilled white vinegar
- 1 white onion, thinly sliced
- 6 garlic cloves
- 1 bay leaf
- Salt and freshly ground black pepper to taste

Pickled Onions (see right)

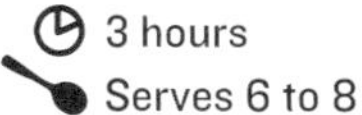

3 hours
Serves 6 to 8

For the Braised Pork Shoulder:

1. Pat the pork dry with paper towels and generously season with salt and pepper on all sides. In a large pot, heat the oil over medium-high heat. Add the pork and sear until browned on all sides, 15 to 20 minutes. Transfer to a large plate.
2. Reduce the heat to medium and remove all but ½ cup fat from the pot. Add the garlic and cook until golden, about 2 minutes. Add the stock, orange juice, lime juice, vinegar, soy sauce, brown sugar, ginger, cinnamon, and star anise. Bring to a boil, then add the pork and bring back to a boil. Reduce the heat, cover, and simmer, turning the pork every 30 minutes, until very tender, 1 ¼ to 2 hours. Remove the pork from the liquid and set aside on a plate. Tent with aluminum foil. Cut into ½-inch-thick slices just before serving.
3. Bring the liquid in the pot back to a boil and cook over medium-high heat until reduced by about half, about 30 minutes. Taste and adjust the flavors, adding more lime juice, soy sauce, or sugar if necessary.

For the Yucca:

1. Peel the yucca, rinse, and slice each piece in half lengthwise. Remove the stringy core in the center. Cut each half crosswise into 2-inch lengths.
2. In a large pot, combine the yucca with the remaining ingredients. Bring to a boil, then reduce the heat and simmer, covered, until tender, 1 to 1 ½ hours, adding more stock or water to cover as needed. Drain.

To Serve:

Divide the yucca among the serving plates. Place pork slices on top and drizzle with mojo sauce. Top with pickled onions and garnish with cilantro. Serve immediately.

ON THE SIDE:
Pickled Onions

- ⅔ cup distilled white vinegar
- ½ cup granulated sugar
- Salt and freshly ground black pepper
- 2 tablespoons extra-virgin olive oil
- 2 large red onions, cut into rings

While you're cooking the pork and yucca, in a medium bowl, combine the vinegar, sugar, and salt and pepper to taste. Whisk to dissolve the sugar, then whisk in the oil. Add the onions and toss to coat. Cover and refrigerate until ready to serve.

Duo of Beef
with Kobe Strip Loin and Braised Kobe Short Ribs, with White Polenta

CHEF: Harold
SEASON 1, EPISODE 12
ELIMINATION CHALLENGE: Cook the best meal of your life.

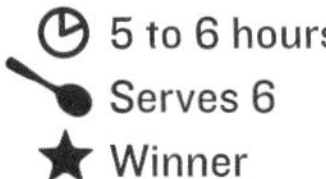

5 to 6 hours
Serves 6
Winner

Braised Kobe Short Ribs:
5 pounds Kobe short ribs, well trimmed
Salt and freshly ground black pepper
¼ cup olive oil
2 medium yellow onions, chopped
1 celery rib, chopped
5 medium tomatoes, seeded and chopped
One 750-ml bottle red wine
2 cups low-sodium chicken stock
1 quart low-sodium veal stock

Kobe Strip Loin:
1 ¼ pounds Kobe strip loin, well trimmed
Salt and freshly ground black pepper
2 tablespoons olive oil
2 tablespoons unsalted butter, melted

White Polenta:
2 cups milk
1 cup heavy cream
1 cup coarse white polenta
2 tablespoons unsalted butter, cut into pieces
¼ cup mascarpone cheese
Salt and freshly ground white pepper

Vegetables:
Salt
24 asparagus tips
1 tablespoon extra-virgin olive oil
1 tablespoon unsalted butter
4 ounces fresh morel mushrooms, quartered
Freshly ground black pepper

To Serve:
Fresh rosemary sprigs for garnish

For the Braised Kobe Short Ribs:

1. Generously season the ribs with salt and pepper.
2. In a large, heavy pot, heat the oil over medium-high heat. Add the beef, in batches, and brown well, turning occasionally, 8 to 10 minutes per batch. Using tongs, remove the ribs and transfer to a large bowl.
3. Reduce the heat to medium, add the onions and celery, and cook until caramelized, 15 to 20 minutes. Add the tomatoes and cook until softened, about 5 minutes. Add the wine, raise the heat, and cook until reduced by about half, about 20 minutes.
4. Return the ribs with their drippings to the pot, along with the chicken and veal stocks. Bring to a simmer, then reduce the heat to low, cover, and cook, stirring occasionally, until the beef is very tender and falling off the bone, 3 to 4 hours.
5. Remove the beef from the pot, cool slightly, then remove the bones and cut into 3-inch pieces. Strain the sauce, then return the sauce to the pot, raise the heat to high, and boil until reduced to about 4 cups, about 30 minutes. Return the beef to the pot.

For the Kobe Strip Loin:

1. Preheat the oven to 375°F. Generously season the strip loin with salt and pepper.
2. In a large skillet, heat the oil over high heat until hot but not smoking. Sear the beef, about 2 minutes on each side. Place the skillet with beef in the oven and cook for about 30 minutes for medium-rare (internal temperature of 130° to 135°F) or about 40 minutes for medium (internal temperature of 140° to 150°F). Baste the beef with the butter about halfway through cooking time.
3. Remove from the oven, let the beef sit for 5 minutes, then slice.

For the White Polenta:

1. In a large saucepan, combine the milk, cream, and 2 cups water and place over medium heat. Heat just until bubbles begin to form around the edges (watch the pot so it doesn't boil over) and slowly whisk in the polenta. Reduce the heat to low and simmer, stirring constantly with a wooden spoon, until the mixture is thick but pourable and leaves the sides of the pan as you stir it, about 20 minutes.
2. Remove from the heat and beat the butter and mascarpone into the polenta. Season with salt and white pepper to taste.

For the Vegetables:

1. Bring a large pot of salted water to a boil. Add the asparagus and cook until just tender, about 3 minutes. Remove the asparagus from the water using a slotted spoon and transfer to a large bowl. Toss with the oil.
2. In a medium skillet, heat the butter over medium heat. Add the mushrooms and sauté until softened, about 5 minutes. Add the asparagus and heat to warm through. Season with salt and pepper to taste.

To Serve:

Spoon the polenta onto serving plates, arrange the steak slices on top, and place the vegetables alongside. Add some of the ribs, along with the sauce, and garnish with the rosemary sprigs. Serve immediately.

TIMESAVER!

Time management is key to the outcome of this dish. Try to enlist an assistant toward the end of cooking to wrap it all up smoothly. The best approach to cooking this meal is:

1. Put your ribs up to braise.

2. Gather your ingredients for all the other components and preheat the oven for the steak.

3. After the ribs are cooked and as you're reducing the sauce, start in with the steak, polenta, and vegetables—in the time that the sauce is reducing, you can have the steak in the oven, and while the steak is cooking, you'll be freed up to stir the polenta while you're cooking the vegetables.

TOM COLICCHIO, HEAD JUDGE "MY FAVORITE DISH OF ALL THREE SEASONS. WHAT I LIKED ABOUT IT WAS HIS RESPECT FOR THE PRODUCTS. I HAVE ABSOLUTELY NO CRITICISMS."

Prosciutto and Cheese Pizza

CHEF: Frank
SEASON 2, EPISODE 4
ELIMINATION CHALLENGE: Create a meal under 500 calories.

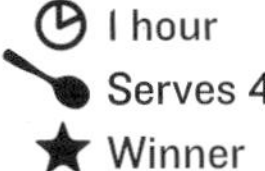

I hour
Serves 4
Winner

Pizza Sauce:

- 1 tablespoon extra-virgin olive oil
- ½ medium yellow onion, minced
- 1 garlic clove, minced
- One 15-ounce can tomato puree
- 1 tablespoon tomato paste
- ¼ cup red wine
- 2 teaspoons finely chopped fresh oregano
- 2 teaspoons finely chopped fresh basil
- 1 teaspoon sugar, or to taste
- Salt and freshly ground black pepper

Crust and Toppings:

- 4 whole wheat pita bread rounds
- ¼ cup extra-virgin olive oil
- Salt and freshly ground black pepper
- 12 ounces fresh mozzarella cheese, thinly sliced
- 2 large tomatoes, thinly sliced
- 8 thin slices prosciutto, torn into pieces
- 12 fresh basil leaves, torn into pieces

For the Pizza Sauce:

1. Preheat the oven to 400°F.
2. In a medium saucepan, heat the oil over medium heat. Add the onion and sauté until soft, about 5 minutes. Add the garlic and sauté until soft, about 1 minute. Add the tomato puree, tomato paste, wine, oregano, basil, sugar, and salt and pepper to taste and stir to combine. Bring to a simmer, cover, then reduce the heat and simmer for 30 minutes for the flavors to blend, stirring occasionally. Set aside to cool slightly.

For the Crust and Toppings:

1. Drizzle the pitas with the oil and season with salt and pepper.
2. Spread the sauce over the pitas, then top with the cheese and tomato slices.
3. Place the pizzas on a baking sheet, transfer to the oven, and bake until the cheese is melted and the crust is crisp, about 20 minutes. Remove from the oven and scatter the prosciutto and basil on top. Cut each pizza into 4 slices and serve immediately.

Note:

In the episode, the team used sausage on their pizza, but you can also make it with prosciutto, as shown here.

FRANK "AS SOON AS WE WALKED INTO THE STORE, BETTY AND I LOOKED AT EACH OTHER AND SAID, 'PIZZA!' I MEAN, WE WERE COOKING FOR KIDS."

Black Truffle Burger
with Taleggio Cheese, Tomato, and Radicchio

CHEF: Howie
SEASON 3, EPISODE 8
QUICKFIRE CHALLENGE: Prepare a burger for Red Robin's line of "Adventuresome Burgers."

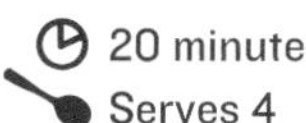

20 minutes
Serves 4

1 ½ pounds ground sirloin
3 ounces black truffle butter
1 teaspoon salt
4 slices pancetta
4 ounces Taleggio cheese, sliced
4 brioche buns, split in half and toasted
1 heirloom tomato, sliced
8 radicchio leaves

1. Preheat the oven to 350°F.
2. In a large bowl, combine the beef, truffle butter, and salt. Mix with a fork or your fingers until the butter is just incorporated. Form the beef into 4 patties. Lay a slice of pancetta over each patty.
3. Preheat a large, ovenproof skillet (preferably cast iron) over medium-high heat until hot. Put the burgers in the skillet, pancetta-side down, and cook for about 4 minutes per side for rare, 5 minutes per side for medium-rare.
4. Put the cheese on top of the burgers and place the skillet in the oven until the cheese is melted, about 5 minutes.
5. Place the burgers on the bottom bun halves, top with the tomato slices and radicchio, and cover with the top bun halves.

WHAT ARE . . .
Truffles

Why is the truffle one of the most expensive foods in the world? For one, this little fungus is extremely hard to find. Truffles never break through the surface of the soil, so specially trained pigs and dogs are used to sniff them out. Add their rich, earthy aroma, and to many this is a delicacy worth going to the ends of the world for. The king of black truffles is the Perigord truffle from France. The white truffle, mainly from Italy, is milder in flavor and usually served raw. Both can cost hundreds of dollars a pound.

Corn Sopes
with Char Siu Pork and Pickled Asian Slaw

CHEFS: Lee Anne and Stephen
SEASON 1, EPISODE 5
ELIMINATION CHALLENGE: Fuse two of San Francisco's culinary cultures in a new kind of street food.

1 hour, plus marinating 1 hour
Serves 6 to 8

- 2 pounds thinly sliced center-cut pork chops
- Half 14-ounce jar char siu barbecue sauce
- 1 Hass avocado
- 2 tablespoons sour cream
- 1 tablespoon chili oil
- Juice of ½ lime
- Salt and freshly ground white pepper
- 3 cups masa harina
- ½ cup lard or vegetable shortening
- 1 cup corn kernels
- Vegetable oil for frying

Pickled Asian Slaw (see right)

1. Put the pork chops in a large bowl and drizzle with the char siu sauce, tossing to coat the chops evenly. Cover and refrigerate for at least 1 hour.
2. In a food processor, combine the avocado, sour cream, chili oil, and lime juice. Process until smooth, then season to taste with salt and white pepper. Cover and refrigerate.
3. In a large bowl, combine the masa harina, lard, corn, and 2 teaspoons salt. Sprinkle in 10 tablespoons water and mix with your hands until the dough is smooth, adding a little more water if the dough is too dry.
4. Roll out half of the dough between two sheets of plastic wrap to ¼ inch thick. Use a 4-inch round cutter or a drinking glass to cut out rounds, gathering up and re-rolling the scraps. Repeat with the remaining dough.
5. Preheat the oven to 250°F.
6. In a large cast-iron skillet or sauté pan, heat ½ inch oil over medium-high heat. When the oil is hot but not smoking, add 5 or 6 of the masa rounds, being careful not to overcrowd the pan. Cook, turning once, for about 3 minutes on each side, reducing the heat to medium-low if necessary to keep the oil from smoking, until the masa is tender and well browned. Transfer to a baking sheet lined with paper towels to drain and season lightly with salt. Repeat with the remaining masa rounds, adding more oil to the pan if necessary. Put the baking sheet in the oven to keep the sopes warm while you grill the pork.
7. Preheat a charcoal grill and set the grate about 8 inches above the coals. Lightly brush the grate with oil. When the flames have died down and the coals are white, place the pork chops on the grill. Cook for about 2 minutes per side, until grill-marked and cooked through. Remove to a cutting board and let rest for 5 minutes.
8. Cut the pork into ¼-inch cubes.
9. To serve, spread a bit of the avocado sauce onto each sope, then top with chopped pork, then slaw. Serve immediately, 3 or 4 sopes per person.

ON THE SIDE:
Pickled Asian Slaw

- ⅔ cup rice vinegar
- 1 ⅓ cups sugar
- ½ jicama, cut into julienne
- ¼ head green cabbage, cored and shredded
- 1 carrot, cut into julienne
- ½ red onion, cut into julienne
- ½ bunch fresh cilantro, stemmed and chopped
- 2 teaspoons sesame oil
- Salt and freshly ground black pepper

1. In a large saucepan, bring 2 cups water, the vinegar, and sugar to a boil, stirring to dissolve the sugar.
2. Add the jicama, cabbage, carrot, and onion and cook, stirring, until the carrot and onion are just tender, 6 to 8 minutes. Drain the vegetables and spread them out in a large baking dish to cool to room temperature.
3. In a large bowl, toss the vegetables with the cilantro and sesame oil. Season with salt and pepper to taste. Cover and refrigerate until ready to serve.

Seared Elk Loin

with Cauliflower and Fingerling Potato Mash, and Pickled Cauliflower

CHEF: Dale
SEASON 3, EPISODE 13
ELIMINATION CHALLENGE: Prepare elk for hungry rodeo cowboys and cowgirls.

3 hours, plus marinating overnight
Serves 6 to 8
Winner

"I liked the way Dale cooked the elk, and the huckleberry sauce was excellent."

CHEF ERIC RIPERT, GUEST JUDGE

Pickled Cauliflower:

- 1 medium head cauliflower, cut into small florets
- 5 shallots, thinly sliced
- ½ cup sherry vinegar
- ¼ cup red wine vinegar
- 1 ½ cups sugar
- 1 tablespoon kosher salt

Elk Loin:

- 5 tablespoons finely chopped fresh rosemary
- 5 tablespoons finely chopped fresh thyme
- 2 tablespoons minced garlic
- 2 teaspoons coarsely crushed black peppercorns
- 2 teaspoons salt
- ½ teaspoon ground allspice
- ½ teaspoon ground cloves
- ½ teaspoon ground star anise
- One 2- to 3-pound elk loin
- 2 tablespoons olive oil

Huckleberry-Blackberry Sauce:

- 15 black peppercorns
- 2 bay leaves
- 5 whole allspice berries
- 1 cinnamon stick
- 7 whole cloves
- 3 pieces star anise
- 1 tablespoon unsalted butter
- ½ cup diced yellow onion
- ½ cup diced carrot
- ½ cup diced celery
- 2 garlic cloves, peeled and left whole
- 4 cups red wine
- 3 thyme sprigs
- 3 cups huckleberries
- 3 cups blackberries
- 1 ½ cups tawny port
- 4 cups lamb demi-glace
- 2 tablespoons sugar, or more to taste
- Salt and freshly ground black pepper

Cauliflower and Fingerling Potato Mash:

- 3 cups cauliflower florets
- 1 pound fingerling potatoes, sliced into ½-inch rounds (about 4 cups)
- About 5 cups milk
- ½ cup chèvre
- ½ cup dried tart cherries
- ¼ cup finely chopped fresh flat-leaf parsley
- Salt and freshly ground white pepper

To Serve:

- Pinch of cinnamon
- Pinch of ground ginger
- Fresh blackberries
- Fresh mint leaves
- Corn shoots
- Radish sprouts
- Chopped toasted pecans

For the Pickled Cauliflower:

1. Put the cauliflower and shallots in a large bowl.
2. In a large saucepan, combine 3 cups water, the vinegars, sugar, and salt and place over high heat. Bring to a boil, whisking to dissolve the sugar and salt. Pour the mixture over the cauliflower and shallots, cool slightly, then cover and refrigerate overnight. Drain just before serving.

For the Elk Loin:

1. Combine the rosemary, thyme, garlic, peppercorns, salt, allspice, cloves, and star

anise in a medium bowl. Spread the mixture over a large plate. Press the elk loin into the spice mixture to coat all sides. Cover the elk and refrigerate overnight.

2. When all the other components of the meal are ready to go, cook the elk. You may need to cut the loin in half to fit in your pan. In a large skillet, heat the oil over medium-high heat. Sear the elk on both sides for about 7 minutes total per inch of meat, or until rare to medium-rare (internal temperature 130° to 140°F).
3. Let the elk rest for 5 to 7 minutes, then cut into serving slices.

For the Huckleberry-Blackberry Sauce:

1. In a large saucepan, combine the peppercorns, bay leaves, allspice berries, cinnamon stick, cloves, and star anise and place over medium-high heat. Toast the spices, stirring, until aromatic, about 3 minutes. Reduce the heat to medium, add the butter, and stir to melt. Add the onion, carrot, celery, and garlic and sauté until lightly browned, 5 to 7 minutes.
2. Add 2 cups of the red wine and stir, scraping up the browned bits from the bottom of the pan. Add the thyme sprigs. Bring to a simmer and cook until the wine is reduced by about half, about 10 minutes.
3. Add the huckleberries and blackberries and cook, breaking the fruit up with the back of a wooden spoon, until the berries are falling apart and the mixture is slightly reduced, about 15 minutes.
4. Add the remaining 2 cups red wine and reduce by about a third, about 15 minutes. Add the port and reduce by about a third, about 15 minutes. Add the demi-glace and reduce by about half, about 10 minutes. Add the sugar and season with salt and pepper to taste.
5. Strain through a fine-mesh sieve, return to the pan, and add more sugar, salt, and pepper as needed. Warm through just before serving.

For the Cauliflower and Fingerling Potato Mash:

1. In a large saucepan, combine the cauliflower and potatoes and add milk to cover. Place over medium heat and bring to a simmer, watching the pot so the milk doesn't boil over. Cook for about 15 minutes, or until the vegetables are tender. Strain, reserving the cooking liquid.
2. Transfer the mixture to a large bowl and add the chèvre and cherries. Mash with a hand masher, breaking the mixture down to a risotto-like consistency and adding some of the cooking liquid as needed.
3. Add the parsley and season with salt and white pepper to taste. Rewarm just before serving if necessary.

To Serve:

Spoon the cauliflower and potato mash onto serving plates. Arrange the elk slices alongside, sprinkle the elk with a pinch of cinnamon and ginger, and top with the huckleberry-blackberry sauce. Add the pickled cauliflower and garnish with blackberries, mint, corn shoots, radish sprouts, and chopped pecans. Serve immediately.

TIMESAVER!

Plan on starting a day ahead for this recipe, as both the pickled cauliflower and elk call for overnight marinating.

Moroccan Cubanos

CHEFS: Dave and Tiffani
SEASON 1, EPISODE 5
ELIMINATION CHALLENGE: Fuse two of San Francisco's culinary cultures in a new kind of street food.

More than 3 hours
Serves 6
Winner

WHAT IS . . .

Ras Al-Hanout?

Ras al-hanout (pronounced "RAS-all-hah-NOOT") is a Moroccan spice blend. It's available in specialty and Middle Eastern markets, or you can make your own. Combine 2 teaspoons each ground cumin, ground ginger, and salt, and 1 teaspoon each freshly ground black pepper, ground cayenne, ground coriander, and ground cinnamon, and ½ teaspoon ground cloves.

Pork:

One 4- to 5-pound bone-in pork butt, trimmed

Salt

2 tablespoons ras al-hanout

1 cup low-sodium veal stock

1 cup low-sodium chicken stock

Pickled Vegetables:

3 cups red wine vinegar

1 cup sugar

1 tablespoon fennel seeds

4 carrots, cut into julienne

1 red onion, cut into julienne

3 fresh jalapeño chiles, thinly sliced

To Serve:

4 fresh pocketless pitas or other flatbread, or fresh corn tortillas

For the Pork:

1. Preheat the oven to 275°F.
2. Season the pork generously with salt and ras al-hanout.
3. Heat a large cast-iron skillet over high heat. Add the pork and cook until well browned on all sides, about 12 minutes total.
4. Put the pork in a large roasting pan and pour in the stocks and ½ cup water. Roast for 4 to 5 hours, until the pork is tender enough to pull apart with a fork.
5. Remove the pork to a cutting board and pour the cooking juices into a small saucepan. Cook the juices over high heat until reduced to about ¾ cup; shred the pork into bite-size pieces, discarding the bones. In a large bowl, toss the pork with the reduced juices.

For the Pickled Vegetables:

1. In a large nonreactive pot, combine the vinegar, sugar, fennel, and 3 cups water and bring to a boil, stirring to dissolve the sugar.
2. Put the carrots, onion, and chiles in a large heatproof bowl. Pour the hot vinegar mixture into the bowl. Cover tightly with plastic wrap and let the vegetables steam for 20 minutes. Pour out all but about 1 cup of the liquid. Keep the vegetables, covered, in the refrigerator; bring to room temperature when ready to serve.

To Serve:

1. In a skillet over medium-high heat, warm the pitas, one at a time.
2. Pile the pork onto the pitas, top with pickled vegetables, and serve immediately.

TOM COLICCHIO, HEAD JUDGE "I LIKED THE IDEA THAT THERE WAS A NICE LITTLE SALAD IN THERE THAT COOLED OFF SOME OF THE HEAT."

Prime New York Strip Steaks
with Foie Gras Sauce and Parsnip Puree

CHEF: Harold
SEASON 1, EPISODE 6
ELIMINATION CHALLENGE: Create a seven-course dinner party for Ted Allen.

2 hours
Serves 4

Foie Gras Sauce:
1 tablespoon olive oil
About 12 ounces beef trimmings and bones
Salt and freshly ground black pepper
2 shallots, chopped
1 carrot, peeled and chopped
2 celery ribs, chopped
2 garlic cloves, smashed
1 cup red Burgundy wine
4 cups low-sodium veal stock
1 fresh thyme sprig
1 bay leaf
4 to 6 ounces foie gras, diced

Parsnip Puree:
2 tablespoons unsalted butter
5 parsnips, peeled and chopped
1 small shallot, chopped
1 garlic clove, chopped
¾ cup heavy cream
About ¾ cup low-sodium chicken stock
Leaves from 1 fresh thyme sprig

Beef:
Four 10- to 12-ounce prime strip steaks
Salt and freshly ground black pepper
2 tablespoons olive oil
4 tablespoons unsalted butter
4 garlic cloves, minced

For the Foie Gras Sauce:

1. In a heavy saucepan, heat the oil over medium-high heat. Add the trimmings and bones, season with salt and pepper, and cook for 8 minutes, or until browned. Add the shallots, carrot, celery, and garlic and sauté for 8 minutes, until lightly browned. Add the wine and cook until it is almost evaporated. Add the stock, thyme, and bay leaf, bring to a simmer, and cook until reduced to 1½ cups, about 1 hour.
2. Using an immersion blender, blend the foie gras into the sauce 1 or 2 pieces at a time, blending until completely incorporated. Season with salt and pepper and set aside.

For the Parsnip Puree:

1. In a medium saucepan, melt the butter over medium heat. Add the parsnips, shallot, and garlic and sauté until the shallot is translucent, 8 to 10 minutes.
2. Add the cream, enough stock to cover the parsnips, and the thyme leaves and bring to a simmer. Cook until the parsnips are very soft, 10 to 15 minutes. Transfer to a food processor and puree until smooth. Set aside.

For the Beef:

1. Preheat the oven to 400°F.
2. Let the steaks warm to room temperature, then season them with salt and pepper.
3. Heat a large, heavy skillet over high heat. Add the oil. When the oil is hot but not smoking, add the steaks. Cook, turning once, until nicely browned on both sides, about 8 minutes total. Put the skillet in the oven and roast the steaks to desired degree of doneness. Transfer to serving plates and brush with the butter and garlic; let rest for 5 minutes. Spoon the sauce around the steaks. Place a mound of parsnips on each plate. Serve immediately.

Spicy Braised Korean Pork
with Kim Chee and Sticky Rice

CHEFS: Marisa, Ilan, Frank, Marcel, Cliff, Elia, Otto (Team Korea)
SEASON 2, EPISODE 2
ELIMINATION CHALLENGE: Prepare a dish using the flavors of either Korea or Vietnam.

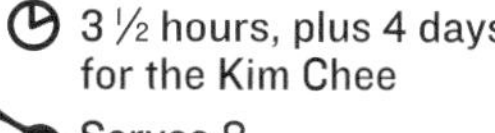

3 ½ hours, plus 4 days for the Kim Chee
Serves 8

Sticky Rice:

4 cups short-grain sticky rice

Spicy Braised Korean Pork:

- One 5- to 6-pound pork shoulder, trimmed, halved if necessary
- 1 tablespoon Korean red pepper or red pepper flakes
- 2 tablespoons paprika
- 2 tablespoons curry powder
- 2 tablespoons minced garlic
- 1 tablespoon salt, plus more to taste
- 1 teaspoon freshly ground black pepper, plus more to taste
- 2 tablespoons vegetable oil
- 2 Bosc pears, peeled, cored, and diced
- 1 cup diced carrots
- 1 cup diced celery
- 1 cup diced yellow onions
- 10 garlic cloves
- 2 tablespoons minced fresh ginger
- 1 quart apple juice
- 2 teaspoons rice vinegar, or to taste

Kim Chee (see right)

For the Sticky Rice:

1. Put the rice in a large bowl and add enough cold water to cover by 3 inches. Soak for about 3 hours (or overnight) while you're preparing the pork.
2. During the last 30 minutes or so of cooking the pork, drain the rice and place it in a steamer basket lined with cheesecloth. Place over a pot of boiling water, cover, and steam until tender, about 20 minutes. Remove from the heat and let stand, covered, for about 5 minutes.

For the Spicy Braised Korean Pork:

1. Preheat the oven to 350°F. Pat the pork dry with paper towels. In a small bowl, combine the red pepper, paprika, curry powder, garlic, 1 tablespoon salt, and 1 teaspoon pepper. Pat the rub all over the pork.
2. In a large, heavy pot, heat the oil over medium-high heat. Add the pork and sear until browned on all sides, 15 to 20 minutes total. Remove the pork from the pan and transfer to a large bowl or platter. Add the pears, carrots, celery, onions, garlic, and ginger to the fat in the pot. Reduce the heat to medium and sauté until tender, about 10 minutes. Add the apple juice, increase the heat to medium-high, and bring to a boil, stirring constantly.
3. Put the pork back in the pot and turn to coat. Bring the liquid back to a boil, then cover, turn off the heat and transfer to the oven. Bake for about 3 hours, turning the pork every 30 minutes, until very tender. Remove the pork and transfer to a platter. Tent with aluminum foil, then cut into thick pieces just before serving.
4. Skim the fat off the cooking liquid, place over medium-high heat, and boil until thickened, about 15 minutes. Add the vinegar and season with salt and pepper.

To Serve:

Spoon the sticky rice onto serving plates. Top with the pork and some sauce. Place the kim chee alongside and serve immediately.

ON THE SIDE:
Kim Chee

- 1 head napa cabbage
- 1 medium daikon radish
- About ½ cup salt
- 3 scallions, thinly sliced
- 3 garlic cloves, minced
- 4 teaspoons minced fresh ginger
- 1 tablespoon red pepper flakes or kim chee spice mix
- 2 teaspoons soy sauce

1. Separate the cabbage into leaves, discarding any damaged outer leaves. Peel the daikon and cut into ¼-inch-thick slices. In a large nonreactive bowl, layer the cabbage and daikon slices, sprinkling salt in between each layer, using about ½ cup salt total. Add water to cover by 1 inch and place a heavy plate on top of the leaves. Set aside overnight.
2. The next day, remove the plate and drain the vegetables. Rinse well under running water and drain. Cut the cabbage into ¼-inch-thick slices. Transfer the vegetables to a large nonreactive bowl. Add the scallions, garlic, ginger, pepper flakes, soy sauce, 2 teaspoons salt, and 1 cup water. Mix gently.
3. Transfer the vegetable mixture and liquid to a large crock. Cover tightly and refrigerate for 3 days, stirring once a day.

Threesome of Colorado Lamb

CHEF: Stephen
SEASON 1, EPISODE 1
ELIMINATION CHALLENGE: Prepare a signature dish to be served to the other contestants.

3 hours
Serves 4

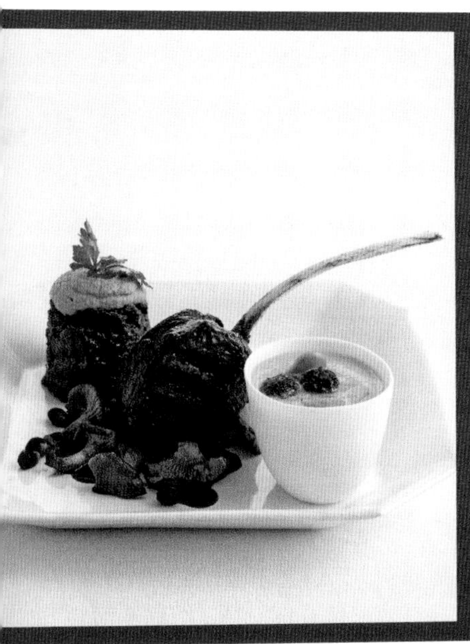

TIMESAVER!

Save time by making elements of each part of the threesome at once: simmer the soup and make the pomegranate reduction while the short ribs cook.

Short Ribs:

1 ¼ pounds lamb short ribs, or 1 lamb breast
½ teaspoon salt
2 garlic cloves
¼ cup red wine such as Tempranillo
1 tablespoon olive oil
2 Medjool dates, pitted
1 pound fresh peas, shelled
Fresh flat-leaf parsley sprigs

Soup:

2 small lamb sausages (about ¼ pound)
1 carrot, cut into ½-inch slices
1 celery rib, cut into ½-inch slices
1 leek, white and light green part only, washed and chopped
1 tablespoon unsalted butter
4 fresh fava bean pods

Rack of Lamb:

1 pomegranate
¼ cup red wine
1 tablespoon sugar
One 1 ½-pound rack of lamb (with 8 bones)
Coarse sea salt
12 to 16 chanterelle mushrooms
1 tablespoon olive oil
½ cup soy sauce
½ cup mirin
½ cup white miso paste

For the Short Ribs:

1. Season the short ribs with the salt. Put them in a gallon-size zip-top bag with the garlic, wine, and oil, press out as much air as possible, and seal the bag.
2. Bring a large pot of water to 180°F—just below a simmer. Lower the bag into the water and cook at 180°F for 2 hours. Remove the ribs from the bag and let them rest until cool enough to handle. Pull the meat from the bones and shred it; discard the bones and the bag.
3. Mince the dates and combine them with the lamb; set aside.
4. In a small saucepan of boiling water, cook the peas for 5 to 7 minutes, until soft; drain in a colander set over a bowl, reserving the cooking liquid. In a food processor, puree the peas, adding some of the reserved cooking liquid to make a smooth, thick puree. Season with salt to taste.

For the Soup:

1. Remove the casings from the sausages and form half of the sausage into miniature meatballs about ⅓ inch in diameter. Heat a small sauté pan or skillet over medium-high heat and cook the meatballs until browned and cooked through. Set aside.
2. Put the remaining sausage, the carrot, celery, leek, and water to cover in a small saucepan. Bring to a boil, then lower the heat and simmer for 1 hour. Pour through a fine-mesh sieve set over a bowl, reserving the cooking liquid. In a blender or food processor, puree the sausage and vegetables, adding the butter and most of the reserved liquid to make a thick, smooth soup. Add salt and pepper and set aside.
3. Open the fava bean pods and remove the beans. In a small saucepan of boiling water, blanch the beans for 2 minutes; drain. Peel the beans and set them aside.

For the Rack of Lamb:

1. Make several cuts in the pomegranate skin from top to bottom. Immerse the pomegranate in a bowl of water and gently break it apart. Pull the seeds away from the pith and they will sink. Pour off the water and pith, leaving the seeds in the bowl. Drain in a colander. Set ¼ cup of the seeds aside for garnish; place the rest in a blender and blend until finely chopped. Strain the liquid through a fine-mesh sieve lined with several layers of rinsed and squeezed cheesecloth set over a large bowl.
2. In a small saucepan, combine the pomegranate juice, wine, and sugar and bring to a boil. Cook for about 25 minutes, until the sauce is reduced by about half and is a syrupy consistency. Set aside.
3. Season the lamb all over with sea salt. Toss the mushrooms with the oil and sea salt to taste.
4. Preheat a charcoal grate and set the grate about 8 inches above the coals.
5. Lightly brush the grate with oil. When the flames have died down and the coals are white, put the lamb on the grill; brush the top of the lamb with soy sauce, cover the grill, and cook for 2 minutes, then turn the lamb over. Brush with soy sauce, cover the grill, cook for 2 minutes, then turn again. Brush with mirin, cover, cook for 2 minutes, then turn again, brush with mirin, cover, and cook for 2 minutes. Repeat with the miso paste, turning and brushing to create a crust, and cooking for 2 minutes on each side. Cover the grill and cook, turning as necessary, until the lamb registers 135°F for medium-rare, about 2 minutes longer, for a total of about 16 minutes. Remove the lamb to a carving board and let rest for 5 minutes. Cut between every other set of 2 bones into double-size chops.
6. Put the mushrooms on the grill and cook until softened, about 2 minutes.

To Serve:

1. Gently warm the lamb and date mixture in a small saucepan over low heat (or put in a glass bowl and heat for 30 seconds in a microwave oven). Place a small ring mold on one side of each of 4 serving plates and pack it with one quarter of the lamb mixture. Remove the mold to form a timbale. Top each timbale with a dollop of the pea puree and garnish with parsley.
2. Reheat the soup in a small saucepan. Divide the meatballs and fava beans among 4 small cups set on the serving plates. Ladle in the soup.
3. Spoon some of the pomegranate sauce into the center of each plate. Place the mushrooms over the sauce. Place a lamb chop on top of the mushrooms on each plate, garnish with the reserved pomegranate seeds, and serve immediately.

"The lamb was an expression of my signature style. There was the pomegranate glacé, which reflects my French training; the lamb based on Japanese wagyu beef, which represents my time at Nobu; and then the traditional lamb soup, which is very Italian."
STEPHEN

CHEF AND RESTAURATEUR HUBERT KELLER, GUEST JUDGE "THIS WAS ALTOGETHER A GREAT DISH. I LIKED IT AS SOON AS IT CAME TO THE TABLE."

Fennel-Crusted Pork Chops
with Three-Apple Fennel Salad and Apple Cider Sauce

CHEF: Howie
SEASON 3, EPISODE 3
ELIMINATION CHALLENGE: Turn traditional family favorites into healthier dishes.

Fennel-Crusted Pork Chops:
- ½ cup olive oil
- 2 large shallots, chopped
- 4 garlic cloves, chopped
- 2 tablespoons Dijon-style mustard
- 4 rosemary sprigs, chopped
- Leaves from 4 thyme sprigs, chopped
- 5 tablespoons fennel seeds, toasted and roughly ground
- Salt and freshly ground black pepper
- 4 boneless pork loin chops (each about ½ inch thick)

Apple Cider Sauce:
- 1 quart apple cider
- 1 cup apple cider vinegar
- 1 cup packed light brown sugar
- 4 shallots, chopped
- 5 garlic cloves, chopped
- One 2-inch piece ginger, thinly sliced
- 1 small bunch fresh thyme
- 2 pieces star anise
- 2 cinnamon sticks
- 1 bay leaf

Three-Apple Fennel Salad (see right)

1 ½ hours, plus marinating overnight
Serves 4
Winner

For the Fennel-Crusted Pork Chops Marinade:

1. Combine the oil, shallots, garlic, mustard, rosemary, thyme, 1 tablespoon of the fennel seeds, and salt and pepper to taste in a blender and puree.
2. Place the pork chops in a heavy-duty zip-top bag, pour in the marinade, seal the bag, and distribute the marinade to coat. Refrigerate overnight to marinate, moving the pork chops around a few times to keep them thoroughly coated.

For the Apple Cider Sauce:

1. Combine all the ingredients in a large saucepan and place over medium-high heat. Bring to a boil, then reduce the heat to medium-high and simmer, uncovered, until the sauce has a rich, glossy consistency and is reduced to about 1 cup, 45 to 60 minutes. Watch carefully toward the end, as the sauce will bubble and start to get syrupy—remove from the heat just before it becomes thick and syrupy.
2. Strain and discard the solids. Set aside and reheat just before serving.

To Cook the Fennel-Crusted Pork Chops:

1. Preheat the grill to medium-high.
2. Combine the remaining 4 tablespoons ground fennel with 1 teaspoon salt and 1 teaspoon pepper. Remove the pork chops from the marinade and wipe off any excess. Press the pork chops into the fennel seeds to coat all sides.
3. Oil the grill rack, then grill the pork chops, covered, turning once, until just cooked through, about 10 minutes, or until the internal temperature reaches 150° to 160°F. Let the pork rest for a few minutes, then cut into thin slices. (Alternatively, the chops can be cooked in a lightly oiled large ridged grill pan over medium-high heat.)

To Serve:

Spoon the sauce onto serving plates, top with the pork slices and fennel salad. Garnish with the reserved fennel fronds and serve immediately.

ON THE SIDE:
Three-Apple Fennel Salad

- ½ cup olive oil
- 3 tablespoons apple cider vinegar, or to taste
- ½ cup golden raisins
- ½ teaspoon ground cumin
- Salt and freshly ground black pepper
- ½ cup julienned Granny Smith apple (about ½ apple)
- ½ cup julienned Golden Delicious apple (about ½ apple)
- ½ cup julienned Braeburn apple (about ½ apple)
- 1 ½ cups julienned fennel (from 1 small bulb), fronds reserved for garnish

1. While you're cooking the apple cider sauce, in a blender, combine the oil, vinegar, 2 tablespoons water, the raisins, cumin, and salt and pepper to taste and blend to combine and chop the raisins.

2. Just before serving, combine the apples and fennel in a large bowl and add the vinaigrette. Toss to coat, taste, and add more vinegar, salt, or pepper if needed.

Veal Medallions

with Cremini and Apple Brandy, with Cauliflower Gratin

CHEF: Casey
SEASON 3, EPISODE 11
ELIMINATION CHALLENGE: Devise a delicious entrée for Continental's BusinessFirst service.

1 hour, 45 minutes
Serves 6
Winner

Compound Butter:

2 cups unsalted butter, at room temperature
1 teaspoon salt
1 teaspoon chopped fresh parsley
1 teaspoon chopped fresh thyme
1 teaspoon zahtar

Apple Brandy Sauce:

1 tablespoon olive oil
½ onion, finely diced
8 ounces bacon, finely diced
12 ounces cremini mushrooms, trimmed and quartered
½ cup brandy
1 Granny Smith apple, peeled and finely diced
1 cup low-sodium chicken stock
½ cup veal demi-glace
Salt and freshly ground black pepper

Cauliflower Gratin:

Salt
1 large head cauliflower, cut into florets
2 ½ cups milk
4 tablespoons unsalted butter
¼ cup all-purpose flour
8 ounces Gruyère cheese, grated
Freshly ground black pepper
¾ cup cracker crumbs

Vegetables:

1 tablespoon olive oil
1 bunch white asparagus, tips only (about 1 pound)
Salt and freshly ground black pepper
6 Brussels sprouts, halved
6 plum tomatoes, halved

Veal:

Olive oil
Twelve 2-ounce slices veal strip

To Serve:

Minced fresh parsley

For the Compound Butter:

In a mixer or food processor, combine the butter, salt, parsley, thyme, and zahtar. Process until smooth; set aside.

For the Apple Brandy Sauce:

1. In a medium saucepan, heat the oil over medium heat. Add the onion, bacon, and mushrooms and sauté until the bacon is browned and the onion is translucent, about 8 minutes. Pour off most of the fat and return the pan to medium heat.
2. Add the brandy to the pan, stirring to scrape up any browned bits. Add the apple, stock, and demi-glace. Simmer for 10 minutes, then season with salt and pepper to taste. Set aside.

For the Cauliflower Gratin:

1. Preheat the oven to 350°F.
2. In a medium saucepan of boiling salted water, cook the cauliflower for 3 minutes. Drain and transfer the cauliflower to a bowl of ice water to cool. Drain and put the cauliflower in a 9-by-11-inch baking dish. Set aside.

WHAT IS . . .

Zahtar?

Zahtar (pronounced "ZAH-tar") is a Middle Eastern spice blend that contains white sesame seeds, dried thyme, and dried ground sumac.

3. In a small saucepan, bring the milk to just below a simmer over low heat.
4. Meanwhile, in a medium saucepan, melt the butter over medium-low heat and add the flour. Cook, stirring constantly, until the mixture is light golden brown, 3 to 5 minutes.
5. Gradually add the milk to the mixture, whisking constantly. Cook until thickened to a sauce consistency. Set 3 tablespoons of the cheese aside and add the remaining cheese to the sauce a little at a time, whisking constantly to incorporate. Season the sauce with salt and pepper to taste, then pour it over the cauliflower.
6. Sprinkle the reserved cheese and the cracker crumbs over the cauliflower and bake for 15 to 20 minutes, until browned and bubbling.

For the Vegetables:

1. In a large sauté pan or skillet, heat the oil over medium-high heat and add the asparagus. Season with salt and pepper to taste and sauté until just tender, 3 to 5 minutes. Set aside.
2. Return the pan to the heat, add more oil if necessary, and add the Brussels sprouts. Season with salt and pepper to taste and sauté until well browned and tender, covering the pan and lowering the heat if they start to brown too quickly, 8 to 10 minutes. Set aside.
3. Return the pan to the heat, add a bit more oil, and add the tomatoes, cut side down. Cook, without turning, until the tomatoes are caramelized and lightly browned but still hold their shape, about 4 minutes. Sprinkle lightly with salt and pepper and set aside.

For the Veal:

1. Preheat a charcoal grill and set the grate about 6 inches above the coals.
2. Lightly brush the grate with oil. When the flames have died down and the coals are white, place the veal on the grill. Cook until just done, about 2 minutes on each side. Remove to a large platter and dot each medallion with compound butter.

To Serve:

1. Reheat the sauce and stir in any accumulated juices from the veal.
2. Divide the asparagus, Brussels sprouts, and tomatoes among 6 serving plates. Place 2 veal medallions on each plate. Spoon a bit of the sauce over each serving and garnish with parsley. Serve immediately, with the gratin on the side.

"I've learned that Tom doesn't really like grilling, and Gail doesn't like to eat veal, so I'm pretty happy I was able to win with this one!"

CASEY

CHEF AND AUTHOR ANTHONY BOURDAIN, GUEST JUDGE "I THINK CASEY SHOWED US THINGS THAT YOU LOOK FOR IN A CHEF: CREATIVITY AND DARING."

Curried Lamb Kabobs

CHEF: Marcel
SEASON 2, EPISODE 10
QUICKFIRE CHALLENGE: Create a snack using mayonnaise, barbecue sauce, or Italian dressing.

2 cups mayonnaise
2 teaspoons honey
¼ cup Madras curry powder
1 pound lamb loin, cut into 1-inch cubes
1 portobello mushroom cap, cut into four 1-inch cubes
4 small tomatoes
Olive oil
Salt and freshly ground black pepper

30 minutes
Serves 2
Winner

1. Preheat a charcoal grill and set the grate about 8 inches above the coals.
2. In a small bowl, whisk the mayonnaise, honey, and curry powder together and set aside.
3. In 3 separate small bowls, toss the lamb, mushroom, and tomatoes with oil to coat and season with salt and pepper to taste.
4. Lightly brush the grate with oil. When the flames have died down and the coals are white, put the mushroom and lamb cubes on the grill and cook for about 5 minutes, turning occasionally, until the mushroom is softened and the lamb is cooked to medium-rare or rare. Place the tomatoes on the grill; cook for 2 to 3 minutes, until blistered and charred.
5. Thread the mushroom squares, tomatoes, and lamb cubes onto skewers and place the kabobs on 2 serving plates with dollops of curry mayonnaise. Serve immediately.

HOW TO:

Spice Up Your Mayonnaise

With a little imagination, mayonnaise can be one of the most versatile sauces at the cook's disposal. Add a bit of lemon juice and crushed garlic and you have a quick aioli to go with crudités or to spread on crusty bread with grilled summer vegetables. Add chopped capers or cornichons, some minced shallot, and a squeeze of lemon juice to make an elegant tartar sauce for lightly fried fish. Stir in any spice blend for an instant dipping sauce: curry powder, Cajun spices, or your own personal blend. The possibilities are limitless. Sitting patiently in the refrigerator door is a miracle waiting to happen.

CHEF AND RESTAURATEUR MIKE YAKURA, GUEST JUDGE "FANTASTIC. TECHNICALLY DONE VERY, VERY WELL. I THOUGHT THE MAYONNAISE REALLY HEIGHTENED THE DISH."

Beware! Bourdain

Guest judges come and guest judges go, but nobody forgets an episode of *Top Chef* when Anthony Bourdain sits at Judges' Table.

He's cranky, opinionated, and a master of the vicious metaphor, but what saves Chef Bourdain from being simply a mean bastard is the genuine love of cooking and chefs that pervades even his nastiest barbs.

Not that that's of much comfort to those on the receiving end. To get scalded by Bourdain's displeasure is to burn for days; to be brushed by his approval may be the highest compliment a *Top Chef* contestant can get.

Of course, it's often hard to tell the difference. As a public service, we present the finely calibrated Insult-O-Meter.

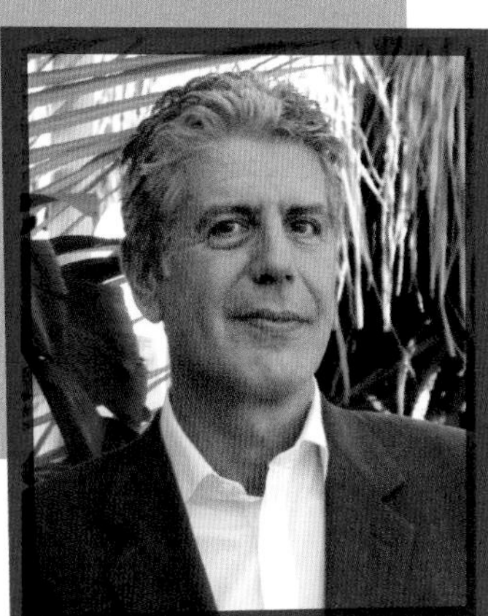

"What kind of crack house are you running here?"

—to Tom Colicchio at Season 2's Thanksgiving dinner

"It's too dry, but I kind of like that he's had the balls to go this far out. Astroboy has balls!"

—on Marcel Vigneron's Turkey Roulade

FEEL THE LOVE

"I love you like a son, already. Your sheer contrariness, your sheer refusal to conform—I kind of like that. Your Twice-Baked Potato, in spite of its absolutely Flintstonian execution, was, for me, the single most enjoyable mouthful of food I had this evening. The taste—it didn't suck."

—on Michael Midgley's Twice-Baked Potato

"I would love this dish if I was drunk. I feel I should be eating it at the bar."

—on Brian Malarkey's Eel Surf and Turf

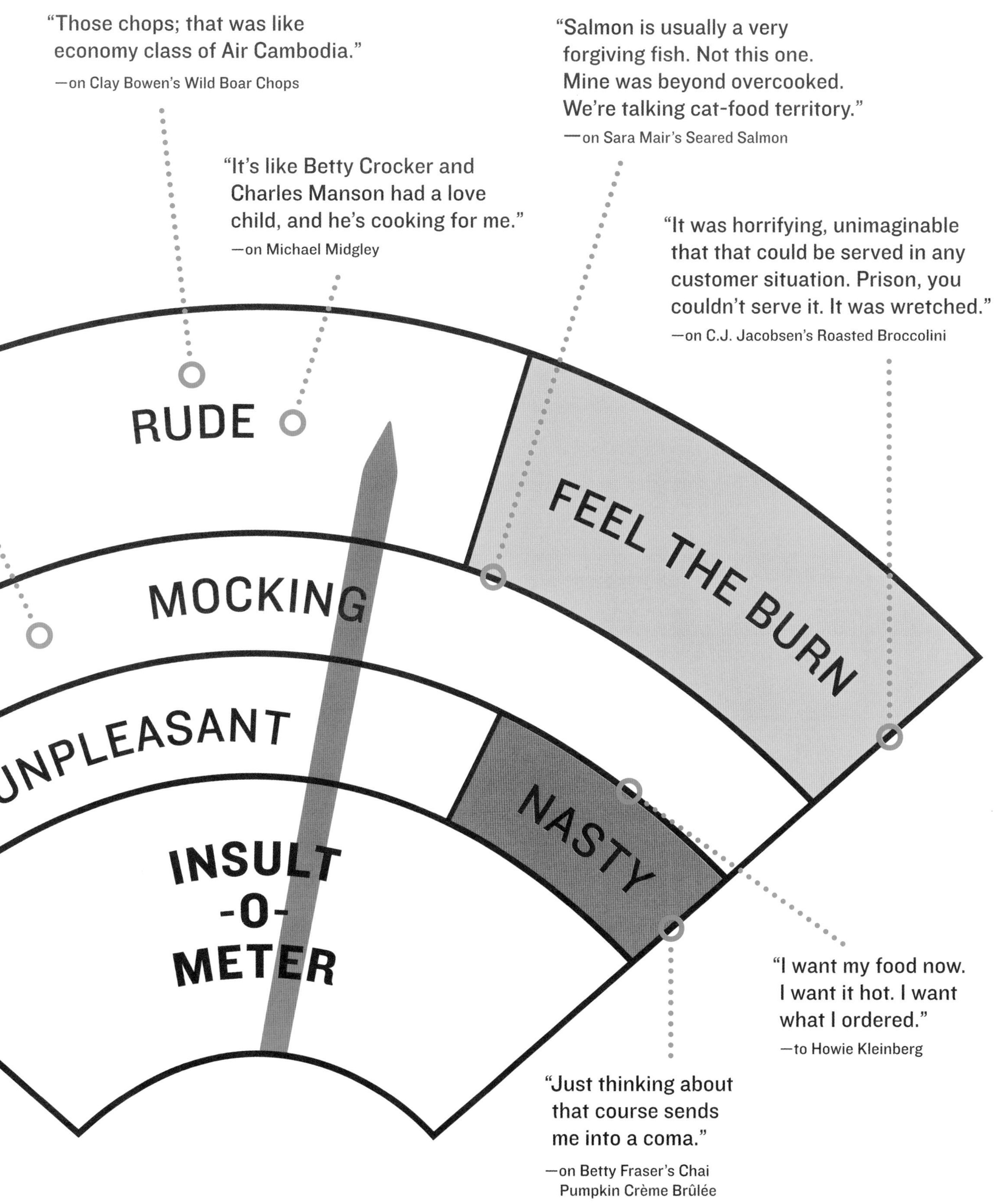
"Those chops; that was like economy class of Air Cambodia."
—on Clay Bowen's Wild Boar Chops
"Salmon is usually a very forgiving fish. Not this one. Mine was beyond overcooked. We're talking cat-food territory."
—on Sara Mair's Seared Salmon
"It's like Betty Crocker and Charles Manson had a love child, and he's cooking for me."
—on Michael Midgley
"It was horrifying, unimaginable that that could be served in any customer situation. Prison, you couldn't serve it. It was wretched."
—on C.J. Jacobsen's Roasted Broccolini
RUDE
FEEL THE BURN
MOCKING
UNPLEASANT
NASTY
INSULT -O- METER
"I want my food now. I want it hot. I want what I ordered."
—to Howie Kleinberg
"Just thinking about that course sends me into a coma."
—on Betty Fraser's Chai Pumpkin Crème Brûlée

Season 2: Elimination Bracket

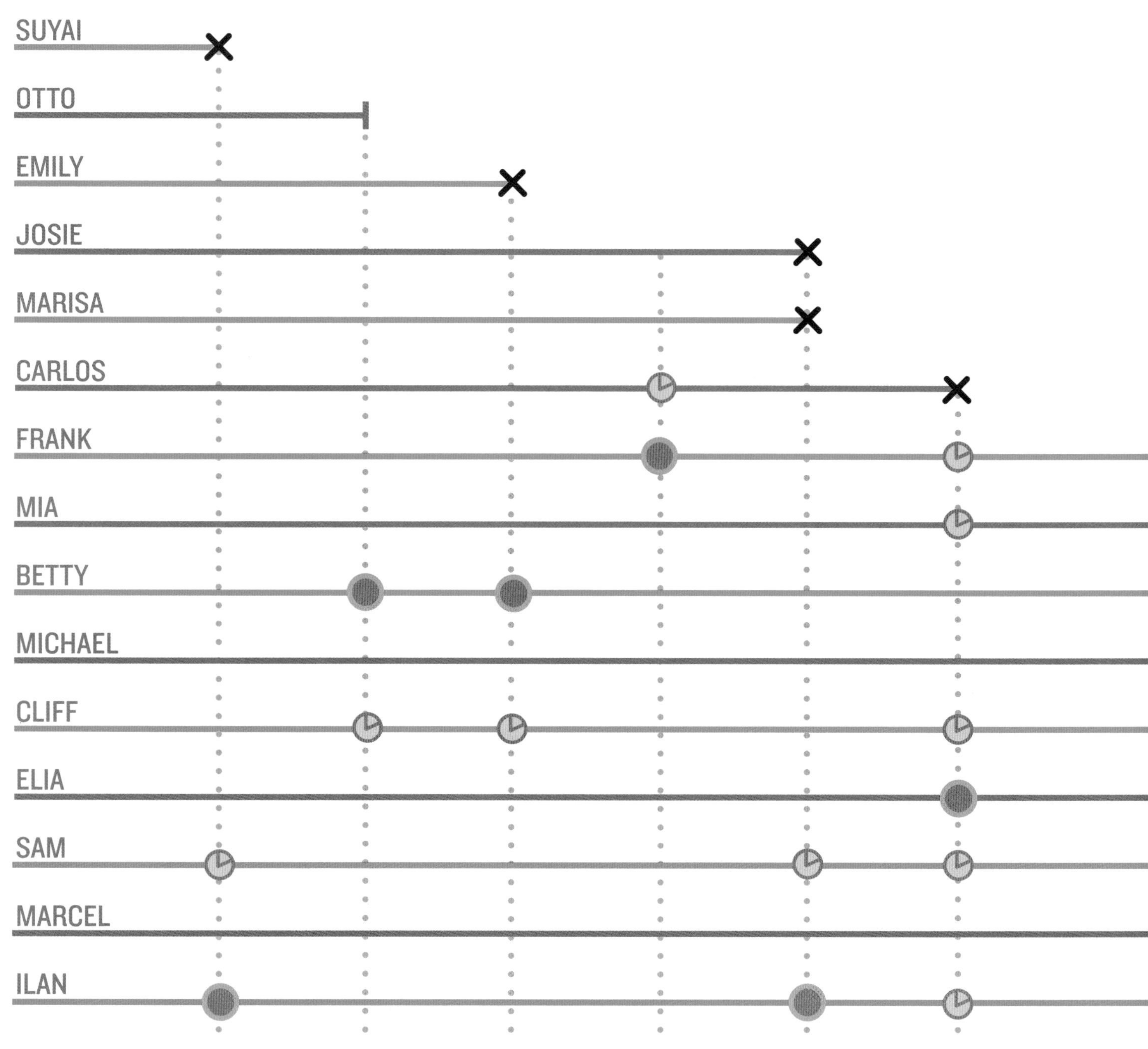

Winner of title "Top Chef"

Winner of Elimination Challenge

Winner of Quickfire

Winner of both Quickfire and Elimination Challenges

Contestant Eliminated

Quit Competition

Disqualified (See page 123)

* No one was eliminated

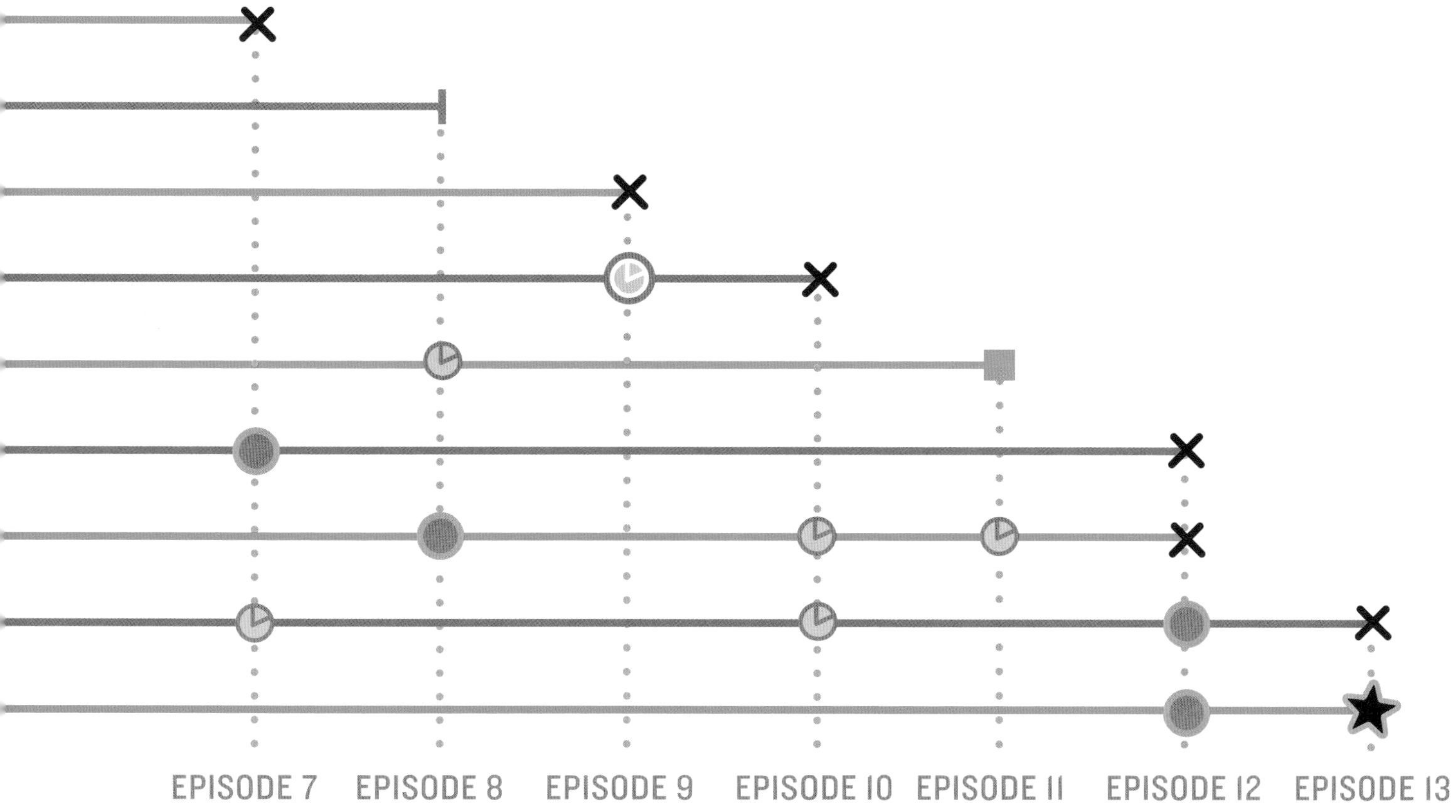

EPISODE 7 EPISODE 8 EPISODE 9 EPISODE 10 EPISODE 11 EPISODE 12 EPISODE 13

Season 2: Episode Guide

 Episode

 Winner of Title "Top Chef"

 Winner of Elimination Challenge

 Winner of Quickfire

 Guest Judge

Contestant Eliminated

Season 2

The Knives Come Out

It didn't take long for Season 2 to establish itself as a wild and wacky ride.

Only two episodes in, Otto walked off with a crate of lychees and then resigned from the competition. With a historic heat wave in Los Angeles and a cast of characters guaranteed to set off sparks, tempers just rose from there. Betty got things going in the Marcel-bashing sweepstakes. Elia seemed perpetually on the verge of cracking. Mike was, well, Mike. And things devolved into a fascinating simulation of a junior high school cafeteria. The finale in Hawaii between Marcel and Ilan was the perfect cap to this emotional season.

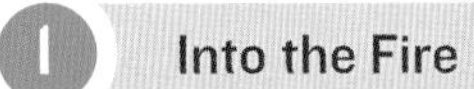

1 Into the Fire

 Create a flambé dish in a limited amount of time.

 Prepare a dish using all the ingredients in a closed crate to be served to the other contestants.

This season starts off with a bang as the chefs flare up flambés for the Quickfire, then cook for each other with cruel and unusual mystery ingredients. Sam and Ilan feel right at home, but Suyai can't take the heat and is the first to go.

 *Top Chef* winner Harold Dieterle

 Sam

 Suyai

 Ilan

2 Far East Feast

 Create a sushi dish for master sushi chef Hiroshi Shima.

 Split into Team Vietnam and Team Korea to prepare dishes using the flavors of each country.

Much to Marcel's dismay, Cliff impresses the "bad-ass" sushi whiz Hiroshi Shima. Later, Betty's superhuman smile woos the judges and Marisa snitches on Otto, who commits hara-kiri over a crate of stolen lychees.

 Chef Hiroshi Shima and Chef Ming Tsai

 Cliff

 Otto (Quits)

 Betty

3 Food for the People

 Create an original ice cream flavor and serve it at the Redondo Beach Seaside Lagoon.

 Update a childhood classic for TGI Friday's.

Marcel's bacon and avocado ice cream gets more grimaces than grins from the kids at Redondo Beach, and Mike is chewed out by Tom for managing to make even a steak sandwich taste awful.

 Chef Stephen Bulgarelli

 Cliff

 Emily

Betty

4 Less Is More

 Create an amuse-bouche using ingredients from a vending machine.

 Create a meal under 500 calories for diabetic and overweight children.

Rolls of quarters in hand, the chefs go shopping in the break room. Ilan fries some corn nuts, Carlos garnishes his veggie loaf with grapefruit soda, and Mike goes more avant-garde than even Marcel. At camp, Frank's pizza gets the kids' seal of approval, while his teammate Betty bends the rules.

 Chef Suzanne Goin

 Carlos

No one

 Frank

5 Social Service

 Create a dish using offal, the leftover parts of animals.

 Cook a six-course lunch for sixty using only leftovers.

Marcel gets vild with pig's blood (is he Dracula in disguise?) while for Ilan it's death by saffron. Still, he and Sam emerge on top again, while miscommunication in the kitchen sends two chefs home.

 Chef Michelle Bernstein

 Sam

 Josie and Marisa

 Ilan

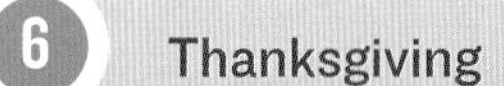

6 Thanksgiving

 Create a dish using three different canned foods.

 Reinvent traditional ingredients for a cutting-edge Thanksgiving dinner.

After a chocolate catharsis, Elia and her mushroom soup give Anthony Bourdain little to sneer at. Frank blows a fuse at "Astroboy," and Carlos hits the road for an uncooked, uninspired salad.

 Chef and author Anthony Bourdain

 Cliff, Frank, Ilan, Mia, and Sam

X Carlos

 Elia

7 The Raw and the Cooked

 Create an uncooked entrée with fresh ingredients from the Redondo Beach Farmers' Market.

 Prepare breakfast on the beach for surfers.

Frank shakes things up in the Quickfire (literally) but he and his quiche fall apart on the beach when the chefs gather round a campfire to cook breakfast. While Marcel chats up surfer babes, Elia gets win number two.

 Chef Raphael Lunetta

 Marcel

X Frank

 Elia

8 Holiday Spirit

 Create a Baileys® mixed drink and an accompanying dish.

 Working in two teams of four, cater a holiday party for *Los Angeles* magazine.

In a team challenge, the chefs split up to cater a Hollywood holiday hoedown. Sam and his team ace it with a huge spread, while Elia's team runs low on food, but not on tension. Mia rants and raves but rescues Elia by sacrificing herself.

 Mixologist Kristin Woodward, Chef Lee Hefter, and Ted Allen

 Cliff

 Mia (Quits)

 Sam

9 Seven

 Create a dish based on a color drawn from the knife block.

 Create a seven-course meal, with each course representing one of the seven deadly sins.

Cliff flies (color) blind in the Quickfire, and is no match for Mike. Down one tooth and hopped up on painkillers, everyone's favorite underdog pulls a *Top Chef* hat trick.

 Ted Allen and Chef Robert Ivan

 Michael

 Betty

 Michael

10 Unhappy Customers

 Create a snack using three Kraft® Foods products: mayonnaise, barbecue sauce, or Italian dressing.

 Divide into two teams and turn an empty space into a restaurant in twenty-four hours.

Oreo hockey pucks and nauseating gnocchi mean no one wins Restaurant Wars. The team leaders get spared for once; it's the sous chefs and wait staff who take the brunt of the judges' wrath.

 Chef Mike Yakura

 Marcel and Sam

 Michael

 No one

11 Sense and Sensuality

 Create a dish using Nestlé Chocolatier® products.

 Create a romantic five-course menu.

It's chaos in the kitchen as Elia, riding high off of a Quickfire thumbs-up from Chef Eric Ripert, stresses over her dessert. Later, Cliff joins the pick-on-Marcel club with a "hair"-brained plan that goes too far and is forced to leave the competition.

 Chef Eric Ripert

 Sam

 Cliff (Disqualified)

 No one

12 Hawaii Finale: Part 1

 Rethink two classic Hawaiian dishes.

The chefs touch down in Hawaii and, for once, get an afternoon off to enjoy a traditional Hawaiian feast. The fun soon ends, though, when they are told to remake what they just ate, adding their own twists to the classic dishes.

 Chef Alan Wong

 Ilan and Marcel

X Elia and Sam

13 Hawaii Finale: Part 2

 Prepare a five-course meal to be served to a table of luminaries from the culinary world.

Marcel and Ilan battle it out on the Big Island. Mike and Sam swallow their pride (kind of) and help Marcel as he asks, "Where's the fish?!" Betty, Elia, and Ilan are one happy family, and Ilan's safe but savory food gets him the crown.

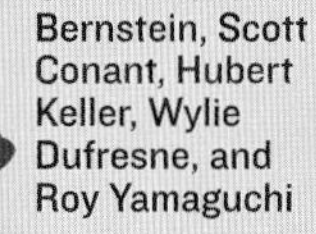 Chefs Michelle Bernstein, Scott Conant, Hubert Keller, Wylie Dufresne, and Roy Yamaguchi

 Marcel

  Ilan

"I wanna be famous."
ILAN

TOP STATS

Age
25

Hometown
Great Neck, NY

Currently
Living in Brooklyn

Favorite piece of equipment
Short plancha spatula

Chefs he most admires
Andy Nussen, Raphael Ray Hall, and Ramiro Tacuri

Favorite judge or guest judge
Gail Simmons

Philosophy
"Every time you change the format in which you're doing your craft, you learn more."

Featured recipes
Spanish Tortilla, p. 45
Pork Shoulder, p. 77
Baked Escargot, p. 80
Lau Lau, p. 81
Korean Pork, p. 109
Gazpacho, p. 162
Fideos, p. 164

Ilan Hall

SEASON 2: WINNER
WINS: 2 ELIMINATION CHALLENGES, 1 QUICKFIRE

Season 2 seemed to be as much about mind games as cooking, and the man who proved himself best at both was winner Ilan Hall, the hipster line cook from New York's Casa Mono.

As good as he was at turning out Spanish-influenced delicacies, he was at least as good at falling into the kind of cliquish drama you might find in a high school cafeteria. Some Marcel fans may have looked at him and seen a bit of a bully, but it's undeniable that Ilan won the loyalty of his housemates and the admiration of the judges. And he scored the ultimate victory by defeating Marcel head-to-head in the finale.

On the very first episode, you said you wanted to be famous. How's that working out?
I think I was just excited to be there. I had all these things running through my head. I said it and I meant it, but it was more important that I be respected for what I was doing. That people liked what I was cooking.

Was it a weird experience to watch yourself on TV?
It was interesting, not weird. For six weeks, you have cameras in your face, so you're already used to a really weird lifestyle. I was prepared. It was exciting. The weirdest part is that people come up and talk to me as though they know who I am.

Are they angry with you about how you treated Marcel?
Yeah. I get some of that. But you have to understand a few things. One, people weren't there, living the experience with us. Two, they're seeing us on television and judging our entire personalities on one or two clips. It's not real life. So I can't take people too seriously. They don't really know what they're talking about.

Do you regret anything that happened?
Not really. You get aggravated sometimes. It's a stressful situation and you react in certain ways. There was no deep-seated hate or anything like that. We just didn't get along. Besides, you can't regret anything in life. You learn something from every experience.

Does it bother you when people complain that you can only cook Spanish food?
Everything I made showed my cooking skill. If anything, I was more challenged than the other chefs because I used only one cuisine. Chefs study their whole lives to master one cuisine. You go to a French restaurant and they're cooking French recipes. So, I thought that was kind of silly.

Your biggest victory was over Sam in the next-to-last episode. And Padma thought your taro was undercooked.
Well, Padma was wrong.

CHEF AND AUTHOR ANTHONY BOURDAIN, GUEST JUDGE "ILAN WAS VERY SHREWD. HE SURVIVED LARGELY ON RECIPES FROM CASA MONO, AND THERE'S NOTHING WRONG WITH THAT. I HAVE NO PROBLEM WITH A SMART PROFESSIONAL WITH A REALISTIC VIEW OF HIS STRENGTHS AND WEAKNESSES BEATING OUT A MORE TALENTED BUT LESS WISE CONTESTANT."

IT'S MORE THAN JUST SAFFRON . . .

If Ilan's rise to the title of Top Chef accomplished one thing, it was making Americans more aware than ever of Spanish food. While less celebrated, the dishes of Spain have much in common with those of Italy. Both focus on the strength of fresh, earthy ingredients and do great things with olive oil, pork, and seafood. Spanish cuisine shows the influence not only of its Mediterranean neighbors, but of nearby Africa and of the Moors who once ruled the Iberian peninsula.

Ilan got his Spanish training at the New York restaurant Casa Mono, and he bristles at the notion that he failed to show range. If anything, he points out, "the fact that I was able to win using Spanish cooking proves what a large and inclusive cuisine it is."

Ironically, by far the most famous and influential Spanish chef of the past decade is Ferran Adrià, who cooks a very different incarnation of Spanish cuisine. In fact, he's most famous for one innovation: Marcel's beloved foam.

[Rapping] "You say my food lacks fundamentals like salt and peppa and I'm like, yo man, whatever!"
MARCEL

TOP STATS

Age
27

Hometown
Bainbridge, WA

Currently
Living in Las Vegas, where he recently helped open Company American Bistro

Favorite piece of equipment
Vita-Prep blender

Chefs he most admires
Ferran Adrià, Thomas Keller, Joel Robuchon, and Alice Waters

Favorite fast food
In-N-Out Burger's Double-Double® Animal® Style

Philosophy
"Studying the science of food ultimately makes me a better cook."

Featured recipes

Marcel Vigneron

SEASON 2
ELIMINATED: EPISODE 13, "HAWAII FINALE: PART 2"
WINS: 1 ELIMINATION CHALLENGE, 2 QUICKFIRES

Through the first three seasons of *Top Chef*, there have been 42 contestants. None has been as memorable, as divisive, as confusing, as infuriating, or as downright strange as Marcel.

Short in stature, large in hair, Marcel arrived on the show promising to blow the competition away with his skills at molecular gastronomy. That he did, making it all the way up to the season finale. But it was his personality that caused the biggest chemical reactions. It wasn't always clear why but, one by one, Marcel's housemates lost their temper with the chef. They called him a gnat, a know-it-all, a cheat, and pretty much everything else under the sun. Eventually, to Cliff's eternal regret, they even tackled him on video. Marcel mostly brushed it off, occasionally venting in defiant culinary raps on the roof. Whether you pitied him as a picked-on geek or wanted desperately to beat him up yourself, Marcel achieved one thing for sure: he was impossible to ignore.

Did you feel like you were accurately portrayed on the show?
A lot of my friends who watched the show got a huge kick out of it. You know, the arrogant, egotistical, antisocial Marcel. Because I'm very social. I get along great with people.

So why do you think people had such a problem with you?
I take what I do very seriously. I have a lot of passion for my craft. And I don't really care what people think about me. When Elia turned against me at the end, I was like, What!? It was totally out of left field. But it's hard to be independent when you have Sam and Ilan whispering in your ears. I think they were kind of desperate because I was killing it.

How could you pick Michael to help you in the finale?
Michael totally went to bat for me. He was like, "What's next, chef? What's next?" He helped a lot more than Sam did.

Are you still making foams?
I don't even use the term "molecular gastronomy" anymore. I felt like I was becoming kind of pigeonholed by that. Like any artist—and I consider myself a culinary artist—I go through phases and when I was on the show I just wanted to be as creative as possible: pile garnish on top of garnish on top of garnish. Since then, I've been becoming more refined. Like, sometimes I just want to make a roast chicken or a classic caprese salad.

Is there anything you would have changed about your time on *Top Chef*?
There were a couple of times when I was sitting at home thinking, Dude, you should have kept your mouth shut. You look like such a prick. But, without being cocky or arrogant, I'm not going to change just because people don't like me. I'm happy with who I am.

TOM COLICCHIO, HEAD JUDGE "MARCEL HAS A VERY QUIRKY PERSONALITY. HE'S NOT A BAD GUY; HE'S JUST A KID WHO DIDN'T ALWAYS KNOW WHAT HE WAS DOING. NOWADAYS, THE FOAMS HAVE BECOME SUCH A MOVEMENT, AND HE REALLY THOUGHT HE WAS DOING IT, BUT MOST OF THE STUFF DIDN'T WORK."

ALL ABOUT FOAM

As Marcel would be the first to tell you, "molecular gastronomy" hardly began with him. All cooking, of course, is based in science—the interaction of heat and protein, acid and base, and so on. In the 1980s, however, chefs and scientists began exploring a new kind of cooking that made use of advanced chemistry in pursuit of new flavors. None is more famous or influential than Ferran Adrià, chef of the restaurant El Bulli in Catalonia, Spain. Adrià closes his restaurant, often called the best in Europe, for six months a year to travel and work in his Barcelona laboratory.

Meanwhile, foams have swept the culinary world. In America, the most famous molecular gastronomist is none other than *Top Chef* guest judge Wylie Dufresne, inventor of deep-fried mayonnaise. Now that would have made one hell of a Quickfire!

"If I could have an IV running mayonnaise through my veins, I probably would."
SAM

TOP STATS

Age
30

Hometown
Charlotte, NC

Currently
Opening a restaurant in New York City

Chefs he most admires
Wylie Dufresne, Tom Douglas, James Burns, and Suzanne Goin

Go-to ingredient
Vinegar

Favorite comfort food
Ranch Dressing

Philosophy
"I cook light and seasonal."

Featured recipes
Pork Shoulder, p. 77
Beignets, p. 96
Espresso Shrimp, p. 167
Fruit Salad, p. 187

Sam Talbot

SEASON 2: FAN FAVORITE
ELIMINATED: EPISODE 12, "HAWAII FINALE: PART I"
WINS: 1 ELIMINATION CHALLENGE, 5 QUICKFIRES

In a season when so many of the characters seemed to fall into high school stereotypes, it was probably inevitable that there be one tall, dark, sensitive chef that indisputably earned the title of "Top Hunk."

That chef was Sam Talbot—he of the sideburns and bandannas, of the soft voice and strong hands, quietly coping with diabetes. Even when he snapped and went on a long tirade against Marcel, it was hard to hate the guy or doubt his abilities. His performance in Hawaii was so strong that Tom, Padma, and Gail argued deep into the night about whether Sam should advance to the finale instead of Ilan. It was one of the most contentious Judges' Tables ever. All in all, not a bad run for a guy whose mom worried he wasn't smiling enough.

Has life changed much since the show aired?
Yes, a year ago I would never have thought so many doors would open or that I'd meet so many great people because of the wide success of the show. It is still very humbling to have people approach me, whether I'm shopping for food or I'm walking down a street. It's just been a great experience, all-around.

Why was there so much drama during Season 2?
For some reason, it was really cliquey. Instantly. You could easily pick up on it at home: there were the cool kids and the dork and the older guys. But that's part of what draws people to watch the show.

Is there any animosity between you and Ilan, since he essentially beat you out for a spot in the finale?
In retrospect, I'm glad I didn't win. I mean, monetarily it would have been nice. But I don't have a giant bull's-eye on my back.

How was the experience of watching yourself on TV?
Before every episode I would literally have a panic attack, because even though you were there, you can't remember everything you said. You know, you've just slept for two hours or you haven't eaten for fifteen hours and they're asking you questions.

Did you see any moments you regretted?
I think I look miserable and unhappy throughout the thing. My mother kept asking why I didn't smile. But I was kind of miserable. I'm an only child, and I'm not used to living and being around so many people, especially seven other guys. It took a little getting used to, and, of course, it was a little nerve-racking sometimes.

To judge by the blogs, you being miserable and nutty is very attractive to women.
I know. Maybe I should keep that look going.

TOM COLICCHIO, HEAD JUDGE "I'VE HUNG OUT WITH SAM, DOING EVENTS. I'VE COOKED WITH HIM. I LIKE HIM; I THINK HE'S A GOOD GUY. HE HASN'T LET THIS STUFF GET TO HIS HEAD."

SAM'S RECIPE FOR A ROMANTIC DINNER

"To me, there's nothing sexier than bringing your date to the green market with you, to get inspired together and plan a menu. Just talk to her: 'What do you like? Doesn't this butternut squash look good? How do you like it prepared?' If you're both involved from the get-go, it's much more intimate.

"Then, instead of her just showing up to a finished meal, have her come to the kitchen and be a part of the cooking experience. Put some music on the iPod. Let her taste things. Food is very sexual, you know, whether you're peeling pomegranates and popping the seeds in her mouth or sharing a strawberry or whatever. In my experience, it tends to lead to different kinds of fun a little later in the evening."

“Smart people decide to do what they like to do, not what the world thinks.”

ELIA

TOP STATS

Age

29

Hometown

Mexico City, Mexico

Currently

Living in Las Vegas

Number of culinary degrees

34

Philosophy

“There has to be definition in your dish, a definite taste that comes out. The others just supplement it.”

Featured recipes

Waffle, p. 39
Korean Pork, p. 109
Roasted Chicken, p. 155
Ahi Tuna Tacos, p. 170
Portobello Crème, p. 193
Cheesecake, p. 240

Elia Aboumrad

SEASON 2
ELIMINATED: EPISODE 12, "HAWAII FINALE: PART I"
WINS: 2 ELIMINATION CHALLENGES, 0 QUICKFIRES

Season 2 of *Top Chef* will probably always be remembered for devolving into a contest of wills and words between boys—Ilan and company on one hand, Marcel on the other. But there was one woman right in the thick of it.

Elia hardly looked like a formidable contestant when the competition began, choosing red wine for the very first flambé Quickfire. But, as the weeks went by, she emerged as a force to be reckoned with, scoring perhaps her biggest triumph with a festive, extravagant roast chicken when asked to embody pride during the seven deadly sins challenge. Elia also showed herself to be temperamental and even a little mischievous. Angry and dispirited after a bad day, she let it all out by smearing chocolate over her face. And, of course, there was the infamous head-shaving incident and her accusations that Marcel was cheating, delivered at Judges' Table moments before she was eliminated. For all that, Elia remains defiant. "Really," she says, "I don't regret anything."

Did you have trouble with the living situation?
I have a huge family, so I grew up sharing everything—apartments, rooms, beds. So that wasn't hard. What's tough is that everything is on the record—you have a camera when you wake up and a camera when you go to bed—and you don't know how it will be used.

There were times when you seemed to be going a little crazy.
I did go off the deep end a little. I was always tired and hungry and I didn't agree with a lot of things—like how long they made us wait. Things you wouldn't go through as a chef. I mean, I know what it's like to work in harsh kitchens, working eighteen-hour days. I've done that. But cook out of a vending machine? I've never been in situations like that.

How did you wind up shaving your head?
I did it because I really wanted to do it, not for any other reason. I don't even drink. I never get drunk. I wanted to do it since I was like fifteen years old. And Ilan said, "If you do it, we'll all do it." So it seemed like good timing.

Did you regret how that night turned out?
No, I do not regret it. We had a lot of fun and I think Marcel should have just let us shave his head, too. He would have had as much fun as we did and would have had that super cool memory of the show. It would have brought him closer to all of us!

It seemed a little mean, like you'd turned on him.
Well, he was mean the whole show. We are friends now, but he was rude. He insulted people. That's why people hated him. He did things that made people want to smack him.

SHAUNA MINOPRIO, EXECUTIVE PRODUCER "I GOT A CALL THAT ELIA HAD SHAVED HER HAIR. I COULDN'T BELIEVE IT. WE STILL HAD TO INTERVIEW HER ABOUT THE LAST TWO SHOWS AND SHE HAD NO BLOODY HAIR! SO I SPOKE TO HAIR AND MAKE-UP AND WE FIGURED OUT HOW WE COULD GET ELIA A WIG TO DO THE INTERVIEWS. IT WAS EXTREMELY ANNOYING."

"It's food, it's not rocket science. It's really just innate; whatever I feel is what I do."
CLIFF

TOP STATS

Age
29

Hometown
New York, NY

Currently
Living in New York City

Lucky charm during the competition
27-year-old T-shirt from his former boss

Secret splurge at the grocery store
Cookies

Philosophy
"Be true to the product."

Featured recipes
Hama Hama Oysters, p. 85
Korean Pork, p. 109
Cookie Ice Cream, p. 234

Cliff Crooks

SEASON 2
DISQUALIFIED: EPISODE 11, "SENSE AND SENSUALITY"
WINS: 0 ELIMINATION CHALLENGES, 4 QUICKFIRES

In his application to be on *Top Chef*, Cliff Crooks noticed that he was usually so intense in the kitchen that his colleagues often thought he was angry. That intensity served him well during Season 2 when—for the first ten episodes at least—in the midst of turbulent drama on every side, he was a rock of poise and consistently excellent cooking.

Then came one bad night, the last night in Los Angeles, when things got out of hand in the *Top Chef* house. By wrestling with Marcel, Cliff violated a contest rule and, after a day of deliberations among the judges, he was disqualified. (It was small consolation that his performance in the previous day's challenge would likely have gotten him sent home anyway.) "Once the decision came down, I didn't argue," Cliff now says. "I was going to take it like a man." That kind of grace makes it possible to remember the sweeter times (like Marshmallow and Cookie Ice Cream) instead of just the way he left.

How do you look back on your *Top Chef* experience now?
It was great. I wouldn't change anything.

Nothing at all?
Cooking is one of the things I'm most passionate about. So to be able to go on and do what I do every day . . . that's what drew me to the show to begin with.

Had you watched the first season?
I wish I'd watched more, in retrospect. I really didn't know how crazy it would get. Like, you get to sleep after midnight and they wake you up at 3:30 a.m. It gets to the point where you're like, "What are you guys doing to me?"

What about living in the house?
I hadn't done anything like that since college. You do start to get a little itchy. The first two weeks, you're getting to know each other, making new friends. By week three, you're thinking, "How am I going to get away from all my new friends?"

Let's talk about the circumstances of you leaving. Did you watch that episode?
I did. It was a little difficult. I don't want to say it looked worse than it was, because it looked pretty bad. What you saw is what happened. It was a joke gone really sour. I've apologized for it numerous times and I think we've all sort of moved on.

Did you make up with Marcel?
After the show, I was in Vegas and I visited him in his restaurant. Everything was great.

Did he serve you some kind of foam?
Yes, he did. Yes, he did.

SHAUNA MINOPRIO, EXECUTIVE PRODUCER "ONE OF THE CREW MEMBERS ASKED ME FOR A CAMERA, AND I SAID, 'YEAH, SURE.' I'D GIVEN CAMERAS TO CASTS BEFORE. HOW MUCH TROUBLE COULD YOU GET INTO? SO I FELT VERY SORRY FOR CLIFF—IT WAS JUST A DUMB MISTAKE."

Betty Fraser

SEASON 2
ELIMINATED: EPISODE 9, "SEVEN"
WINS: 2 ELIMINATION CHALLENGES, 0 QUICKFIRES

It was always hard to know what to make of Betty. At first glance, she was the sweet, maternal type: quick with the bright smile, the nurturing word, and the commonsense solution. So it was a bit of a shock, after a few episodes, to see her start to mix it up with other contestants—whether that meant fighting back when accused of slipping extra sugar into a "healthy kids" menu (she still claims it wasn't cheating) or, most famously, blowing up at Marcel.

There was never any question that this sunny Californian had a stormy side. Perhaps it came from the toughness required to change jobs later in life than most and become a caterer. But whether you thought Betty was a Mean Girl or Earth Mother, what you could say for sure is that she lasted longer in the *Top Chef* competition than many would have guessed, deploying a combination of charm, kitchen chops, and what she proudly calls comfort food.

A year and a half on, how do you feel about your *Top Chef* experience?
Overall, it's been great. I had no idea what the world of reality television was all about, and I'm still amazed by how often I'm approached by fans of the show. They usually want to know what it was like around the set and I let them know that, while it was a lot of fun, we were often hot, tired, and under a lot of self-imposed pressure to win.

Is that what made you so testy?
My "testy level" is actually pretty high. I work in a high-energy environment everyday and I couldn't make it unless I had some balance. But there were a couple of "perfect storms" during the show and I spoke my mind. Marcel and I are actually thinking about creating an act and taking it on the road. We'll just cook and argue for an hour and say good night.

Is Ilan really a nice guy?
Ilan is a nice guy as well as being a very talented, focused chef. Nothing but kudos for Ilan.

Was it weird being one of the older contestants and living with a bunch of kids?
I've noticed that when people who love what they do get together, age becomes irrelevant. Of course, it wasn't so irrelevant that I wasn't usually the first to go to bed.

Did you feel like it was really you up there on-screen?
Oh, it was me all right! Because the cameras are always around, they just kind of meld into the background and you forget they're there. There were a couple of moments that were a little embarrassing. I was watching with my ex-husband the night I blew up at Marcel and he turned to me and said, "I know that voice." I guess they don't call it "reality TV" for nothing!

TOP STATS

Age
46

Hometown
San Francisco, CA

Currently
Co-owner of Grub Restaurant and As You Like It Catering in Hollywood, CA

Chefs she most admires
Jamie Oliver and Nigella Lawson

Person she'd most like to make a meal for
Harrison Ford

What she would serve
Root vegetable risotto with an herb-rubbed T-bone steak

Philosophy
"Be happy . . . it's better than the alternative."

Featured recipes
Ham and Egg, p. 47
Pork Shoulder, p. 77
Mussels, p. 176
Grilled Cheese, p. 194

Carlos Fernandez

SEASON 2
ELIMINATED: EPISODE 6, "THANKSGIVING"
WINS: 0 ELIMINATION CHALLENGES, 1 QUICKFIRE

Season 2 of *Top Chef* may be best remembered for interpersonal turmoil and drama, but somebody forgot to send Carlos Fernandez the memo. Maybe it was just that he was older than most of his fellow contestants. Or maybe years living and running a restaurant, Hi-Life Café, in South Florida better prepared him for dealing with different personalities in the midst of a Los Angeles heat wave.

Whatever the reason, while his fellow contestants sniped and squabbled around him, Carlos floated above it all, smiling the whole way. If anything, his only beefs were with the judges, as when he memorably told Tom Colicchio that one of his dishes might not have been great but it wasn't "crap on a plate."

Carlos also displayed a keen eye for summing up his competitors. (On Sam Talbot: "He's blessed. He could sneeze on a plate and it would come out gorgeous.") Since leaving the show, he's put that skill to good use on the Spanish-language cooking video webcast he hosts for BravoTV.com. And he's just as sunny now as he was on the show. "I came here from Cuba when I was one year old," he says. "I feel like I'm living the American dream."

Why do you think you wound up getting along with people so well?

My fellow contestants just charmed me. I came planning to compete and run everyone else into the ground, but by the time I left I just fell in love with each and every one of them.

Everybody else seemed to have trouble with Marcel.

I just thought Marcel was a little immature. So my strategy was to treat him kindly. I wish I had been there for the video incident. I would have put an end to that immediately.

What about Mike?

Mikey was a hoot. There was one point when he lost a bet to Frank and had to sing the national anthem. Imagine Roseanne Barr, but larger and uglier. That's Mikey.

Was it weird living with so many young people?

I'm thirty-seven. I hadn't shared a bedroom since college! You know, when you get home from the show, you go through "*Top Chef* depression." You kind of need to be reintegrated into society. For me, I spent a lot of time wondering, "What would it have been like if I was twenty-five? If I had more energy and stamina?" Because it's really physically and mentally exhausting.

What would you tell a contestant going on the show?

By all means, go ahead, but don't think it's as easy as it looks. It's much easier to play armchair chef.

"It's not about you, it's about the competition."

TOP STATS

Age
38

Hometown
Hoboken, NJ

Currently
Co-owner and executive chef of Hi-Life Café in Fort Lauderdale, FL

Chefs he admires
Julia Child and Graham Kerr

Philosophy
"I never want to be pigeonholed. My gimmick is affordable, contemporary American cuisine."

Featured recipes
Carrot Loaf, p. 191

Suyai Steinhauer

"I have never cooked so badly in my life."

BIO BITE

Packed her knives

Episode 1, "Into the Fire"

During her oh-so-short stay on Season 2, no one can say Suyai wasn't entertaining to watch. A bizarrely devious Elimination Challenge sent her into a **downward spiral of tears, frustration, and panic** before she finally threw up her hands in desperation. She was the first victim of the most tumultuous season yet.

Otto Borsich

"What do I know about sushi? I'm just a round-eye from Cleveland, Ohio."

BIO BITE

Packed his knives

Episode 2, "Far East Feast"

Otto was the focus of Season 2's **Great Lychee Scandal**, in which he may or may not have walked out of the supermarket with a stolen case of the tropical fruit. Plenty of drama and tattling followed, until Otto, trying to save face, chose to remove himself from the competition.

Featured recipe

Korean Pork, p. 109

Emily Sprissler

"I'm not a mass-producer. I'm not a turn-and-burner."

BIO BITE

Packed her knives

Episode 3, "Food for the People"

Emily might not have made it to the end of the season, but she sure had the right attitude. From insulting her customers in the ice cream challenge to bad-mouthing her fellow contestants, Emily was **as high-minded as the best of them**. It's too bad she never had the chance to face off with Stephen.

Marisa Churchill

"Do I use my sexuality to my advantage? Damn right."

BIO BITE

Packed her knives

Episode 5, "Social Service"

Marisa might have been more of a gossip than a gourmand, spending too much time backstabbing and too little watching her own knives. A sliced finger made her one of the season's first injured, but it was a **spoon full of Pepto-Bismol** that sent her home.

Featured recipe

Korean Pork, p. 109

Josie Smith-Malave

"I'm the chef's hit man."

BIO BITE

Packed her knives

Episode 5, "Social Service"

Josie was almost as much of a **brash Brooklyn bulldog** as Joey and Howie from Season 3, letting Betty have it when she slipped extra sugar into her supposedly diet-friendly cookies. Maybe she should have re-thought the muddled intermezzo that sent her home.

Frank Terzoli

"A true chef is a gentleman, and shall remain that way."

BIO BITE

Packed his knives

Episode 7, "The Raw and the Cooked"

For a nice guy, Frank sure was at the center of a lot of controversies, whether it was defending Otto or **threatening to kill Marcel for touching his toothbrush**. Asked if he had any regrets looking back on the season, he didn't hesitate to invoke that last incident: "I should have hit him."

Featured recipes

Mini Quiches, p. 76

Pizza, p. 100

Korean Pork, p. 109

Mia Gaines-Alt

"I'm a professional barbecue-ologist."

BIO BITE

Packed her knives

Episode 8, "Holiday Spirit"

Best remembered for her cowboy hats and cornflake battered frog legs, Mia brought a **Southern sense of style**—and honor—to the competition. Tough as nails, she chewed out Cliff for bossing her around and put her own neck on the chopping block to save Elia from an early exit.

Featured recipe

Crabcakes, p. 49

Michael Midgley

"I don't care about other chefs. I cook good food."

BIO BITE

Packed his knives

Episode 10, "Unhappy Customers"

From his phallic chocolate Cheetos to his **painkiller-fueled Quickfire/Elimination stunner**, Mike was a contestant for the ages. Who knows how this burly frat boy got as far as he did, but it's a good thing the judges kept him around so long. Where would we be without lines like, "It's cool to be cool"?

Featured recipe

Trout and Salmon, p. 168

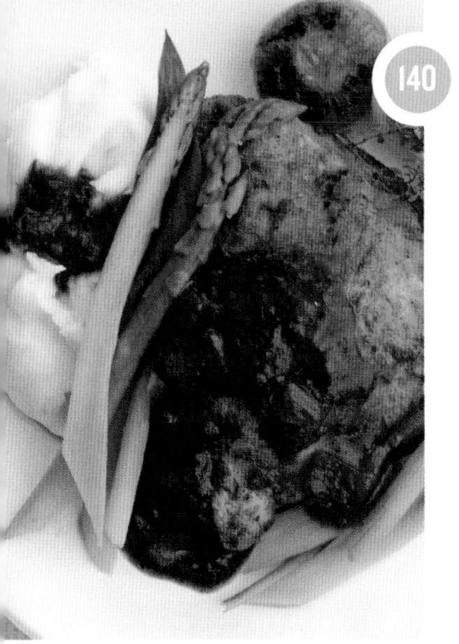

Entrées: Poultry

149

152

155

Coq au Vin
with Whipped Potatoes, Sautéed Ramps, and Asparagus

CHEF: Casey
SEASON 3, EPISODE 12
ELIMINATION CHALLENGE: Turn an onion, a potato, and a chicken into a meal for chefs at the French Culinary Institute.

2 hours, 45 minutes
Serves 6

> "This wasn't pretentious. It was well done, and it had a lot of flavor."
>
> JACQUES TORRES, FRENCH CULINARY INSTITUTE DEAN, GUEST JUDGE

- 6 skinless chicken thighs
- Salt and freshly ground black pepper
- 2 tablespoons plus 1 teaspoon grapeseed oil
- 8 ounces bacon, finely chopped
- 1 small white onion, chopped
- 1 tablespoon tomato paste
- 1 tomato, roughly chopped
- 1 bay leaf
- 3 cups red wine
- 3 sprigs fresh thyme, plus more for garnish
- 1 ½ to 2 cups low-sodium chicken stock
- 4 russet potatoes, peeled and cut into 1-inch pieces
- 1 cup heavy cream
- 9 tablespoons cold salted butter
- 1 tablespoon mascarpone
- 12 cipollini onions, blanched and peeled
- 1 tablespoon olive oil
- 1 bunch ramps (optional)
- 1 bunch asparagus (1 ½ pounds), halved lengthwise
- 1 tablespoon chopped fresh dill
- Juice of ½ lemon

1. Preheat the oven to 350°F. Season the chicken with salt and pepper. In a large oven-safe sauté pan or skillet, heat 2 tablespoons of the grapeseed oil over medium-high heat. Add the chicken and cook until browned on both sides, about 10 minutes. Remove the chicken from the pan and set aside.

2. Pour off all but 1 tablespoon of the fat from the pan. Add the bacon and cook over medium-high heat, stirring, for about 5 minutes; pour off most of the fat. Add the onion and cook, stirring, for 1 minute. Add the tomato paste, tomato, and bay leaf. Reduce the heat to medium-low and cook, stirring constantly, for 5 minutes.

3. Add the wine and stir to scrape up any browned bits. Cook for 10 minutes. Return the chicken to the pan, add the thyme and enough stock to cover the chicken, and cover the pan. Place the pan in the oven and bake for 1 hour. Turn the thighs over. Bake, uncovered, for 15 minutes longer.

4. Cook the potatoes in a pot of boiling water for 15 to 20 minutes, until tender. Drain and return the potatoes to the pot; place over low heat for 1 to 2 minutes, shaking the pot, until the potatoes are dry. Pass through a ricer into a large bowl and use a wooden spoon to gradually beat in the cream and 7 tablespoons of the butter, beating until the potatoes pull away from the sides of the bowl. Stir in the mascarpone and season with salt and pepper. Set aside.

5. In a sauté pan or skillet, melt 1 tablespoon of the butter with the remaining 1 teaspoon grapeseed oil over medium-high heat. Add the cipollini onions and season with salt and pepper. Cook, stirring frequently, for about 5 minutes, until browned and cooked through.

6. In a second sauté pan or skillet, heat the olive oil and the remaining 1 tablespoon butter over medium-high heat. Add the ramps, if using, and asparagus. Cook, stirring, until just tender, 3 to 4 minutes. Add the dill and lemon juice. Season with salt and pepper to taste.

7. Spoon the potatoes onto serving plates. Put 1 thigh on each plate and spoon some of the sauce over it. Arrange the cipollini, asparagus, and ramps on the plates, garnish with thyme, and serve immediately.

Pan-Roasted Quail
with Herb Spaetzle, Cherries, and Foie Gras

CHEF: Harold
SEASON 1, EPISODE 12
ELIMINATION CHALLENGE: Cook the best meal of your life.

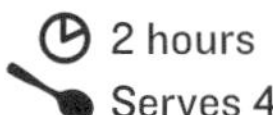

2 hours
Serves 4

ON THE SIDE:
Herb Spaetzle

- 2 ¼ cups all-purpose flour
- 1 teaspoon salt
- Large pinch of white pepper
- Large pinch of freshly grated nutmeg
- 3 large eggs, beaten
- ¾ cup milk
- 3 tablespoons minced fresh basil, parsley, and thyme
- Olive oil (optional)

1. In a large bowl, whisk together the flour, salt, white pepper, and nutmeg. Stir in the eggs, milk, and herbs, mixing until the batter is just combined.

2. Bring a large pot of water to a boil. Working with about ½ cup of the batter at a time, use a rubber spatula to push the batter through a colander with ¼-inch holes (or a flat coarse cheese grater) directly into the boiling water. Stir gently with a slotted spoon, and lift the spaetzle out of the water as they float to the surface, transferring them to a bowl of ice water to cool. Drain. If making the spaetzle in advance, toss with a little oil to prevent sticking.

- 4 quail
- 3 cups low-sodium chicken stock
- 2 ½ tablespoons unsalted butter
- Salt and freshly ground black pepper
- 1 cup pitted fresh cherries
- ¼ cup port
- Four ½-inch-thick slices foie gras, veins and imperfections trimmed off
- 2 tablespoons olive oil

- Herb Spaetzle (see left)

1. Debone the quail: using poultry shears or kitchen scissors, cut out the backbone of each quail (reserve the bones); lay the quail out skin side down. With a sharp boning knife, cut just under the ribs on each side and remove the ribs. Remove the breast cartilage by sliding the knife underneath it and pulling it out. Cut out any remaining small bones, leaving the legs and thighs intact. Set the quail aside.

2. In a medium sauté pan or skillet over high heat, cook the reserved bones, turning frequently, until well browned on all sides, about 5 minutes. Add the stock, bring to a boil, and cook for 15 to 20 minutes, until the liquid is reduced to about ½ cup. Pour through a fine-mesh sieve set over a bowl and whisk in 1 tablespoon of the butter. Season with salt and pepper to taste and set the jus aside.

3. In a medium sauté pan or skillet, melt ½ tablespoon of the butter over medium-high heat and add the cherries. Sauté until softened, about 3 minutes. Add the port and cook for 1 minute. Add the jus and cook for about 5 minutes, until reduced to a sauce consistency. Pour into a bowl and set aside, covered to keep warm.

4. Score the foie gras in a shallow diamond pattern on each side. Cover and put in the freezer for a few minutes.

5. In each of 2 large sauté pans or skillets, heat 1 tablespoon oil over medium-high heat. Season the quail with salt and pepper and add 2 quail to each pan, skin side down. Cook, turning once, until well browned and cooked through, 7 to 10 minutes total, lowering the heat if the quail are browning too quickly. Remove to a large plate and tent with aluminum foil.

6. Put the remaining 1 tablespoon butter in a medium sauté pan or skillet over medium-high heat. When the foam has subsided and the butter is just starting to brown, add 1 cup of the spaetzle (reserve the rest for another use). Cook, tossing to coat with the butter, until heated through, about 2 minutes.

7. Meanwhile, heat a medium sauté pan or skillet over high heat for 1 minute. Add the foie gras and cook for 30 to 45 seconds on each side, until golden brown.

8. Divide the spaetzle among 4 serving plates. Put a quail and a slice of foie gras on each plate. Spoon a few cherries and sauce around the plate. Serve.

Spring Harvest Pheasant's Pie
with Chicken, Pheasant Sausage, Potato, and Ramp Puree

CHEF: Brian M.
SEASON 3, EPISODE 12
ELIMINATION CHALLENGE: Turn an onion, a potato, and a chicken into a meal for chefs at the French Culinary Institute.

- 6 bone-in chicken thighs (about 2 ½ pounds)
- Salt and freshly ground black pepper
- 5 ramps
- 2 tablespoons extra-virgin olive oil
- 3 russet potatoes (about 1 ¾ pounds), peeled and cut into 1-inch pieces
- 1 large parsnip, peeled and cut into 1-inch pieces
- 12 tablespoons unsalted butter
- 1 cup heavy cream
- 1 onion, chopped
- 6 shiitake mushrooms, cut into ½-inch dice
- 1 spicy pheasant sausage, cut into ½-inch cubes
- 1 cup chicken stock
- 2 teaspoons fresh thyme leaves
- 3 scallions, white and green parts, chopped

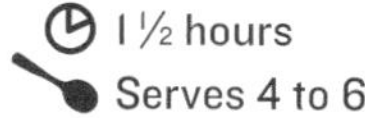
1 ½ hours
Serves 4 to 6

"Very rich, very smoky."
GAIL SIMMONS, JUDGE

1. Preheat the oven to 350°F.
2. Season the chicken with salt and pepper and place in a baking dish. Roast for 40 to 45 minutes, until cooked through. Remove from the oven (leave the oven on). When cool enough to handle, pull the meat off the bones. Roughly chop the meat and set aside.
3. Meanwhile, bring a medium pot of water to a boil and add the ramps. Cook until just tender, about 1 minute, then drain and transfer the ramps to a bowl of ice water to cool. Drain and puree the ramps in a food processor with the oil. Set aside.
4. Put potatoes and parsnip in a medium pot and cover with cold water. Add a large pinch of salt and bring to a boil over medium-high heat. Simmer until tender, about 15 minutes. Drain and return the vegetables to the pot. Place over low heat for 1 minute, shaking the pan so they dry evenly. Pass through a potato ricer into a large bowl.
5. In a small saucepan, heat 6 tablespoons of the butter and the cream until the butter is melted and the cream is steaming. Beat the cream mixture into the potatoes and parsnips until smooth. Stir in the pureed ramps and season with salt and pepper to taste. Set aside.
6. In a medium skillet, melt 4 tablespoons of the butter over medium heat. Add the onion and cook, stirring occasionally, until very soft, about 8 minutes, lowering the heat if necessary to keep the onion from browning. Add the mushrooms and sausage and sauté until the mushrooms are just tender, about 3 minutes. Add the stock and chicken and bring to a simmer over medium-high heat. Simmer for 8 to 10 minutes, until reduced slightly. Stir in the thyme and scallions and season with salt and pepper to taste.
7. Spoon the chicken mixture onto 4 to 6 ovenproof serving dishes (or a 9-by-11-inch baking dish) and spread the potato mixture over the top. Dot with the remaining 2 tablespoons butter. Bake for 10 to 15 minutes, until heated through and bubbling. Serve.

Black Truffle and Parmesan Linguine
with Kale, Tomato Confit, and Grilled Chicken

CHEFS: C.J. and Tre
SEASON 3, EPISODE 6
ELIMINATION CHALLENGE: Split into pairs to create a frozen pasta meal.

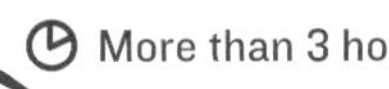 More than 3 hours
 Serves 4
Winner

Sauce:

One 3- to 3 ½-pound whole chicken, cut into 8 pieces
1 tablespoon olive oil
1 large yellow onion, chopped
1 carrot, chopped
2 celery ribs, chopped
4 ounces mushrooms, sliced
3 garlic cloves, chopped
Half 750-ml bottle white wine
3 quarts low-sodium chicken stock
2 bay leaves
3 fresh thyme sprigs
1 ½ teaspoons black peppercorns
1 tablespoon sherry vinegar
4 ounces Parmesan cheese, freshly grated
Drizzle of truffle oil
4 tablespoons unsalted butter
Salt to taste
½ cup packed fresh basil leaves

Pasta:

4 small tomatoes (about ½ pound)
1 bunch fresh basil
1 whole garlic head, cloves peeled
About 3 cups plus 5 tablespoons olive oil
Salt
12 ounces dried linguine pasta
1 bunch Tuscan kale (about ½ pound), thick stems removed
8 ounces cremini mushrooms, cut into ½-inch slices
Freshly ground black pepper
4 boneless, skinless chicken breast halves (1 ¼ pounds)
2 tablespoons chopped fresh rosemary
2 tablespoons chopped fresh oregano
½ teaspoon cracked black pepper

To Serve:

1 ½ ounces black truffle butter
Salt and freshly ground black pepper
Shaved Parmesan cheese

For the Sauce:

1. Preheat the oven to 400°F.
2. Put the chicken in a large roasting pan and roast for 45 minutes, or until well browned. Set aside.
3. In a large stockpot, heat the olive oil over medium heat. Add the onion, carrot, and celery and cook, stirring, for 5 to 7 minutes, until softened.
4. Add the mushrooms and garlic and cook over medium-high heat, stirring, for 5 minutes. Add the wine and stir, scraping up any browned bits from the bottom of the pot. Bring to a boil and cook for 8 to 10 minutes, until the wine is reduced by about half.
5. Add the stock, bay leaves, thyme, and peppercorns. Add the browned chicken, bring to a boil over high heat, then lower the heat to maintain a simmer. Simmer for 1 hour, occasionally skimming the foam from the surface of the broth.
6. Remove the chicken from the pot and pour the broth through a fine-mesh sieve set over a clean pot; discard the chicken and vegetables or reserve them for another use, and return the broth to high heat. Bring to a boil, then lower the heat and simmer, skimming the foam occasionally, for about 45 minutes, until reduced by half.

7. Add the vinegar, then whisk in the cheese, truffle oil, butter, and salt. Cook for 5 minutes, then add the basil and remove from the heat. Let the sauce steep for 2 to 3 minutes, then pour through a fine-mesh sieve into a medium bowl. Set aside.

For the Pasta:

1. To make the tomato confit: with a small knife, core the tomatoes. Cut a small X in the bottom of each tomato and blanch in a saucepan of boiling water for 1 to 2 minutes. Drain and transfer the tomatoes to a large bowl of ice water to cool. Slip the skins off the tomatoes.
2. Put the tomatoes in a medium saucepan, along with the basil and garlic. Pour in enough oil to just cover the tomatoes, then bring just to a simmer over low heat. Simmer for 20 to 30 minutes, until the tomatoes are soft but still hold their shape. Using a slotted spoon, remove the tomatoes from the oil and put them in a bowl.
3. Pour the oil through a fine-mesh sieve lined with 3 layers of rinsed and squeezed cheesecloth into a medium bowl or jar; set aside.
4. When cool enough to handle, cut each tomato into 6 wedges. Set aside.
5. Bring a large pot of salted water to a boil. Add the pasta and cook according to package directions until almost al dente. Drain, then transfer the pasta to a bowl of ice water to cool. Drain again and toss with a little of the oil from the tomato confit to prevent sticking. Set aside.
6. Bring a large pot of salted water to a boil. Add the kale and cook for 2 minutes. Drain, then transfer the kale to a bowl of ice water to cool. Drain again and cut into wide strips. Set aside.
7. In a large sauté pan or skillet, heat 2 tablespoons of the olive oil over medium-high heat. Add the mushrooms and cook, stirring frequently, for 4 minutes, or until they give up their moisture. Season with salt and pepper to taste.
8. Preheat a charcoal grill and set the grate about 8 inches above the coals.
9. In a large bowl, toss the chicken breasts together with 3 tablespoons of the olive oil, the rosemary, oregano, 1 teaspoon salt, and the cracked black pepper.
10. Lightly brush the grate with oil. When the coals are white, put the chicken on the grill and cook for about 2 minutes on each side, depending on the thickness of the breasts, until cooked through. Transfer to a cutting board and let rest for 5 minutes. Cut the chicken breasts crosswise into ½-inch-wide strips and set aside.

To Serve:

1. In a large sauté pan or skillet, heat 1 tablespoon of the oil from the tomato confit over medium heat. (Reserve the remaining oil for another use.)
2. Add the chicken, sauce, kale, and pasta. Bring to a simmer and cook for 3 minutes. Add the tomatoes and truffle butter and cook for 2 minutes longer. Add salt and pepper if necessary. Divide among 4 plates, sprinkle with shaved cheese, and serve.

HOW TO:
Save Some for Later

This recipe yields more sauce than you'll need for four servings. (In this case it's actually easier to make more sauce than you need.) Put the leftover truffle-Parmesan sauce in small plastic containers and freeze them for later use; the sauce reheats nicely in a small saucepan over low heat.

Sous-Vide Duck with Truffle-Scented Broth
and Mushroom Ragout

CHEF: Hung
SEASON 3, EPISODE 14
ELIMINATION CHALLENGE: Cook the best meal of your life.

2 hours
Serves 4

"I really wanted to showcase French techniques with a Vietnamese flavor profile. The Asian flavor is all the herbs I put in—lime leaves, lemon-grass. With the truffle and the foie gras, it's just, 'Wow.'"
HUNG

- 4 bone-in duck breast halves (about 12 ounces each)
- 1 tablespoon vegetable oil
- Salt and freshly ground black pepper
- 1 celery rib, cut into ½-inch dice
- 1 carrot, peeled and cut into ½-inch dice
- ½ onion, cut into ½-inch dice
- 2 stalks lemongrass, bottom parts only, crushed and chopped
- 1 kaffir lime leaf, plus 4 leaves for garnish
- 12 ounces black truffle juice
- 4 ounces foie gras, cut into ½-inch dice
- 1 cup chanterelle mushrooms
- 1 cup lobster mushrooms
- 1 tablespoon minced shallot
- 2 tablespoons minced fresh chives
- 1 tablespoon minced fresh flat-leaf parsley
- 1 tablespoon balsamic vinegar

1. Debone and skin the duck breasts. Set the meat aside in the refrigerator.
2. In a large, heavy pot, heat the oil over high heat and add the duck bones. Season lightly with salt and pepper and cook, turning occasionally, until well browned on all sides, 6 to 8 minutes. Add the celery, carrot, and onion and cook until slightly softened, then add the lemongrass, lime leaf, and 3 quarts water. Bring to a boil, then skim the foam from the surface. Lower the heat and simmer briskly for about 1 hour, until the liquid is reduced to 1 quart.
3. Pour the broth through a fine-mesh sieve into a small saucepan and add the truffle juice. Simmer for about 40 minutes longer, until reduced to 2 cups. Turn the heat to very low to keep the broth warm.
4. Bring a medium pot of water to about 135°F—hot, but well below a simmer.
5. Season the duck breasts with salt and pepper. Arrange them flat in a heavy-duty zip-top bag and press out as much air as possible, then seal the bag. Lower the bag into the hot water and cook for 20 minutes, checking the water temperature often and adjusting the heat to maintain it at 135°F. Remove the duck breasts from the bag and let rest for 10 minutes on a cutting board, tented loosely with aluminum foil.
6. Meanwhile, heat a medium sauté pan or skillet over high heat. Add the foie gras and cook, stirring gently, until just beginning to color, 2 to 4 minutes. With a slotted spoon, immediately transfer the foie gras to a bowl and set aside. Pour the fat into a cup and set aside.
7. Return the pan to medium-high heat and add the mushrooms and shallot. Cook, stirring frequently, until softened, about 4 minutes. Season with salt and pepper to taste and stir in the chives and parsley. Gently fold in the foie gras and vinegar.
8. Divide the mushroom mixture among 4 deep serving plates. Thinly slice the duck breasts and place the slices on top of the mushroom mixture. Using an immersion blender or a whisk, blend the reserved foie gras fat into the warm broth, blending until froth forms on the surface. Spoon some of the broth and froth over each serving and garnish with a fresh lime leaf. Serve immediately.

Chicken in Red Curry Sauce

CHEF: Lee Anne
SEASON 1, EPISODE 4
ELIMINATION CHALLENGE: Create a gourmet entrée that can be reheated in the microwave.

- 2 tablespoons vegetable oil
- 1 medium yellow onion, thinly sliced
- One 2-inch piece ginger, peeled and chopped
- One 1-inch piece galangal, peeled and chopped
- 6 garlic cloves, chopped
- 4 fresh kaffir lime leaves, chopped
- 2 lemongrass stalks, bottom parts only, crushed and minced
- 2 whole dried red chiles
- 2 cups low-sodium chicken stock
- Salt
- 1 cup thinly sliced carrots
- 1 cup snow peas, trimmed
- One 14-ounce can unsweetened coconut milk
- 1 tablespoon palm sugar
- 2 to 3 teaspoons red curry paste, or to taste
- Freshly ground white pepper
- 1 ½ pounds boneless, skinless chicken breast, cut into 1-inch cubes
- 2 tablespoons minced fresh Thai basil, plus basil leaves for garnish
- 2 tablespoons minced fresh cilantro
- Steamed jasmine rice for serving

1. In a large pot, heat the oil over medium heat. Add the onion, ginger, galangal, garlic, lime leaves, lemongrass, and chiles and sauté until the vegetables have softened, about 5 minutes. Add the stock, bring to a simmer, and cook until reduced by three-quarters, about 15 minutes.
2. While the stock is reducing, fill a large bowl with ice water. Bring a large pot of salted water to a boil, add the carrots and blanch for 1 minute, then add the snow peas and blanch 1 minute more, then drain and transfer to the ice-water bath. Drain and set aside on paper towels.
3. Add the coconut milk, palm sugar, and curry paste to the stock and cook, stirring to dissolve the curry paste and sugar, until reduced by half, about 10 minutes. Strain the mixture through a fine-mesh sieve into a clean pot, discarding the solids. Season with salt and white pepper to taste.
4. Place the pot over medium heat and bring to a simmer. Add the chicken pieces and cook until the chicken is just cooked through, about 5 minutes. Add the snow peas and carrots and cook for about 2 minutes to warm through. Add the basil and cilantro and adjust the seasonings, adding more salt and pepper as needed.
5. Serve with steamed jasmine rice and garnish with the basil leaves. Serve immediately.

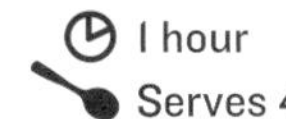
1 hour
Serves 4

WHAT IS . . .
Curry?

The word *curry* (probably from the South Indian word *khari*, "sauce") most commonly refers to hot dry- or wet-sauced dishes of Indian, Pakistani, or Bangladeshi origin that contain a mixture of spices such as cumin, coriander, and turmeric (which is what gives standard curry powder—developed by the British—its characteristic yellow color). Other spices that could be included depending on the region and the individual cook are yellow and black mustard seeds, cardamom, fenugreek, ground ginger, ground cinnamon, ground cloves, nutmeg, mace, black pepper, dried chiles, poppy seeds, and curry leaves.

7. Add the vinegar, then whisk in the cheese, truffle oil, butter, and salt. Cook for 5 minutes, then add the basil and remove from the heat. Let the sauce steep for 2 to 3 minutes, then pour through a fine-mesh sieve into a medium bowl. Set aside.

For the Pasta:

1. To make the tomato confit: with a small knife, core the tomatoes. Cut a small X in the bottom of each tomato and blanch in a saucepan of boiling water for 1 to 2 minutes. Drain and transfer the tomatoes to a large bowl of ice water to cool. Slip the skins off the tomatoes.
2. Put the tomatoes in a medium saucepan, along with the basil and garlic. Pour in enough oil to just cover the tomatoes, then bring just to a simmer over low heat. Simmer for 20 to 30 minutes, until the tomatoes are soft but still hold their shape. Using a slotted spoon, remove the tomatoes from the oil and put them in a bowl.
3. Pour the oil through a fine-mesh sieve lined with 3 layers of rinsed and squeezed cheesecloth into a medium bowl or jar; set aside.
4. When cool enough to handle, cut each tomato into 6 wedges. Set aside.
5. Bring a large pot of salted water to a boil. Add the pasta and cook according to package directions until almost al dente. Drain, then transfer the pasta to a bowl of ice water to cool. Drain again and toss with a little of the oil from the tomato confit to prevent sticking. Set aside.
6. Bring a large pot of salted water to a boil. Add the kale and cook for 2 minutes. Drain, then transfer the kale to a bowl of ice water to cool. Drain again and cut into wide strips. Set aside.
7. In a large sauté pan or skillet, heat 2 tablespoons of the olive oil over medium-high heat. Add the mushrooms and cook, stirring frequently, for 4 minutes, or until they give up their moisture. Season with salt and pepper to taste.
8. Preheat a charcoal grill and set the grate about 8 inches above the coals.
9. In a large bowl, toss the chicken breasts together with 3 tablespoons of the olive oil, the rosemary, oregano, 1 teaspoon salt, and the cracked black pepper.
10. Lightly brush the grate with oil. When the coals are white, put the chicken on the grill and cook for about 2 minutes on each side, depending on the thickness of the breasts, until cooked through. Transfer to a cutting board and let rest for 5 minutes. Cut the chicken breasts crosswise into ½-inch-wide strips and set aside.

To Serve:

1. In a large sauté pan or skillet, heat 1 tablespoon of the oil from the tomato confit over medium heat. (Reserve the remaining oil for another use.)
2. Add the chicken, sauce, kale, and pasta. Bring to a simmer and cook for 3 minutes. Add the tomatoes and truffle butter and cook for 2 minutes longer. Add salt and pepper if necessary. Divide among 4 plates, sprinkle with shaved cheese, and serve.

HOW TO:

Save Some for Later

This recipe yields more sauce than you'll need for four servings. (In this case it's actually easier to make more sauce than you need.) Put the leftover truffle-Parmesan sauce in small plastic containers and freeze them for later use; the sauce reheats nicely in a small saucepan over low heat.

Sous-Vide Duck with Truffle-Scented Broth and Mushroom Ragout

CHEF: Hung
SEASON 3, EPISODE 14
ELIMINATION CHALLENGE: Cook the best meal of your life.

2 hours
Serves 4

"I really wanted to showcase French techniques with a Vietnamese flavor profile. The Asian flavor is all the herbs I put in—lime leaves, lemon-grass. With the truffle and the foie gras, it's just, 'Wow.'"
HUNG

- 4 bone-in duck breast halves (about 12 ounces each)
- 1 tablespoon vegetable oil
- Salt and freshly ground black pepper
- 1 celery rib, cut into ½-inch dice
- 1 carrot, peeled and cut into ½-inch dice
- ½ onion, cut into ½-inch dice
- 2 stalks lemongrass, bottom parts only, crushed and chopped
- 1 kaffir lime leaf, plus 4 leaves for garnish
- 12 ounces black truffle juice
- 4 ounces foie gras, cut into ½-inch dice
- 1 cup chanterelle mushrooms
- 1 cup lobster mushrooms
- 1 tablespoon minced shallot
- 2 tablespoons minced fresh chives
- 1 tablespoon minced fresh flat-leaf parsley
- 1 tablespoon balsamic vinegar

1. Debone and skin the duck breasts. Set the meat aside in the refrigerator.
2. In a large, heavy pot, heat the oil over high heat and add the duck bones. Season lightly with salt and pepper and cook, turning occasionally, until well browned on all sides, 6 to 8 minutes. Add the celery, carrot, and onion and cook until slightly softened, then add the lemongrass, lime leaf, and 3 quarts water. Bring to a boil, then skim the foam from the surface. Lower the heat and simmer briskly for about 1 hour, until the liquid is reduced to 1 quart.
3. Pour the broth through a fine-mesh sieve into a small saucepan and add the truffle juice. Simmer for about 40 minutes longer, until reduced to 2 cups. Turn the heat to very low to keep the broth warm.
4. Bring a medium pot of water to about 135°F—hot, but well below a simmer.
5. Season the duck breasts with salt and pepper. Arrange them flat in a heavy-duty zip-top bag and press out as much air as possible, then seal the bag. Lower the bag into the hot water and cook for 20 minutes, checking the water temperature often and adjusting the heat to maintain it at 135°F. Remove the duck breasts from the bag and let rest for 10 minutes on a cutting board, tented loosely with aluminum foil.
6. Meanwhile, heat a medium sauté pan or skillet over high heat. Add the foie gras and cook, stirring gently, until just beginning to color, 2 to 4 minutes. With a slotted spoon, immediately transfer the foie gras to a bowl and set aside. Pour the fat into a cup and set aside.
7. Return the pan to medium-high heat and add the mushrooms and shallot. Cook, stirring frequently, until softened, about 4 minutes. Season with salt and pepper to taste and stir in the chives and parsley. Gently fold in the foie gras and vinegar.
8. Divide the mushroom mixture among 4 deep serving plates. Thinly slice the duck breasts and place the slices on top of the mushroom mixture. Using an immersion blender or a whisk, blend the reserved foie gras fat into the warm broth, blending until froth forms on the surface. Spoon some of the broth and froth over each serving and garnish with a fresh lime leaf. Serve immediately.

Roasted Chicken with Vegetables

CHEF: Elia
SEASON 2, EPISODE 9
ELIMINATION CHALLENGE: Create a seven-course meal inspired by the seven deadly sins.

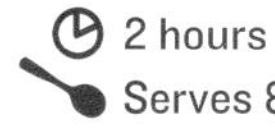
2 hours
Serves 8

- One 7-pound organic roasting chicken, rinsed and patted dry
- 4 tablespoons unsalted butter, softened, plus ½ cup (1 stick) unsalted butter, melted
- Salt and freshly ground black pepper
- 3 medium carrots, cut into chunks on the diagonal
- 2 zucchini, thickly sliced
- 8 ounces button mushrooms, stemmed and halved
- 1 pound fingerling potatoes, halved
- ½ cup low-sodium chicken stock
- 4 fresh rosemary sprigs, plus more for garnish
- 8 fresh thyme sprigs, plus more for garnish

1. Preheat the oven to 400°F.
2. Brush the chicken with the softened butter. Sprinkle generously with salt and pepper. Tie the legs loosely together.
3. In a large bowl, combine the carrots, zucchini, mushrooms, and potatoes. Add the melted butter and toss to coat. Add salt and pepper to taste.
4. Put the chicken in a roasting pan and scatter the vegetables around the chicken. Pour in the stock and top with the herb sprigs.
5. Roast the chicken for 1½ to 2 hours, turning the vegetables a few times to evenly brown, until the chicken is golden brown and an instant-read thermometer inserted into the thickest part of the thigh reads 180°F.
6. Remove the chicken from the roasting pan and cut it into serving pieces. Place on plates and, using a slotted spoon, remove the vegetables from the pan and place them alongside the chicken. Garnish with fresh thyme and rosemary sprigs. Serve immediately.

WHAT ARE . . .

Other Ways to Roast a Chicken?

Elia's recipe for roasted chicken is classic: medium oven temperature, longish roasting time, and plenty of butter. Many people swear by a high-heat method popularized by Barbara Kafka: the whole bird is seasoned simply and stuffed with aromatics, then roasted at a blistering 500°F for less than an hour. (If you haven't cleaned your oven lately, do it before you roast to avoid a very smoky kitchen.) Still others prefer to *spatchcock* the chicken to reduce roasting time: cut out the backbone, open the chicken out like a book, breast side up, and flatten it with your palm. Lay it over sliced lemons and roast at 450°F for about 45 minutes.

TED ALLEN, GUEST JUDGE "I'M SPENDING MOST OF MY COOKING LIFE TRYING TO PERFECT ROAST CHICKEN. I APPRECIATED THE RUSTIC HOMINESS OF IT. SPECTACULAR. IT HAD SOUL."

Top Coif

"I am always suspicious of a chef who is too well groomed," says Anthony Bourdain. "It's like, 'Are you here to cook or to show us your hair?'" Presumably he has to suspend that judgment while watching (and guest judging) *Top Chef.*

It's often been said that chefs are the new rock stars, and *Top Chef*'s contestants have done their best to look the part. It's been the male chefs who have sported the most memorable coifs—from Stephen's spiky look to Marcel's art deco torch of hair to Dale's mohawk (which handily defeated Sandee's mohawk in the Mohawk-Off). Here we present some of our favorite looks.

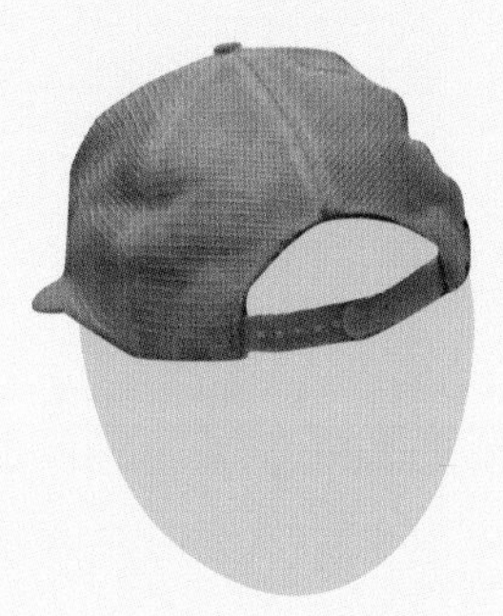

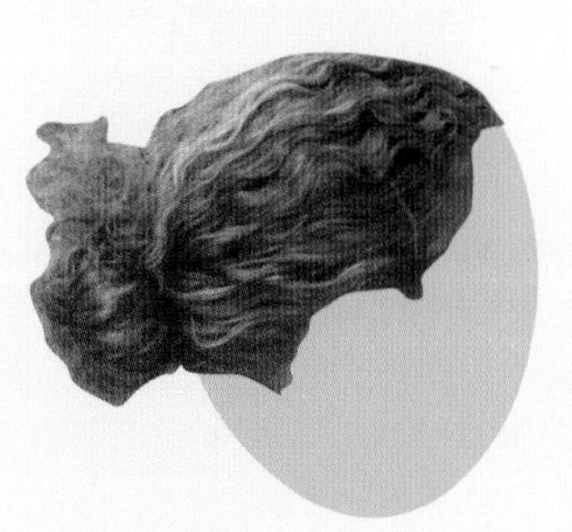

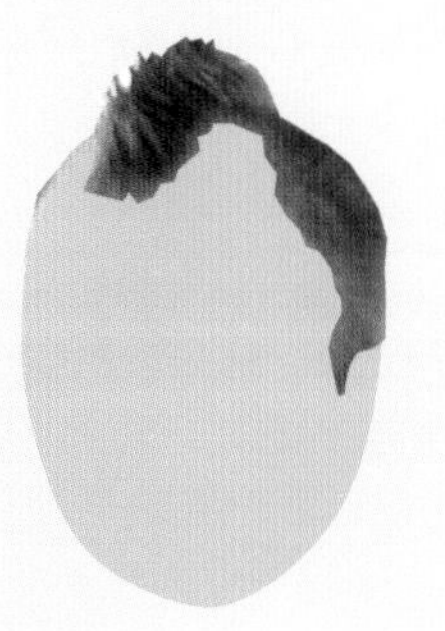

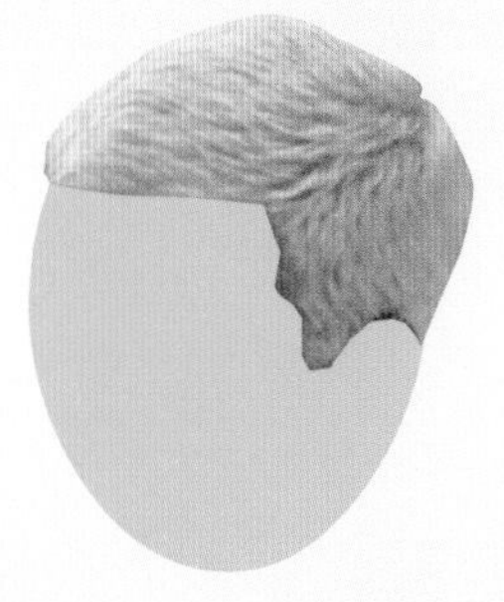

- ■ BETTY
- ■ CASEY
- ■ CLIFF
- ■ DALE
- ■ DAVE
- ■ ELIA
- ■ HOWIE
- ■ ILAN
- ■ MARCEL
- ■ MICHAEL
- ■ MIGUEL
- ■ OTTO
- ■ SAM
- ■ SANDEE
- ■ STEPHEN
- ■ TIFFANI
- ■ TOM
- ■ TRE

ANSWERS: A. Tiffani; B. Marcel; C. Dale; D. Michael; E. Tom, Howie, Tre, Cliff, Elia, Ilan; F. Stephen; G. Sandee; H. Otto; I. Sam; J. Miguel; K. Dave; L. Elia; M. Casey; N. Betty; O. Marcel

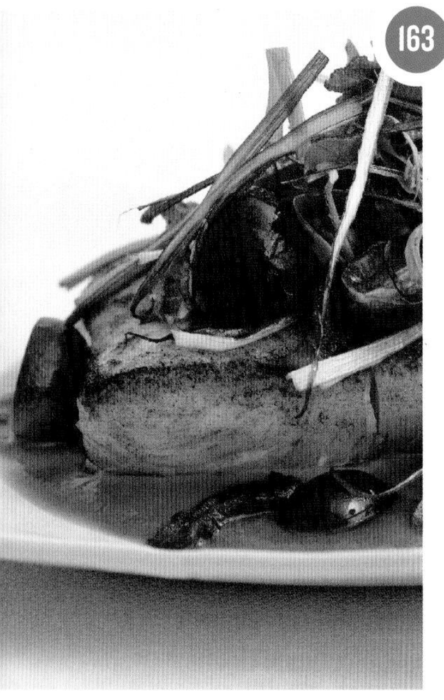

Entrées: Fish

168

175

178

Steamed Red Snapper
with Roasted Butternut Squash Puree

CHEF: Harold
SEASON 1, EPISODE 1
ELIMINATION CHALLENGE: Prepare a signature dish to be served to the other contestants.

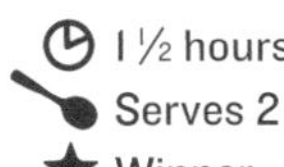

1 ½ hours
Serves 2
Winner

"A real restaurant dish. The flavors were spot on. This was altogether extraordinary."

TOM COLICCHIO, HEAD JUDGE

Roasted Butternut Squash Puree:

- ½ large butternut squash, peeled, seeded, and cut into 1-inch cubes
- 1 tablespoon olive oil, plus more for the pan
- Salt and freshly ground black pepper
- 2 tablespoons unsalted butter
- 1 shallot, finely chopped
- 1 garlic clove, finely chopped
- 1 cup low-sodium chicken stock, plus more if needed

Vegetables:

- 1 tablespoon unsalted butter
- 6 rock shrimp, peeled and deveined
- 3 ounces chanterelle mushrooms, chopped (about ½ cup)
- ¾ cup Brussels sprouts leaves
- Salt and freshly ground black pepper

Red Snapper:

- Two 6- to 8-ounce red snapper fillets with skin
- 1 teaspoon minced fresh chives
- 1 teaspoon minced fresh flat-leaf parsley

For the Roasted Butternut Squash Puree:

1. Preheat the oven to 375°F and grease a medium baking pan.
2. Put the squash in a medium bowl, add the oil, and toss to coat. Sprinkle with salt and pepper and toss. Place the squash in the baking pan in one layer and bake until browned and tender when pierced with a fork, stirring occasionally, about 45 minutes. Remove from the oven and place back in the bowl.
3. In a large sauté pan or skillet, melt 1 tablespoon of the butter over medium heat. Add the shallot and sauté until softened, about 3 minutes. Add the garlic and sauté until softened, about 1 minute more. Add the squash and stock, bring to a simmer, cover, reduce the heat to low, and cook for 10 minutes to blend the flavors.
4. Transfer the mixture to a food processor, add the remaining 1 tablespoon butter, and puree, adding more stock if necessary. Season with salt and pepper to taste.

For the Vegetables:

In a medium sauté pan or skillet, melt the butter over medium heat. Add the shrimp, mushrooms, and Brussels sprouts leaves and cook until the shrimp are just opaque and the vegetables are softened, about 2 minutes. Season with salt and pepper. Remove from the heat.

For the Red Snapper:

Pour enough water into a large pot with a steamer insert to come about 1 inch up the sides. Position a steamer rack or basket in the pot and top with a 9-inch pie plate. Bring the water to a boil and place the snapper on the pie plate. Cover the pot and steam the snapper until opaque in the center, about 5 minutes.

To Serve:

Reheat the vegetables and squash puree if necessary. Spread the squash puree over serving plates, top with the fish, and scatter the vegetables over the fish. Garnish with the chives and parsley and serve immediately.

Macadamia Nut Gazpacho
with Pan-Roasted Moi

CHEF: Ilan
SEASON 2, EPISODE 13
ELIMINATION CHALLENGE: Cook the best meal of your life.

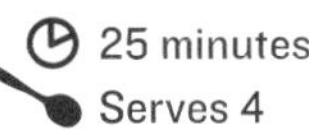
25 minutes
Serves 4

WHAT IS . . .
Moi?

Moi (pronounced "MOY"), a delicate, oily, white-fleshed fish native to tropical areas of the Pacific, was supposedly so highly prized by Hawaiians that a whole industry was devoted to raising the fish in coastal farms (rock walls jutting out into the ocean, with strategically placed gates made of sticks), with fast runners at the ready to carry fish to be cooked fresh for members of the royal family. Wild-caught moi is rare, usually eaten by those who catch it, but moi is now being farmed in deep-sea cages in Hawaii and is becoming more common in mainland fish markets. Chefs compare moi, also known as Pacific threadfin, to pompano, sea bass, and barramundi.

6 garlic cloves
5 tablespoons extra-virgin olive oil
1 cup macadamia nuts
5 slices bread, cubed
1 tablespoon champagne vinegar
⅓ English cucumber
Salt and freshly ground black pepper
8 ounces moi or sea bass fillet with skin, cut into 4 portions
Grated zest of ¼ Buddha's hand citron
Smoked Spanish paprika for garnish

1. Thinly slice 4 of the garlic cloves. In a small sauté pan or skillet, heat 1 tablespoon oil over medium heat. Add the sliced garlic and sauté until browned and crisp, about 3 minutes; be sure the garlic does not burn. Transfer the garlic to paper towels to drain, and set aside.
2. Chop about ¼ cup of the macadamia nuts and toast them in a dry skillet over medium heat until browned in spots, about 2 minutes, stirring constantly. Remove from the heat and set aside.
3. In a blender, combine the remaining 2 garlic cloves and ¾ cup macadamia nuts, the bread, vinegar, 2 tablespoons oil, and ¾ cup water. Blend, starting at a low speed and increasing the speed to high as the mixture is pureed, adding more water a little at a time and scraping down the sides of the blender frequently, until very smooth. The gazpacho should be the consistency of a thick cream soup. Put in the refrigerator until ready to serve.
4. Peel the cucumber and cut it into ⅛-inch-thick strips, then cut into ⅛-inch cubes. Put in a small bowl and toss with a drizzle of oil and salt and pepper to taste. Divide the cucumber among 4 soup plates and set aside.
5. In a medium sauté pan or skillet, heat the remaining 2 tablespoons oil over high heat. Season the fish with salt and pepper. Put the fish in the pan skin side down and cook without turning, carefully spooning hot oil from the pan over the top of the fish as it cooks, for about 4 minutes, until well browned and crisp on the bottom and just cooked through. Using a thin metal spatula, lift the fish from the pan and place 1 piece in each soup plate on top of the cucumber, browned side up.
6. Ladle gazpacho around the fish and cucumber, then garnish each serving with the fried garlic, toasted nuts, citron zest, and a pinch of smoked paprika. Serve immediately.

CHEF AND RESTAURATEUR SCOTT CONANT, GUEST JUDGE "THIS IS EXACTLY WHAT I LOOK FOR IN A YOUNG CHEF. HE GETS IT."

Halibut with Grapes and Fried Leeks

CHEF: Sara M.
SEASON 3, EPISODE 9
ELIMINATION CHALLENGE: Reopen your restaurant from the previous episode.

5 ounces slab bacon, diced
4 leeks, white parts only
3 cups plus 3 tablespoons vegetable oil
5 shallots, sliced
Salt
One 375-ml bottle Sauternes wine
Half 750-ml bottle white wine such as Chardonnay
½ bag seedless red grapes (about 12 ounces)
4 tablespoons cold unsalted butter, cut into pieces
Six 6-ounce pieces halibut fillet with skin
Freshly ground black pepper
About 2 ounces arugula, washed, dried, and cut into chiffonade

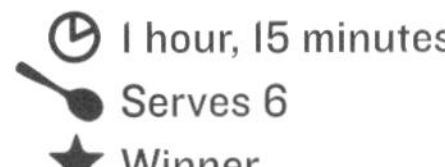
1 hour, 15 minutes
Serves 6
Winner

1. In a heavy skillet over medium heat, cook the bacon for about 15 minutes, until crisp. Using a slotted spoon, transfer to paper towels to drain. Strain the bacon fat through a fine-mesh sieve and set aside.
2. Meanwhile, cut the leeks in half lengthwise and cut into thin julienne strips. Wash well in cold water, drain, and thoroughly pat dry with paper towels.
3. In a large, heavy pot, heat 3 cups of the oil to 375°F. Carefully add a small handful of the leeks and fry for 30 to 45 seconds, until golden brown. Using a slotted spoon, remove the leeks from the oil, transfer to paper towels to drain, and set aside. Repeat with the remaining leeks.
4. Preheat the oven to 450°F.
5. Heat 1 tablespoon of the remaining oil in a medium saucepan over medium-high heat. Add the shallots, season lightly with salt, and cook for about 5 minutes, stirring frequently, until browned and soft. Add the wines, scraping up the browned bits from the bottom of the pan. Set aside 12 grapes and add the remaining grapes to the pan. Raise the heat to high and bring to a boil; cook for about 20 minutes, until the sauce is reduced by half. Working in two batches, transfer the sauce to a blender and puree until smooth. Strain all the pureed sauce through a chinois or a fine-mesh sieve set over a clean saucepan. Bring to a boil over high heat and cook for about 12 minutes, until reduced to 1 ½ cups. Whisk in the bacon fat, then whisk in the butter one piece at a time. Remove from the heat and cover to keep warm.
6. In a large ovenproof sauté pan or skillet, heat the remaining 2 tablespoons oil over high heat until hot. Season the fish on both sides with salt and pepper, then put the fish in the pan, skin side down, and cook without turning for 1 ½ to 2 minutes, until well browned on the bottom. Using a thin metal spatula, turn the fish over and cook for 30 seconds, then transfer the pan to the oven and roast for 2 minutes, until the fish is just cooked through and flakes easily when prodded with a fork.
7. Cut the reserved grapes in half. In a large bowl, toss the grapes, arugula, bacon, and leeks together. Season the salad with salt and pepper to taste.
8. Spoon some of the sauce onto each of 6 serving plates and place the fish on top of the sauce. Top with the salad and serve immediately.

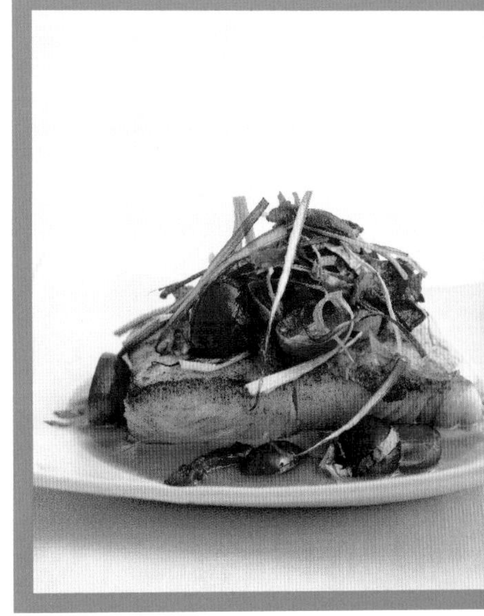

"I like this recipe because it's really light and yet really flavorful. And it's easy to make, too. The grape sauce is very classically French, but it's usually used with chicken."

SARA M.

Fideos with Clams and Saffron

CHEF: Ilan
SEASON 2, EPISODE 11
ELIMINATION CHALLENGE: Create a romantic five-course menu.

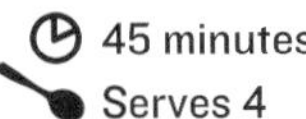

45 minutes
Serves 4

"This is a very traditional dish inspired by something I used to cook at the restaurant where I worked. I think it's one of the most delicious things on Earth."
ILAN

1 pound fideos or capellini pasta
2 cups heavy cream
1 teaspoon saffron threads, crumbled
Salt
1 cup small cauliflower florets
1 cup small broccoli florets
⅓ cup extra-virgin olive oil
10 garlic cloves, peeled and left whole
½ cup white wine or seafood stock
1 pound fresh medium clams, cleaned
Freshly ground black pepper
Chopped fresh flat-leaf parsley for garnish

1. Preheat the oven to 375°F.
2. Break the fideos into 3-inch pieces. Arrange the pieces in an even layer on a rimmed baking sheet. Place in the oven and bake until golden brown, 8 to 10 minutes. Remove from the oven and set aside to cool.
3. In a medium saucepan, combine the cream, saffron, and salt to taste and place over medium heat. Bring just to a boil, whisking and watching the pot so the cream doesn't boil over. Remove from the heat, stir in the cauliflower and broccoli, and set aside.
4. Preheat the broiler.
5. In a large saucepan, heat the oil and garlic over low heat, stirring, until the garlic begins to soften and turn golden, about 15 minutes. Break the garlic up with the back of a wooden spoon, then add the wine, clams, and fideos. Season with salt and pepper to taste and stir to combine.
6. Increase the heat to medium-high and cover the pan. Cook for about 4 minutes, shaking the pan, until the clams have opened. Discard any unopened clams. Stir in the cauliflower and cream mixture and remove from the heat.
7. Divide the clam and pasta mixture among 4 ovenproof dishes. Place the dishes in the oven and broil until golden brown, 2 to 4 minutes.
8. Garnish with the chopped parsley and serve immediately.

CHEF ERIC RIPERT, GUEST JUDGE "THIS WAS REALLY PERFECTION. AT FIRST I THOUGHT IT WAS TOO MUCH FOOD BUT THEN WE ENDED UP FINISHING IT AND PADMA EVEN WANTED MORE."

Scallop Mousse and Shrimp Burger
with Tangerine

CHEF: C.J.
SEASON 3, EPISODE 8
QUICKFIRE CHALLENGE: Prepare a burger for Red Robin's line of "Adventuresome Burgers."

1 ½ minutes
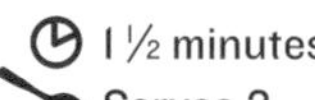
Serves 2
Winner

WHAT ARE . . .
Shrimp Burgers?

The burger, that great American icon, is always associated with ground beef, but the potential of a grilled or fried patty on a bun extends far beyond Wimpy Burger and White Castle. The shrimp burger is an old tradition from the shrimping towns of South Carolina's Lowcountry and holds together best when fresh shrimp is used.

Scallop Mousse and Shrimp Burger:
4 bay scallops
1 teaspoon minced serrano chile
2 teaspoons minced scallion
1 tablespoon fresh lime juice
Salt and freshly ground black pepper
2 tablespoons canola oil
12 large shrimp, peeled, deveined, and cut in half lengthwise

Sauce:
¼ cup pickled ginger
3 tablespoons pickled ginger juice (from the pickled ginger jar)
2 tablespoons fresh lime juice
2 tablespoons rice vinegar
1 tablespoon canola oil
½ cup chopped fresh cilantro
2 scallions, roughly chopped
Salt and freshly ground black pepper to taste

To Serve:
2 crosswise slices honey tangerine
2 brioche buns
2 tablespoons chopped fresh cilantro
¼ cup thinly sliced radicchio
¼ cup thinly sliced spinach leaves

For the Scallop Mousse and Shrimp Burgers:

1. Place the scallops, chile, scallion, lime juice, and salt and pepper to taste in a food processor and pulse to combine, scraping the sides once or twice. With the motor running, pour in 1 tablespoon of the oil through the hole in the lid to emulsify the mixture.
2. Line two 3-inch aspic molds with enough plastic wrap to generously cover the burgers. Arrange 12 shrimp halves in a circular formation in the bottom of the molds. Add the scallop mousse and press down. Top with the remaining shrimp and press down again. Wrap the plastic tightly over the burgers and twist over the top to enclose and seal the burgers. Refrigerate for 1 hour to firm up.
3. In a large skillet, heat the remaining 1 tablespoon oil over medium-high heat. Unwrap the burgers and place them in the skillet; cook until cooked through and lightly browned on both sides, about 5 minutes total. Remove from the skillet and transfer to paper towels to drain.

For the Sauce:

While the burgers are chilling, combine all the sauce ingredients in a blender and blend until smooth. Pour into a bowl and set aside.

To Serve:

Place a honey tangerine slice on each bottom bun. Place the burgers on top, drizzle with the sauce, and sprinkle with the cilantro, radicchio, and spinach. Top with the top bun and serve immediately.

Espresso Shrimp Flambéed with Sambuca
with Roasted Hazelnut and Peanut Paste

CHEF: Sam
SEASON 2, EPISODE 1
QUICKFIRE CHALLENGE: Create a flambé dish in a limited amount of time.

- 20 minutes
- Serves 4
- Winner

3 tablespoons unsalted butter
¼ cup unsalted peanuts
¼ cup blanched hazelnuts
1½ teaspoons sugar
1 scallion, cut into julienne strips
½ red bell pepper, cored, seeded, and cut into julienne strips
1 teaspoon olive oil
1 teaspoon fresh lemon juice
Salt and freshly ground black pepper
1 teaspoon sriracha hot sauce
2 garlic cloves, minced
12 large shrimp, peeled and deveined
2 teaspoons finely ground espresso beans
6 tablespoons Sambuca

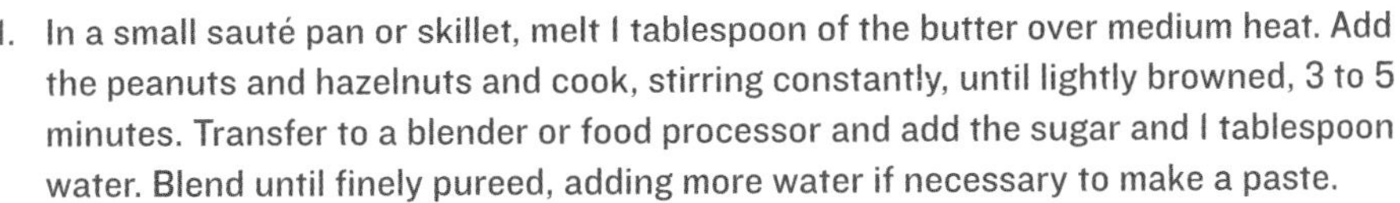

1. In a small sauté pan or skillet, melt 1 tablespoon of the butter over medium heat. Add the peanuts and hazelnuts and cook, stirring constantly, until lightly browned, 3 to 5 minutes. Transfer to a blender or food processor and add the sugar and 1 tablespoon water. Blend until finely pureed, adding more water if necessary to make a paste.
2. Spoon or brush a small amount of the paste onto each of 4 serving plates.
3. In a small bowl, toss the scallion and red pepper with the oil and lemon juice and season with salt and pepper to taste. Place a small pile of the mixture on each serving plate.
4. Garnish the plates with sriracha sauce and set aside.
5. In a medium sauté pan or skillet, melt the remaining 2 tablespoons butter over medium heat. Add the garlic and cook, stirring, until light brown. Add the shrimp and ground espresso beans and cook over medium-high heat, turning the shrimp constantly to coat them with the espresso, for 30 seconds. Add the Sambuca and carefully ignite it, then cook until the sauce coats the shrimp and becomes syrupy, 1 to 2 minutes.
6. Put 3 shrimp on each plate and serve immediately.

CHEF AND SEASON 1 WINNER HAROLD DIETERLE, GUEST JUDGE "THIS DISH WAS OUT OF CONTROL. THE FLAVOR PROFILES WERE RIGHT ON."

Trout and Salmon
with Lemon-Thyme Cream Sauce and Basil Oil

CHEF: Michael
SEASON 2, EPISODE 9
ELIMINATION CHALLENGE: Create a seven-course meal inspired by the seven deadly sins.

 1 hour
 Serves 4
★ Winner

"Our Michael did this? What the hell? He should get his tooth pulled every day."

TOM COLICCHIO,
HEAD JUDGE

Trout and Salmon:

- 2 plum tomatoes, cut into 4 wedges each
- 4 fresh basil leaves
- 3 tablespoons extra-virgin olive oil
- Salt and freshly ground black pepper
- 4 thin asparagus spears, peeled and cut into 2-inch lengths
- 4 tablespoons unsalted butter
- ½ cup heavy cream
- 2 fresh thyme sprigs
- 1 teaspoon fresh lemon juice, or to taste
- One 4-ounce trout fillet, skin removed
- One 8-ounce salmon fillet, skin removed
- 1 medium portobello mushroom cap, chopped
- 4 button mushrooms, stemmed and chopped
- 4 shiitake mushrooms, stemmed and chopped

Basil Oil:

- ¼ cup extra-virgin olive oil
- ½ cup packed fresh basil leaves

For the Trout and Salmon:

1. Preheat the oven to 400°F. Place the tomato wedges in a small baking dish and top with the basil. Drizzle with 1 tablespoon of the oil and sprinkle with salt and pepper. Place in the oven and roast, turning once or twice, until softened and lightly browned, about 15 minutes. Remove from the oven and set aside.
2. Bring a medium saucepan of water to a boil. Add salt and the asparagus. Cook for 30 seconds, or until the asparagus is just tender. Drain and transfer to an ice-water bath until cool. Drain and pat dry with paper towels. Set aside.
3. In a small saucepan, melt 2 tablespoons of the butter over medium-low heat. Add the cream and thyme. Heat until the cream is warm, stirring occasionally. Remove the thyme sprigs and discard. Stir in the lemon juice and season with salt and pepper to taste. Add additional lemon juice if needed. Cover and set aside.
4. Sprinkle the salmon and trout with salt and pepper on both sides. Using a 2- to 3-inch metal cookie cutter, cut each fish fillet into 4 circles.
5. In a medium skillet, heat 1 tablespoon of the butter with 1 tablespoon of the remaining oil over medium heat. Add the fish and cook on both sides until cooked through, 3 to 4 minutes total for the trout and 6 to 9 minutes total for the salmon. Remove from the pan, tent with foil to keep warm, and set aside.
6. Wipe the skillet with a paper towel and heat the remaining 1 tablespoon butter with the remaining 1 tablespoon oil. Add the mushrooms. Cook until the mushrooms are tender, about 5 minutes. Season with salt and pepper to taste.

For the Basil Oil:

Combine the oil and basil in a blender and puree. Strain minced basil through a fine-mesh sieve into a medium bowl. Discard the solids. Cover and refrigerate.

To Serve:

Spoon the cream sauce over serving plates, then top with the mushrooms. Arrange the asparagus over the mushrooms and top with one piece of trout and one piece of salmon. Add some roasted tomato wedges, drizzle with basil oil, and serve.

Ahi Tuna and Shrimp Tacos

CHEF: Elia
SEASON 2, EPISODE 3
ELIMINATION CHALLENGE: Update a childhood classic for T.G.I. Friday's.

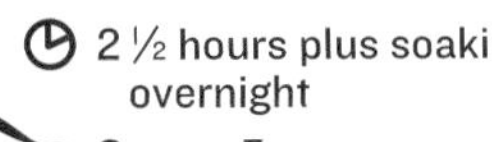

2 ½ hours plus soaking overnight

Serves 5

ON THE SIDE:

Guacamole

- 5 Hass avocados
- 2 plum tomatoes, diced
- 1 large onion, chopped
- 1 cup fresh flat-leaf parsley, chopped
- Juice of 3 limes, or to taste
- 2 tablespoons olive oil
- Salt and freshly ground black pepper

1. In a large bowl, use a potato masher to gently mash the avocados until the largest chunks are the size of the diced tomato pieces.

2. Stir in the tomatoes, onion, parsley, lime juice, and oil. Mix well to combine. Season with salt and pepper to taste, and add more lime juice if necessary.

Black Beans:
- 2 cups dried black beans
- 2 slices bacon
- 2 slices jarred roasted red pepper
- Salt and freshly ground black pepper

Salsa:
- 6 plum tomatoes
- 2 tablespoons olive oil
- 1 onion, chopped
- 2 shallots, chopped
- ¼ teaspoon tomato paste
- ¾ cup fresh cilantro, chopped
- Salt and freshly ground black pepper

Tacos:
- 2 tablespoons olive oil
- 2 tablespoons unsalted butter
- 10 ½ ounces ahi tuna
- 10 ½ ounces large shrimp, peeled and deveined
- Salt and freshly ground black pepper
- 10 corn tortillas

Guacamole (see left)

For the Black Beans:

Soak the beans overnight in enough cold water to cover. Drain the beans and put them in a large pot; cover with cold water. Add the bacon and red pepper and bring to a simmer. Simmer for about 1 ½ hours, until the beans are tender but not falling apart, adding more water if necessary to keep the beans covered, and occasionally skimming the foam from the surface. Season with salt and pepper to taste. Drain off any excess liquid and set aside.

For the Salsa:

1. Put the tomatoes in a blender and puree until smooth.
2. In a medium sauté pan or skillet, heat the oil over medium heat. Add the onion and shallots and cook until just beginning to soften, about 5 minutes. Add the tomato paste and puree to the skillet. Bring to a simmer and cook over medium heat for about 10 minutes, until the mixture begins to thicken and turns a darker shade of red. Remove from the heat. Stir in the cilantro and season with salt and pepper to taste. Cover and keep warm.

For the Tacos:

1. In a large sauté pan or skillet, heat the oil and butter over medium heat. Add the beans and cook, turning them over with a spatula occasionally, until the beans are well coated in the oil and butter and are slightly crisp, about 5 minutes.
2. Season the tuna and shrimp with salt and pepper to taste.
3. Preheat a charcoal grill and set the grate about 8 inches above the coals. Lightly brush the grate with oil. When the coals are white, put the tuna on the grill; cook for about 2 minutes on each side, until medium-rare. Transfer to a carving board and let rest for 5 minutes. Thinly slice.
4. Grill the shrimp for 1 to 2 minutes per side, until pink and opaque.
5. On the grill or in a steamer over boiling water, warm the tortillas. Divide the tuna and shrimp among the tortillas. Top with the beans, guacamole, and salsa and serve.

Sautéed Shrimp
with Corn Pudding, Bacon and Corn Salad, and Shrimp Foam

CHEF: Hung
SEASON 3, EPISODE 4
ELIMINATION CHALLENGE: In teams of three, create a trio of one ingredient.

8 large shrimp, unpeeled
2 tablespoons extra-virgin olive oil
¼ cup finely chopped onion
¼ cup finely chopped celery
¼ cup finely chopped carrot
1 plum tomato, finely chopped
1 tablespoon white wine
About 1 cup low-sodium chicken stock
3 teaspoons unsalted butter
Salt and freshly ground white pepper
10 ears corn
2 slices bacon, diced
1 tablespoon minced fresh chives

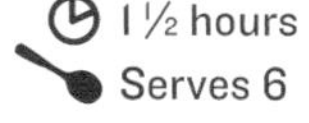
1 ½ hours
Serves 6

1. Peel the shrimp, keeping the shells and refrigerating the shrimp bodies until ready to use. In a medium saucepan, heat 1 tablespoon of the oil over medium heat. Add the onion, celery, and carrot and sauté until lightly caramelized, about 15 minutes. Add the tomato and cook until softened, about 2 minutes. Add the shrimp shells and cook for 2 minutes to break down a little. Add the wine and stir to release any bits stuck to the bottom of the pan. Add enough stock to cover the mixture, raise the heat, and cook until the liquid is reduced to about ¼ cup, about 10 minutes. Strain through a fine-mesh sieve, pressing down on the solids to release all the liquid. Return the liquid to the pot, stir in 1 teaspoon of the butter, and season with salt and pepper to taste. Transfer to a bowl, and just before you're ready to serve, use an immersion blender to blend to make the foam.
2. While the shrimp liquid is reducing, remove the corn kernels from the cobs. Run the kernels from 8 of the ears through a juice extractor and discard the pulp. Reserve the kernels from 2 ears for the salad. Place the corn juice in a medium saucepan over medium heat. Bring to a simmer. Simmer, stirring continuously, until the mixture has a puddinglike consistency, about 5 minutes. (If you don't stir continuously, it will become gummy very quickly.) Add the remaining 2 teaspoons butter and salt and pepper to taste. Remove from the heat and set aside.
3. Put the bacon in a small skillet over medium heat until crisp, about 5 minutes. Add the reserved corn kernels and cook for 1 to 2 minutes, or until just cooked through. Add the chives and season with salt and pepper to taste. Remove from the heat and set aside.
4. Heat the remaining 1 tablespoon oil in a medium sauce-pan over medium heat. Add the shrimp bodies and sauté on both sides until just cooked through, 3 to 5 minutes. Season with salt and pepper to taste. Remove from the heat.
5. Spoon the corn pudding onto serving plates and top with the shrimp. Place the bacon and corn salad alongside and finish with the shrimp foam.

HOW TO:
Juice Kernels

Run the corn kernels through a juice extractor and then discard the pulp.

TED ALLEN, JUDGE "IT WAS A FLAVORFUL FOAM, AND IT BROUGHT A LUSHNESS TO THE PLATE."

Sea Bass, Scallop, and Shrimp Sausage
with Jicama Slaw, Sweet Chili Glaze, and Asian Chimichurri

CHEF: Brian M.
SEASON 3, EPISODE 2
ELIMINATION CHALLENGE: Create an upscale barbecue dish for a summer party.

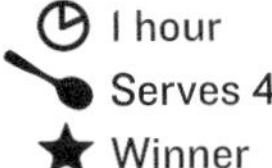
1 hour
Serves 4
Winner

TIMESAVER!

If you prefer not to poach and grill the sausages, chill the seafood mixture well in the freezer, then shape it into patties on a lightly oiled baking sheet and chill again to firm them up slightly. Broil the sausages in the oven on the baking sheet, brushing them with the glaze occasionally and turning them with a thin metal spatula, until browned and cooked through.

Sausage:
- 1 pound Corvina or any other sea bass fillet, cut into 1-inch pieces
- ½ pound black tiger shrimp, peeled and deveined
- ½ pound scallops
- 1 garlic clove, minced
- One 1-inch piece fresh ginger, peeled and minced
- 4 scallions, finely chopped
- 1 bunch fresh cilantro, stemmed and chopped
- ½ cup vegetable oil
- 1 teaspoon sesame oil
- 2 teaspoons red wine vinegar
- 2 teaspoons soy sauce
- Salt and freshly ground black pepper to taste

Sweet Chili Glaze:
- ½ cup sambal chili paste, or more to taste
- ½ cup honey, or more to taste
- ¼ cup red wine vinegar
- 2 teaspoons cornstarch

Jicama Slaw:
- 1 small jicama, peeled
- 1 small red bell pepper, cored and seeded
- 1 carrot
- ½ bunch fresh cilantro, stemmed and chopped

Asian Chimichurri:
- ½ shallot
- ½ cup peeled chopped fresh ginger
- ½ bunch fresh cilantro, stemmed
- ¼ cup sriracha hot sauce
- 2 teaspoons soy sauce
- 1 teaspoon sesame oil
- ¼ cup red wine vinegar
- ¾ cup vegetable oil

For the Sausage:

1. Put the fish, shrimp, and scallops in a food processor and pulse until smooth. Add all the remaining ingredients for the sausage and pulse to combine. Transfer the sausage mixture to a piping bag (or a heavy-duty zip-top bag; cut off one corner with scissors).
2. Place a large pot of water over high heat and bring to a boil; fill a large bowl with ice water and set aside.
3. Lay a 12-inch-long piece of plastic wrap on a work surface and pipe a 1-inch-diameter strip of the sausage mixture down the center of the plastic, about 6 inches long. Wrap the sausage mixture tightly, forming it into a smooth sausage shape, and twist the ends of the plastic tightly. Set aside and repeat with the remaining sausage mixture.
4. When the water is boiling, carefully lower half of the plastic-wrapped sausages into the water. Bring to a simmer and cook for 6 to 8 minutes, until firm to the touch. Using tongs, transfer the sausages to the ice-water bath. Repeat with the remaining sausages. Set aside while you make the chili glaze and jicama slaw.

For the Sweet Chili Glaze:

1. In a small saucepan, combine the chili paste, honey, and vinegar and bring to a boil over high heat.
2. In a cup, combine the cornstarch with 2 teaspoons water, stirring until smooth. Whisk the cornstarch slurry into the chili paste mixture and boil for 3 minutes. Taste; if the glaze is too spicy, add more honey; if you prefer it hotter, add more chili paste. Set aside.

For the Jicama Slaw:

Cut the jicama, pepper, and carrot into julienne strips. In a large bowl, toss the vegetables together with the cilantro. Set aside.

For the Asian Chimichurri:

1. Put all the ingredients except the vegetable oil in a blender and blend on high speed until combined. With the motor running, slowly add the vegetable oil in a thin stream through the hole in the lid.
2. Reserve ¼ cup of the chimichurri and use most of the remaining chimichurri to dress the jicama slaw, tossing to coat well.

To Grill and Serve:

1. Preheat a charcoal grill and set the grate about 8 inches above the coals.
2. Remove the plastic wrap from the sausages.
3. Lightly brush the grate with oil. When the flames have died down and the coals are white, place the sausages on the grill and cook for about 10 minutes, turning with a thin metal spatula and brushing them with the chili glaze as they cook, until well browned and grill-marked.
4. Divide the jicama slaw among 4 serving plates. Place 2 sausages on each plate and serve immediately.

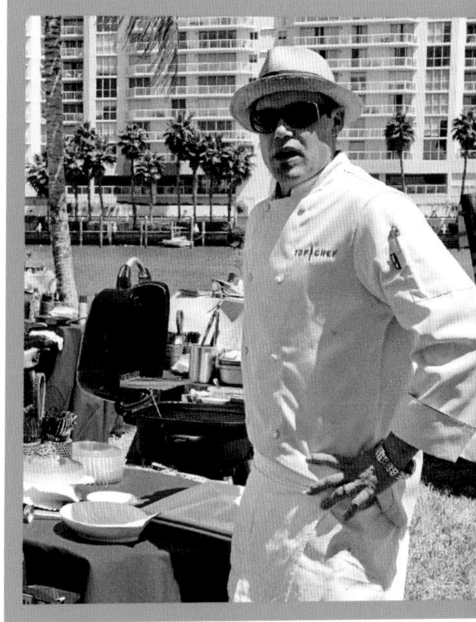

"This had Latin and Asian flavors that really worked nicely together. It was perfect to be served outdoors for the upscale barbecue."

BRIAN

Ecuadorian Ceviche
with Popcorn Cakes

CHEF: Harold
SEASON 1, EPISODE 9
QUICKFIRE CHALLENGE: Re-create a classic junk-food item.

Ecuadorian Ceviche:

3 large tomatoes, quartered
¼ cup fresh orange juice
½ cup fresh lime juice
2 teaspoons sugar
1 red onion, diced
Salt and freshly ground black pepper
1 pound large shrimp, peeled and deveined
1 pound squid, cleaned, tentacles separated and chopped, bodies cut into ¼-inch rings
¼ cup chopped fresh cilantro, plus more for garnish

Popcorn Cakes:

½ cup seltzer water
1 large egg
½ teaspoon salt, plus more for sprinkling
½ teaspoon freshly ground black pepper
2 teaspoons minced fresh chives
½ cup all-purpose flour
1 bag salted microwave popcorn, popped, cooled, and roughly broken up with your hands
Vegetable oil for frying

30 minutes, plus straining overnight and marinating 3 hours

Serves 6 to 8

"The fact of the matter is, I'm not here to cook junk food. I'm going to take the healthiest thing up there and make something with it."

HAROLD

For the Ecuadorian Ceviche:

1. Put the tomatoes in a food processor and puree until smooth. Line a fine-mesh sieve with a double layer of cheesecloth and place over a bowl large enough to hold the liquid from the tomatoes without letting the sieve touch the liquid. Place the sieve on top of the bowl, pour in the tomato puree, cover, and refrigerate overnight without stirring or pressing down on the solids.
2. Discard the tomato puree and transfer the tomato liquid to a measuring cup. Measure out 1 cup liquid and save the rest for another use.
3. In a large bowl, whisk together the tomato liquid, orange juice, lime juice, sugar, onion, and salt and pepper to taste.
4. Bring a large pot of water to a simmer. Add the shrimp and cook until just cooked through, about 1 minute. Add the squid and cook until just tender, about 40 seconds.
5. Drain the shrimp and squid well and add to the marinade. Place in the refrigerator for at least 3 hours or up to 8 hours to marinate, stirring occasionally. Just before serving, stir in the cilantro.

For the Popcorn Cakes:

1. Whisk the seltzer water, egg, salt, and pepper in a large bowl until frothy. Whisk in the chives, then whisk in the flour. Stir in the popcorn until just coated with the batter.
2. In a large skillet, heat ½ inch of oil over medium heat until hot but not smoking. In batches, drop the batter by tablespoons into the oil and fry until nicely browned on both sides, about 2 minutes.
3. Remove the popcorn cakes with a slotted spoon and transfer to paper towels to drain. Sprinkle lightly with salt.

To Serve:

Using a slotted spoon, place the ceviche in small bowls, then spoon the marinade on top. Garnish with cilantro. Place the popcorn cakes alongside and serve.

Spicy Coconut Curry Steamed Mussels
with Mango Couscous

CHEF: Betty
SEASON 2, EPISODE 1
QUICKFIRE CHALLENGE: Create a flambé dish in a limited amount of time.

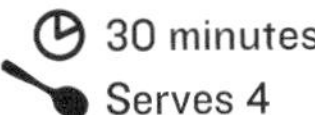

30 minutes
Serves 4

WHAT IS . . .
Good Fat?

Coconut milk contains both the oils and the flavors found in coconut. Though saturated, the fats in coconut oil form shorter molecules than the fatty acids in foods such as meat and eggs. These medium-length fatty acids actually help lower the risk of heart disease. Lauric acid, the main fatty acid in coconut oil, has antiviral, antibacterial, and antifungal properties.

4 pounds fresh mussels, scrubbed and debearded
2 tablespoons vegetable oil
One 2-inch piece fresh ginger, peeled and minced
1 small red onion, minced
1 tablespoon red curry paste, or to taste
One 13 ½-ounce can unsweetened coconut milk
3 cups low-sodium vegetable stock
Juice and finely minced zest of 2 limes
1 teaspoon ground coriander
½ teaspoon salt
Freshly ground black pepper
2 cups instant couscous
1 mango, peeled and diced
¼ cup cognac
2 tablespoons sugar
¼ cup chopped fresh basil
¼ cup chopped fresh cilantro

1. Discard any mussels with cracked shells, and those that do not close when tapped gently.
2. In a large sauté pan or skillet with a lid, heat 1 tablespoon of the oil and add the ginger and onion. Cook over medium heat, stirring frequently, until the onion is just starting to soften, about 3 minutes. Add the curry paste and stir well to coat the ginger and onion. Add the coconut milk and 1 cup of the stock and raise the heat to high; bring to a boil and cook for 5 minutes, or until reduced slightly. Add the lime zest and mussels, then put the lid on and cook over medium-high heat for 6 to 8 minutes, until all the mussels are open. Discard any unopened mussels after 8 minutes.
3. Meanwhile, in a medium saucepan, bring the remaining 2 cups stock, the remaining 1 tablespoon oil, the ground coriander, the salt, and a pinch of pepper to a boil. Add the couscous and stir. Cover the pan and remove from the heat. Let stand for 5 minutes, then fluff with a fork and gently fold in the mango.
4. In a small sauté pan or skillet, combine the lime juice, cognac, and sugar. Cook over low heat, stirring frequently, until the sugar is dissolved, then carefully ignite the mixture and pour it over the mussels. Stir in the basil and cilantro and serve immediately with the couscous.

CHEF AND SEASON 1 WINNER HAROLD DIETERLE, GUEST JUDGE "EVERYTHING WAS SPOT ON. I WANTED TO SIT DOWN AND EAT THE WHOLE BOWL."

Red Wine–Braised Angel Hair Pasta
with Cold Octopus and Tomato Succo with Octopus Frit

CHEF: Tiffani
SEASON 1, EPISODE 3
QUICKFIRE CHALLENGE: Prepare octopus for Chef Laurent Manrique.

Red Wine–Braised Angel Hair Pasta:
One 3-pound octopus, cleaned
6 cups red wine
3 cups chicken stock
6 garlic cloves, peeled and left whole
2 shallots, chopped
½ bunch fresh thyme
½ pound angel hair pasta
4 tablespoons extra-virgin olive oil
1 tablespoon fresh lemon juice, or to taste
1 tablespoon finely chopped fresh basil
1 tablespoon finely chopped fresh flat-leaf parsley
Salt and freshly ground black pepper

Cold Octopus:
Octopus body, braised
About 1 tablespoon extra-virgin olive oil
Salt and freshly ground black pepper

Octopus Frit:
Canola oil for frying
About ½ cup all-purpose flour
Salt and freshly ground black pepper
Octopus tentacles, braised

¼ cup pine nuts for garnish

Tomato Succo (see right)

 3 hours, plus marinating at least 2 hours
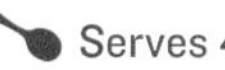 Serves 4
★ Winner

For the Red Wine–Braised Angel Hair Pasta:

1. Submerge the octopus in a large pot of boiling water for 5 minutes. Drain. Remove the head and discard it. Cut the body into 1-inch chunks and cut the tentacles in half. Remove the outer layer of skin from the octopus. In a large bowl, combine the octopus body and tentacles, the wine, stock, garlic, and shallots. Cover and refrigerate to marinate for at least 2 hours or overnight.
2. Put the octopus and marinade in a large saucepan and place over medium-high heat. Add the thyme and bring to a simmer. Reduce the heat, cover the pot, and simmer for about 2 hours, or until the meat is fork-tender. Remove the octopus from the braising liquid, strain the liquid, then return the liquid to the pot and bring to a boil.
3. Add the pasta to the braising liquid and cook to al dente, about 2 minutes. Drain and toss with the oil, lemon juice, basil, parsley, and salt and pepper to taste.

For the Cold Octopus:

Preheat a grill or stovetop grill pan to medium-high. Place the octopus body pieces in a bowl and toss with oil to coat. Season with salt and pepper. Place on the grill and sear until browned on all sides, about 5 minutes total. Remove from the heat and thinly slice. Cover and refrigerate until ready to serve.

For the Octopus Frit:

In a large, heavy pot, heat 3 inches of oil to 375°F. Spread the flour on a plate and season with salt and pepper. Toss the tentacles in the flour, shake to remove excess flour, and fry until golden brown, 3 to 5 minutes. Remove with a slotted spoon to paper towels to drain. Season with salt and pepper.

To Serve:

Place the pasta on serving plates, top with the sliced octopus, and garnish with the pine nuts. Serve the succo in dipping bowls with the tentacles alongside.

ON THE SIDE: Tomato Succo

4 tablespoons extra-virgin olive oil
1 shallot, sliced
2 garlic cloves, sliced
5 ripe yellow tomatoes, peeled, cored, and chopped
1 tablespoon capers, drained
1 tablespoon fresh lemon juice, or to taste
Salt and freshly ground black pepper

1. While the octopus is braising, in a medium saucepan, heat 2 tablespoons of the oil over medium heat. Add the shallot and garlic and sauté until the vegetables are softened, about 3 minutes. Add the tomatoes and capers and cook until the tomatoes start to break down, about 5 minutes. Add the lemon juice and salt and pepper to taste.
2. Transfer the sauce to a blender and pulse until smooth with a few chunks remaining. Set aside until ready to serve.

Mirin-Glazed Sea Bass

CHEF: Tiffani
SEASON 1, EPISODE 4
ELIMINATION CHALLENGE: Create a gourmet entrée that can be reheated in the microwave.

10 minutes, plus marinating overnight
Serves 2
Winner

6 tablespoons mirin
¼ cup white miso paste
¼ cup teriyaki sauce
¼ cup Shaoxing wine
Two 6-ounce pieces sea bass fillet
1 tablespoon vegetable oil
2 fresh purple shiso sprigs
2 fresh salad burnet sprigs

1. In a container large enough to hold the fish, combine the mirin, miso paste, teriyaki sauce, and Shaoxing. Put the fish in the marinade and refrigerate, covered, overnight.
2. In a medium sauté pan or skillet, heat the oil over medium-high heat. Remove the fish from the marinade, scraping off the excess, and pat dry. Put the fish in the pan and cook, without turning, for 3 minutes, until well browned on the bottom; turn and cook the other side for about 3 minutes, until browned and just cooked through—the fish will flake easily when prodded with a knife; turn the heat down to medium if the fish is browning too quickly.
3. Place the fish on serving plates and garnish with purple shiso and salad burnet sprigs. Serve immediately.

WHAT IS . . .
Sea Bass?

The perplexing nomenclature surrounding certain varieties of oily, firm white-fleshed fish could make one swear off seafood altogether—if the fish weren't all so delicious. Here's a cheat sheet:

Sea bass: One of the most common bass in fish markets, harvested along the East Coast.

Striped bass: Caught along the East Coast, though some states have banned commercial fishing of striped bass. Farmed striped bass is usually at the market fresher than wild.

European bass: Most commonly found in the Mediterranean; known as *loup de mer* ("sea wolf") in France and *branzino* in Italy.

Chilean sea bass: Not a true bass, this fish is more accurately known as Patagonian toothfish.

Escolar: Deep-water fish that lives in tropical and temperate climates. Not a bass but a snake mackerel, escolar is sometimes referred to as "white tuna."

Knives Out! Top Feuds

When executive producer Andy Cohen imagined a show about aspiring chefs, he might have imagined something sedate and civil.

That illusion lasted until Ken Lee began pissing off all his fellow contestants *and* the guest chef, Hubert Keller, *and* the judges. "I don't think I realized just how dramatic chefs are," Cohen says. "Then Candice Kumai was suddenly calling Stephen Asprinio 'a tool and a douche bag.' I was like, 'Are you kidding me? This is happening on our chefs' show?!'" That certainly wouldn't be the last of the great *Top Chef* showdowns.

"When we cast Howie and Joey we thought, 'Well, they have similar backgrounds, maybe they'll get along well,'" says executive producer Dan Cutforth. Um, try again.

"Next time I'm in that room, I'll walk out. Next time you're in there, you better step up and be a man."

"You've been blaming everybody else for your bull@#$!. Shake somebody's @#$!ing hand and be a man. You be a @#$!ing man. You wanna know what? I would've been a @#$!ing man about it and you would've @#$!ing bitched about it like a little girl like you've been doing all day."

"Want me to go home now?"

"I don't give a @#$! what you do. I'm here to do my best. You do your best. We'll see what happens. Alright?"

Season 3, Episode 2

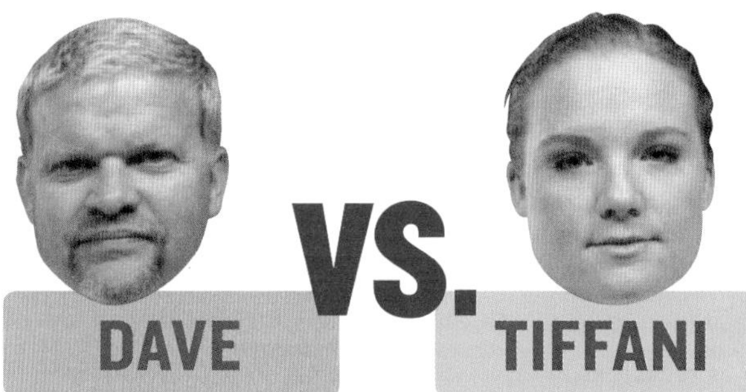

The first and maybe greatest of the *Top Chef* feuds, this battle started with a great line ("I'm not your bitch, bitch") but ended with real consequences when Dave wound up in the position to help or hurt Tiffani as her sous-chef in the finale.

"Tiffani had her vision, and that's great, but you can't be everything in a team of three."

"No—"

"It's my turn to talk, OK? I've heard you talk for the last twenty-four hours so let's just zip it."

"I didn't bash you."

"You've been bashing me for the last twenty-four hours. 'Don't touch that, don't touch that...'"

"When did I ever say that?"

"Every time! I'm not your bitch, bitch. Let's get through it. I don't need to be talked to and treated like @#$!."

Season 1, Episode 7

ILAN

FRANK

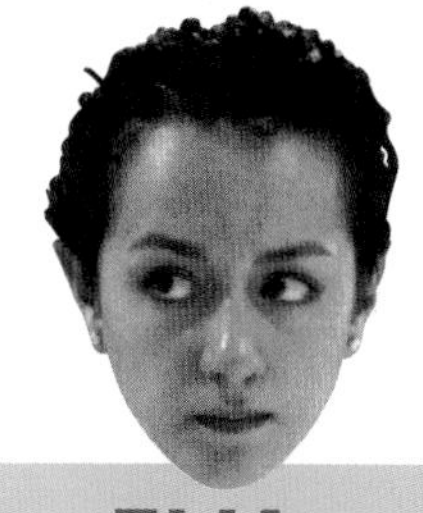

ELIA

CLIFF

VS. VS. VS. VS.

MARCEL

VS.

BETTY

"It was really strange," says executive producer Shauna Minoprio. "We kept hearing about how, one by one, Marcel was getting under everybody's skin. But then we'd look back at the tape and we couldn't find what he was doing." Still, one has to believe the numbers. Something was going on between the molecular gastronomist and the rest of the house.

"You never once offered to help me. I offered to help you. How could you ever tell me that I'm selfish?"

"You never helped to set up that kitchen."

"Did you help me set up my kitchen?"

"I help you all the time."

"Did you ask me for help today? Did you ask me? It's a yes or no question."

"No, it's not a yes or no question, it's an explanation, so sit the @#$! down and, if you're asking me a question, let me tell you the answer."

"Did I have to help you?"

"No, and I kind of wish you didn't."

"I'm still selfish, and you're still a bitch. I hope you go home."

Season 2, Episode 6

STEPHEN VS. CANDICE

A feud with a happy ending. Stephen may have crossed the line when he told Candice, the culinary school student, that she would "fail. Horribly." But his heartfelt apology at the reunion mended all fences. Still, it was shocking at the time.

"I have standards unlike you do. Obviously."

"Obviously you're a tool and a douche bag."

"Can you think of anything smarter?"

"No, you're a tool."

"You will not succeed and you will fail. Horribly. The competition is called *Top Chef*. I don't accept mediocrity."

"Fine, then go ahead and call me mediocrity. Use your fancy, stupid @#$!ing words. Get over yourself!"

Season 1, Episode 3

Entrées: Vegetarian

193

196

198

Truffle and Cognac Cream Macaroni and Cheese

CHEF: Dave
SEASON 1, EPISODE 9
ELIMINATION CHALLENGE: Prepare a dish with expensive black truffles.

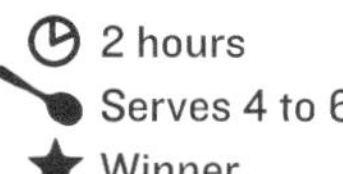

2 hours
Serves 4 to 6
Winner

- Unsalted butter for the baking dishes
- 1 cup cognac
- 1 tablespoon extra-virgin olive oil
- 1 small shallot, minced
- 6 roasted garlic cloves (see page 197), minced
- 1 tablespoon sherry
- 6 ounces Perigord black truffles: 3 ounces finely chopped, 1 ½ ounces thinly sliced with a truffle slicer, mandoline, or very sharp knife, and 1 ½ ounces finely grated
- 4 cups heavy cream
- 2 teaspoons minced fresh oregano
- 2 teaspoons fresh thyme leaves
- 6 ounces Parmesan cheese, finely grated (about 2 cups), plus more for sprinkling
- 2 teaspoons chipotle Tabasco® sauce
- Salt and freshly ground black pepper
- 1 pound fresh penne or other pasta, cooked al dente
- 8 ounces fontina cheese, finely grated (about 2 ½ cups)
- 2 cups seasoned sourdough croutons

1. Generously butter the bottom and sides of 4 to 6 medium baking dishes. Set aside.
2. Place the cognac in a small saucepan or skillet over medium heat. Bring to a simmer and cook until reduced by half, 10 to 15 minutes. Remove from the heat and set aside.
3. In a large saucepan, heat the oil over medium heat. Add the shallot and garlic and cook until the vegetables are softened but not browned, about 3 minutes. Add the sherry and stir until evaporated. Add the chopped truffles, cream, reduced cognac, oregano, and thyme.
4. Bring to a simmer, reduce the heat to medium-low, and cook, stirring occasionally, until the mixture is reduced by half and the truffle flavor is infused, about 20 minutes. Watch the pot carefully so the cream doesn't boil over. Add the Parmesan cheese, Tabasco®, and salt and pepper to taste. Add the cooked pasta and fontina cheese and stir until the cheeses are melted. Taste and adjust the seasoning if necessary. Set aside.
5. Place the croutons in a food processor and process until broken down into crumbs.
6. Arrange a layer of truffle slices on the bottom of each baking dish.
7. Divide the pasta among the baking dishes and top with the crouton crumbs, grated truffles, and a sprinkling of Parmesan cheese. Bake for about 20 minutes, or until bubbly and browned on top.

"This is my signature dish. Everyone knows me for it."
DAVE

Tempura Vegetables and Mozzarella
with Cornichon Mayonnaise

CHEF: Marcel
SEASON 2, EPISODE 10
ELIMINATION CHALLENGE: Divide into two teams and turn an empty space into a restaurant in 24 hours.

1 hour, 15 minutes
Serves 8

"Marcel's dish was crispy and well seasoned. I thought it was nice."

CHEF AND RESTAURATEUR MIKE YAKURA, GUEST JUDGE

1 eggplant
1 zucchini
2 yellow squash
2 shallots
Salt
1 cup mayonnaise
3 cornichons, chopped
2 garlic cloves, finely chopped
Freshly ground black pepper
2 ½ cups all-purpose flour
1 cup cornstarch
2 teaspoons baking powder
3 cups sparkling water
Vegetable oil for frying
1 large bunch fresh flat-leaf parsley, tough stems removed
1 pint bocconcini (mozzarella balls), drained
2 large eggs, beaten
1 ¼ cups dry bread crumbs

1. Cut the eggplant, zucchini, and squash into ¼-inch-thick rounds. Cut the shallots lengthwise into quarters. Sprinkle the eggplant slices on both sides with salt and set aside for 1 hour.
2. In a small bowl, stir together the mayonnaise, cornichons, and garlic. Season with salt and pepper to taste and set aside.
3. In a medium bowl, whisk together 2 cups of the flour, the cornstarch, and baking powder. Add the sparkling water and stir gently until just combined. Refrigerate the batter until ready to use.
4. Preheat the oven to 200°F.
5. In a large, heavy pot, heat 2 to 3 inches of oil to 300°F.
6. Hold a few sprigs of parsley in your fingers or with tongs and dip them into the batter, letting the excess drain off. Carefully lower the parsley into the hot oil and cook until crisp, about 5 seconds. Using a slotted spoon, transfer to paper towels to drain. Sprinkle with salt while still warm. Put the baking sheet in the oven to keep warm.
7. Increase the heat and heat the oil to 350°F.
8. Pat the eggplant dry with paper towels. One at a time, dip the vegetables in the batter, letting the excess drain off. Carefully lower the vegetables into the hot oil and cook, turning occasionally, until golden brown, 1 to 2 minutes, taking care not to overcrowd the pot. Using the slotted spoon, transfer the vegetables as they brown to the baking sheet in the oven. Sprinkle with salt while still warm. Repeat with the remaining vegetables.
9. Dredge the bocconcini in the remaining flour. Dip in the beaten eggs, then in the bread crumbs. Fry for 30 seconds, or until browned. Sprinkle with salt while still hot.
10. Pile the fried parsley, vegetables, and bocconcini on a serving platter. Serve immediately with the cornichon mayonnaise.

Summer Fruit Salad
with Spicy Mint Chimichurri and Spinach

CHEF: Sam
SEASON 2, EPISODE 3
ELIMINATION CHALLENGE: Update a childhood classic for T.G.I. Friday's.

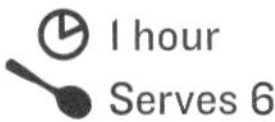
1 hour
Serves 6

Spicy Mint Chimichurri:
½ cup extra-virgin olive oil
2 tablespoons fresh lime juice
2 tablespoons fresh lemon juice
½ cup chopped fresh mint leaves
2 tablespoons chopped fresh cilantro
2 tablespoons chopped fresh flat-leaf parsley
1 teaspoon chopped shallot
1 tablespoon chopped garlic
¾ teaspoon red pepper flakes
Salt to taste

Summer Fruit Salad:
1 cup chopped fresh pineapple
1 cup chopped fresh watermelon, seeds removed
1 cup chopped fresh cantaloupe
¼ cup seedless green grapes, halved
¼ cup seedless red grapes, halved
½ cup diced roasted red peppers

Spinach Salad:
6 cups chopped baby spinach
3 tablespoons extra-virgin olive oil
Juice of 1 lemon, or to taste
Salt and freshly ground black pepper

To Serve:
½ cup grated Gouda cheese

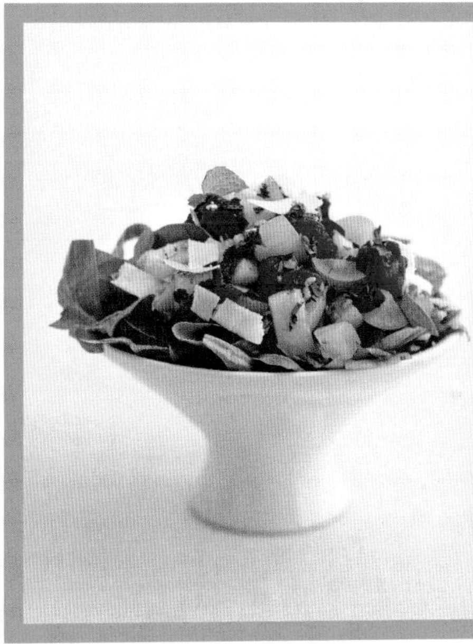

For the Spicy Mint Chimichurri:

In a food processor, combine all the ingredients and process until smooth.

For the Summer Fruit Salad:

1. In a large bowl, combine all the ingredients.
2. Add the chimichurri sauce and mix well to coat the fruit. Cover and refrigerate for about 30 minutes for the fruit to marinate.

For the Spinach Salad:

Place the spinach in a large bowl and toss with the oil. Add the lemon juice and salt and pepper to taste and toss.

To Serve:

Divide the spinach among serving plates. Arrange the fruit mixture on top of the spinach and garnish with the cheese.

"I loved that it was sophisticated and fun, easy and light. So cool on a hot day."

GAIL SIMMONS, JUDGE

CHEF STEPHEN BULGARELLI, GUEST JUDGE "TREMENDOUS FLAVOR. EXCITING AND HEALTHY AND CRAVEABLE."

Chiles Rellenos

CHEF: Sara M.
SEASON 3, EPISODE 5
ELIMINATION CHALLENGE: Prepare a Latin lunch for the cast of a telenovela.

2 hours, plus soaking overnight

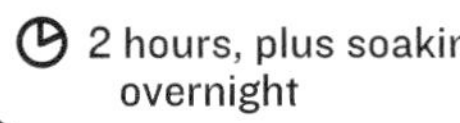
Serves 10

ON THE SIDE:

Roasted Pepper Sauce

- 3 red bell peppers, seeded and quartered
- 1 red onion, quartered
- 2 tomatoes, quartered
- 4 garlic cloves, smashed
- 2 tablespoons olive oil
- Salt and freshly ground black pepper
- Juice of ½ lime, or more to taste

1. Preheat the oven to 500°F.

2. In a large roasting pan, toss the red peppers, onion, tomatoes, and garlic with 1 tablespoon of the oil and season with salt and pepper. Roast until the vegetables are very soft, about 25 minutes.

3. Transfer to a blender and puree until smooth. Add the remaining 1 tablespoon oil and the lime juice. Taste and season with more salt and pepper or lime juice if necessary. Set aside.

Black Beans:
- 1 pound dried black beans
- 1 tablespoon olive oil
- 1 white onion, diced
- 4 garlic cloves, chopped
- 1 tablespoon chili powder
- 1 tablespoon ground cumin
- 3 ½ quarts low-sodium vegetable stock or water, or more if needed
- 1 bay leaf
- Salt and freshly ground black pepper

Poblanos:
- 10 medium poblano chiles
- 1 tablespoon olive oil
- ½ onion, chopped
- 1 zucchini, finely diced
- 1 yellow squash, finely diced
- 3 garlic cloves, chopped
- Salt and freshly ground black pepper
- 2 cups cooked long-grain white rice
- ¼ cup raisins
- ½ bunch fresh cilantro, chopped, plus more leaves for garnish

Avocado Butter:
- 4 Hass avocados
- 1 cup milk
- ½ cup olive oil
- Salt to taste

Roasted Pepper Sauce (see left)

For the Black Beans:

Soak the beans overnight in enough cold water to cover; drain. In a large pot, heat the oil over medium heat. Add the onion and garlic and sauté until translucent, about 5 minutes. Add the chili powder and cumin and cook, stirring, until fragrant. Add the stock, beans, and bay leaf. Bring to a boil, then reduce the heat. Simmer for about 1 ½ hours, until the beans are tender but not falling apart, adding more stock if necessary to keep the beans covered, and occasionally skimming the foam from the surface. Season with salt and pepper to taste.

For the Poblanos:

1. Roast the chiles directly over a gas flame, turning with tongs until blackened. Place in a heat-proof bowl, cover with plastic wrap, and set aside for 20 minutes. Remove the blackened skin. Make a lengthwise slit and remove the seeds and ribs.

2. Preheat the oven to 350°F. In a large sauté pan or skillet, heat the oil over medium-high heat. Add the onion, zucchini, squash, and garlic and sauté until just softened. Season with salt and pepper to taste. Let cool to room temperature, then transfer to a large bowl and fold in the rice, raisins, and cilantro. Stuff the poblanos with the rice mixture and place them in two 9-by-11-inch baking dishes. Cover the dishes with aluminum foil. Bake for 20 minutes, or until heated through.

For the Avocado Butter:

Puree 3 of the avocados, the milk, oil, and salt in a blender until smooth.

To Serve:

Spoon some of the pepper sauce onto each of 10 serving plates. Spoon on some beans, then place the stuffed peppers on the plates and put a dollop of the avocado butter and a slice of avocado on each plate. Serve, garnished with cilantro leaves.

Deconstructed Falafel

CHEF: Miguel
SEASON 1, EPISODE 7
QUICKFIRE CHALLENGE: Build a sandwich for Tom's 'wichcraft restaurants.

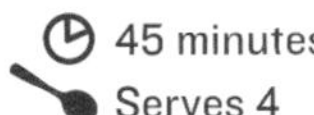
45 minutes
Serves 4

"Miguel would have won this challenge hands down if he had made a sandwich. The flavors were great. If it had bread, it would've been on my menu."

TOM COLICCHIO, HEAD JUDGE

Falafel Bun:

One 15-ounce can chickpeas, rinsed and drained
1 tablespoon minced fresh flat-leaf parsley
1 garlic clove, minced
½ teaspoon ground cumin
Salt and freshly ground black pepper
2 teaspoons fresh lemon juice, or to taste
2 tablespoons all-purpose flour
½ teaspoon baking soda
1 large egg
Vegetable oil for frying

Vegetables:

4 teaspoons extra-virgin olive oil
1 portobello mushroom cap, thinly sliced
Salt and freshly ground black pepper
1 small zucchini, thinly sliced horizontally
8 pickle slices
½ cup alfalfa sprouts

For the Falafel Bun:

1. In a food processor, combine the chickpeas, parsley, garlic, cumin, and salt and pepper to taste and puree until smooth. Remove 3 tablespoons of the hummus mixture, combine it with the lemon juice, and reserve for the sandwich. Add the flour, baking soda, and egg to the mixture in the food processor and pulse to combine. Transfer to a bowl and shape into 4 patties. Place the patties on a plate and let stand for 15 minutes.

2. In a large skillet, heat ½ inch of oil over medium heat until hot. Add the patties and fry until cooked through, crisp, and nicely browned, about 4 minutes on each side. Transfer to paper towels to drain.

For the Vegetables:

In a small skillet, heat 2 teaspoons of the oil over medium-high heat. Add the mushroom and cook, stirring, until lightly browned, about 5 minutes. Season with salt and pepper to taste. Remove from the pan and place on a plate. Add the remaining 2 teaspoons oil to the skillet, add the zucchini, and cook until lightly browned on both sides, about 5 minutes. Transfer to the plate with the mushrooms. (Alternatively, cook over a medium-hot outdoor grill.)

To Serve:

Place a falafel patty on each serving plate. Top with the mushrooms, followed by the zucchini, reserved hummus, and pickles. Finish with the alfalfa sprouts and serve immediately.

Sunflower Seed and Carrot Loaf
with Cilantro, Sesame Oil, and Squirt®

CHEF: Carlos
SEASON 2, EPISODE 4
QUICKFIRE CHALLENGE: Create an amuse-bouche using ingredients from a vending machine.

One 5-ounce bag sunflower seed kernels
½ bunch fresh cilantro, stemmed, plus 4 leaves for garnish
Two 2-ounce packages peeled carrots (about 2 regular-size carrots)
4 drops toasted sesame oil
1 teaspoon fresh lime juice
Pinch of salt
Pinch of white pepper
Ground cayenne
1 hard-cooked egg, white only
1 tablespoon Squirt® soda

20 minutes
Serves 4
Winner

1. In a small bowl, soak the sunflower seeds in enough water to cover for 15 minutes. Drain and put in a food processor.
2. Chop the ½ bunch cilantro and add it to the food processor, along with the carrots, oil, lime juice, salt, white pepper, and a pinch of cayenne. Process until finely ground.
3. Using your hands, form the mixture into 4 small loaves on individual serving plates. Garnish each loaf with a few pieces of chopped egg white, a cilantro leaf, and a pinch of cayenne. Sprinkle the top with soda. Serve immediately.

CHEF AND RESTAURATEUR SUZANNE GOIN, GUEST JUDGE "NICE AND BRIGHT AND CLEAN. CARLOS WAS REALLY GOING BY THE GUIDELINES OF WHAT AN AMUSE-BOUCHE SHOULD BE."

Portobello and Button Mushroom Crème
with Walnuts

CHEF: Elia
SEASON 2, EPISODE 6
ELIMINATION CHALLENGE: Reinvent traditional ingredients for a cutting-edge Thanksgiving dinner.

- 3 tablespoons olive oil
- 1 pound button mushrooms, sliced
- Salt and freshly ground black pepper
- 4 ¼ cups heavy cream
- 2 cups low-sodium vegetable stock
- 1 tablespoon unsalted butter
- 3 portobello mushroom caps, cut into cubes
- 1 cup chopped walnuts, toasted
- 2 tablespoons chopped fresh chives

1 hour, 15 minutes
Serves 4 to 6
Winner

1. In a large saucepan, heat 2 tablespoons of the oil over medium heat. Add the button mushrooms and cook, stirring occasionally, for about 5 minutes, until beginning to soften. Season with salt and pepper to taste.
2. Add the cream and stock and bring to a boil. Lower the heat and simmer for 20 minutes. Cover and simmer for 20 minutes longer. Remove from the heat and let stand, covered, for 20 minutes. Pour the soup through a fine-mesh sieve set over a clean saucepan; discard the mushrooms.
3. Meanwhile, in a small skillet, heat the remaining 1 tablespoon oil and the butter over medium-high heat. Add the portobello mushrooms and cook for about 3 minutes, until beginning to soften. Remove from the heat.
4. Rewarm the soup over low heat if necessary. Divide the soup among 4 to 6 serving bowls and top with the portobello mushrooms, walnuts, and chives. Serve immediately.

GAIL SIMMONS, JUDGE "I LOVED THE TEXTURE, I LOVED THE NUTTINESS. THEY COMPLEMENTED THE MUSHROOMS REALLY WELL."

Grilled Cheese with Portobello Mushrooms
and Roasted Red Pepper Soup

CHEF: Betty
SEASON 2, EPISODE 3
ELIMINATION CHALLENGE: Update a childhood classic for T.G.I. Friday's.

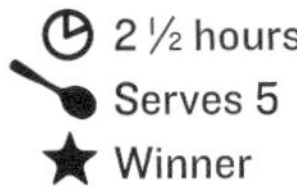

2 ½ hours
Serves 5
Winner

ON THE SIDE:
Roasted Red Pepper Soup

- 3 medium red bell peppers
- ¼ cup extra-virgin olive oil
- 1 medium carrot, diced
- 1 medium celery rib, diced
- 1 large red onion, diced
- Two 28-ounce cans whole tomatoes in juice
- ½ cup chopped fresh basil leaves, plus more for garnish
- 1 tablespoon balsamic vinegar
- Salt and freshly ground black pepper
- ½ cup heavy cream

1. Roast the red peppers and coarsely chop.
2. In a large pot, heat the oil over medium-high heat. Add the carrot, celery, and onion. Cook until they begin to soften, about 5 minutes. Add the peppers, tomatoes, basil, vinegar, and salt and pepper to taste. Bring to a simmer, lower the heat, and simmer until the tomatoes begin to break down, 25 to 30 minutes.
3. Remove from heat, transfer to a blender, in batches, and blend until smooth.
4. Return the mixture to the pot, add the cream, and stir until combined. Serve, garnished with basil.

- 5 tablespoons extra-virgin olive oil
- 1 large red onion, thinly sliced
- Salt and freshly ground black pepper
- 1 pint grape tomatoes, halved
- 1 tablespoon balsamic vinegar, or to taste
- 3 large portobello mushroom caps, thinly sliced
- ¼ cup white wine
- 4 tablespoons unsalted butter
- 3 fresh thyme sprigs
- 10 slices sourdough bread
- 1 ¼ cups coarsely grated provolone cheese
- 1 ¼ cups coarsely grated Monterey Jack cheese

Roasted Red Pepper Soup (see left)

1. Preheat the oven to 350°F.
2. In a medium skillet, combine 2 tablespoons of the oil and the red onion and place over medium heat. Cook until the onion starts to soften, about 5 minutes. Season with salt and pepper to taste and transfer to a roasting dish big enough to fit the onion, tomatoes, and mushrooms.
3. In the same skillet, combine the tomatoes with 1 tablespoon of the oil and the vinegar over medium heat. Cook until the tomatoes start to soften, about 5 minutes. Transfer to the roasting dish with the onions.
4. In a medium bowl, gently toss the mushrooms with the remaining 2 tablespoons oil. Transfer to the roasting dish with the other ingredients. Add the wine and stir to combine.
5. Place the roasting dish in the oven and bake for 25 to 30 minutes, until the vegetables are softened and lightly caramelized and the liquid is absorbed. Remove from the oven and cool to room temperature.
6. While you're roasting the vegetables, in a small saucepan, combine the butter with the thyme sprigs and place over low heat. Heat until the butter is melted. Remove from the heat.
7. Remove the thyme sprigs from the melted butter and brush one side of each slice of bread with the butter. Place the slices buttered side down on a baking sheet or other clean surface. Spread half of the slices with ¼ cup provolone cheese and ¼ cup Monterey Jack cheese each. Top the cheese with the mushroom mixture, dividing evenly among the slices. Place the remaining bread slices on top, buttered side up.
8. Preheat a griddle or skillet over medium-high heat until hot. Place each sandwich on the griddle and cook until golden brown, 2 to 3 minutes, pressing down on the sandwiches with a metal spatula to help them sear. Flip and cook the other side until golden brown and the cheese is melted, 2 to 3 minutes more.
9. Serve the soup, garnished with basil, with the sandwiches, cut in half, on the side.

Lasagna with Two Sauces
and a Colorful Vegetable Medley

CHEF: Dave
SEASON I, EPISODE 4
ELIMINATION CHALLENGE: Create a gourmet entrée that can be reheated in the microwave.

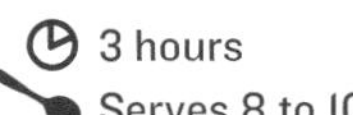

3 hours
Serves 8 to 10

Alfredo Sauce:

2 teaspoons extra-virgin olive oil
3 roasted garlic cloves (see opposite)
1 quart heavy cream
½ teaspoon freshly grated nutmeg
1 teaspoon dried basil
1 teaspoon dried oregano
½ cup finely grated Parmesan cheese
¼ cup finely grated Romano cheese
Salt and freshly ground black pepper

Fire-Roasted Marinara Sauce:

3 tablespoons extra-virgin olive oil
6 roasted garlic cloves (see opposite)
2 medium carrots, finely diced
1 medium white onion, finely diced
2 celery ribs, finely diced
1 shallot, finely diced
1 tablespoon fresh thyme leaves
1 small bunch basil, cut into chiffonade
½ cup sherry
½ cup brandy
Two 28-ounce cans whole fire-roasted tomatoes with juices
3 plum tomatoes, peeled, seeded, and diced
2 cups low-sodium vegetable stock
1 tablespoon sugar
Salt and freshly ground black pepper

Layering Ingredients:

1 pound dried lasagna noodles, cooked al dente
8 ounces mozzarella cheese, coarsely grated (about 2 cups)
8 ounces provolone cheese, coarsely grated (about 2 cups)
1 cup finely grated Parmesan cheese
½ cup finely grated Romano cheese
Freshly ground black pepper

To Serve:

Steamed white, orange, green, and purple cauliflower florets
Fresh thyme sprigs for garnish

For the Alfredo Sauce:

1. In a large saucepan, heat the oil over medium heat. Add the garlic and cook for 2 minutes, breaking it apart with the back of a wooden spoon. Add the cream and bring to a simmer (do not boil). Add the nutmeg, basil, and oregano and cook until reduced by about half, about 45 minutes, watching the pot carefully so the cream doesn't boil over.

2. Lower the heat, add the grated cheeses, and stir until incorporated. Season with salt and pepper to taste. Set aside.

For the Fire-Roasted Marinara Sauce:

1. While you're making the Alfredo sauce, in a large saucepan, heat the oil over medium heat. Add the garlic and cook for 2 minutes, breaking it apart with the back of a wooden spoon. Add the carrots, onion, celery, and shallot and cook until the vegetables are caramelized, about 20 minutes. Add the thyme and basil and cook for 1 minute, stirring.

2. Add the sherry and brandy and cook for 5 minutes, scraping any browned bits from the bottom of the pan. Add the canned and fresh tomatoes, the stock, sugar, and salt and pepper to taste. Bring to a simmer, then reduce the heat and cook for 1 hour, stirring occasionally, to thicken and concentrate the flavors.
3. Using an immersion blender, blend the sauce directly in the pot. Taste and adjust the seasonings, adding salt and pepper to taste as needed. Cook for an additional 15 minutes, stirring occasionally, then taste again and adjust the seasonings if needed. Set aside.

For Layering Ingredients:

1. Preheat the oven to 350°F.
2. Spread a thin layer of marinara sauce over the bottom of a 13-by-9-by-3-inch baking pan or lasagna pan. Follow with a layer of lasagna noodles, overlapping the noodles slightly. Spread a layer of Alfredo sauce over the noodles and top with a layer of marinara sauce. Sprinkle with some of the mozzarella, provolone, Parmesan, and Romano cheeses, followed by a dusting of pepper.
3. Repeat the layers, reserving some of the marinara sauce and some of the Parmesan and Romano cheeses to cover the final layer of pasta.
4. Cover loosely with aluminum foil and bake for 50 minutes, or until starting to bubble, then remove the foil and bake for another 15 to 20 minutes, or until heated through and bubbly on top. Remove from the oven and let stand for 10 minutes before serving.

To Serve:

Cut into serving portions and serve with the cauliflower alongside, garnished with the thyme sprigs.

HOW TO:

Roast Garlic

To roast a head of garlic, preheat the oven to 375°F. Peel off the papery outer layers of the garlic head and cut off the top ½ inch. Place the garlic on a piece of aluminum foil large enough to wrap the garlic. Drizzle with a little olive oil and sprinkle with salt. Wrap in the foil and roast for 30 to 40 minutes, or until the garlic is soft enough to slide out of the skin when pressed.

GAIL SIMMONS, JUDGE "THIS WAS THE BEST WE HAD SEEN FROM DAVE. I THOUGHT IT HAD A LOT OF FLAVOR. I REALLY LIKED THE USE OF CAULIFLOWER TO ADD COLOR."

Quinoa Pilaf
with Curried Sweet Potato Mash

CHEF: Andrea
SEASON 1, EPISODE 4
ELIMINATION CHALLENGE: Create a gourmet entrée that can be reheated in the microwave.

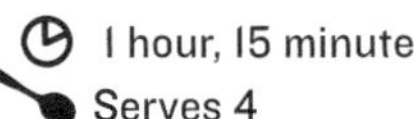
1 hour, 15 minutes
Serves 4

WHAT IS . . .
Quinoa?

Quinoa (pronounced "KEEN-wah"), lately proclaimed as the "supergrain of the future," has in fact been around since the times of the ancient Inca of South America, six thousand years ago. Quinoa was considered the "mother grain"—the nutritional backbone to a rich and powerful civilization, and it is still an important food to the native people of Peru, Chile, and Bolivia. Recently it has made its way onto the menus of upscale restaurants, though health-conscious folk have been benefiting from its rich nutritional profile for some time now. Quinoa is low in carbohydrates, high in fiber, and higher in protein than any other grain. In fact, it's a complete protein in itself—a big plus for vegetarians. It has a light, slightly nutty taste and cooks up in under 20 minutes. Try it as an alternative to rice or pasta.

Curried Sweet Potato Mash:

- 2 large sweet potatoes
- 3 tablespoons extra-virgin olive oil, plus more for the pan
- 1 teaspoon mild curry powder
- Salt
- 1 tablespoon unsalted butter
- 1 tablespoon fresh lemon juice, or to taste

Quinoa Pilaf:

- 1 ⅓ cups quinoa
- Salt
- 1 tablespoon extra-virgin olive oil
- 1 medium yellow onion, diced
- 1 medium leek, cleaned and diced
- 1 garlic clove, minced
- 2 vegetarian sausage links, diced
- 4 shiitake mushrooms, thinly sliced
- 2 tablespoons minced fresh sage, plus sage leaves for garnish
- Freshly ground black pepper
- ½ cup dried cranberries

For the Curried Sweet Potato Mash:

1. Preheat the oven to 375°F. Peel the sweet potatoes and cut into 1-inch cubes. Put the sweet potato cubes in a large bowl and coat with the oil. Add the curry powder and salt to taste. Place in a greased baking pan, cover with aluminum foil, and bake for 50 minutes, or until softened. Remove the foil and bake for an additional 10 minutes, or until lightly browned on top.
2. Remove the sweet potatoes from the oven and transfer to a food processor. Add the butter and lemon juice and process until smooth.

For the Quinoa Pilaf:

1. While the sweet potatoes are roasting, rinse the quinoa until the water runs clear. Put the quinoa in a medium pot over medium heat and add 2 cups of boiling water. Add salt to taste, then reduce the heat, cover the pot, and cook for about 18 minutes, or until the water has been absorbed and the spiral germ separates from the grain. Set aside for 5 minutes, then fluff the quinoa with a fork. Transfer to a large bowl.
2. In a medium sauté pan or skillet, heat the oil over medium heat. Add the onion, leek, and garlic and sauté for about 5 minutes, or until softened. Add the sausage, mushrooms, sage, and salt and pepper to taste and cook for about 5 minutes, or until the sausage is cooked through and the mushrooms have softened.
3. Add the cooked vegetables and dried cranberries to the quinoa and stir to combine.

To Serve:

Spoon the quinoa onto serving plates, along with the mashed sweet potatoes, and garnish with the sage leaves. Serve immediately.

They Oughta Know by Now

You would think the one basic piece of preparation chefs would do before going on *Top Chef* would be, well, watching *Top Chef*. Nevertheless, some of the same culinary mistakes recur season after season. Here are eight of the biggest.

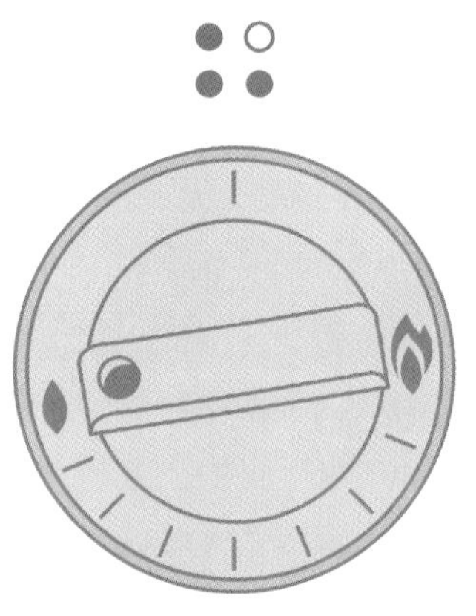

Flame goes on, flame goes off.

It's the most basic act in cooking: applying heat to something and removing it at the right time. So, let's refresh: overcooked steak, bad; overcooked eggs, bad; undercooked chicken, very, very bad.

Taste your food.

You would think this could go without saying; every season someone proves the contrary. A remarkable number of chefs could have saved themselves by sipping their soups and adding a little salt.

The power of one.

Chefs are always tempted to do "duets," showcasing two techniques with the same ingredient, but one stellar dish will always beat two mediocre ones.

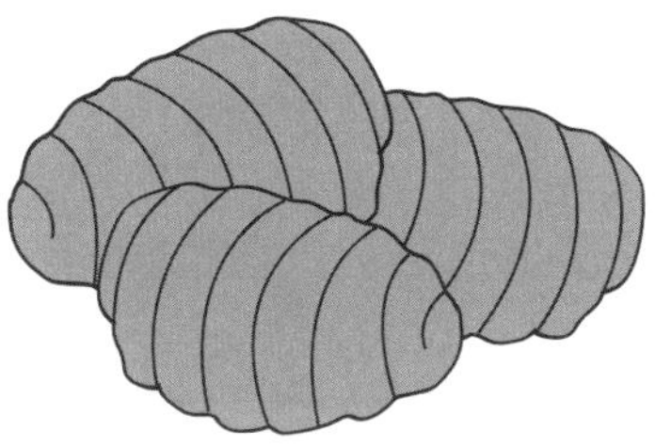

Gnocchi gno-gnos.

For whatever reason, these light, potato-flour dumplings have nearly always fared poorly on *Top Chef*. Avoid, if possible.

Location, location, location.

Not every dish suits every environment: pork belly might not braise well at altitude, vinaigrette "droplets" may ooze in the Hawaiian humidity, broccolini may not hold up to an airplane oven. Point is, take a look around before you start cooking.

Even your dad could make one dessert.

"It boggles my mind that contestants don't show up with at least one simple dessert in their back pocket," says Tom Colicchio. That said, if you aren't armed with a simple flan or cake, and the challenge doesn't require dessert, here's an idea: don't make one.

"Pack your kn... zzzzzz...."

Try not to put the judges to sleep. As Anthony Bourdain says, "Do you really think Tom Colicchio needs to taste one more filet mignon or tuna tartare?"

The icing on the cake.

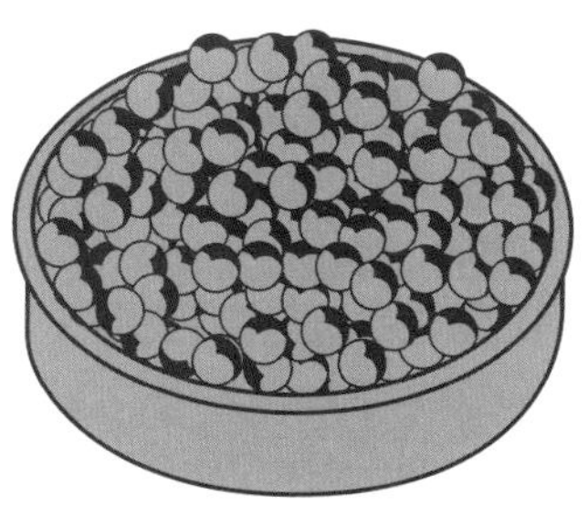

Your parents may be impressed by such luxe ingredients as foie gras, truffles, and caviar. Tom, Gail, and Padma aren't. If anything, they're likely to judge them with an even sharper critical eye. And while we're at it, never ever use truffle oil. "It should be banned," says Colicchio.

Season 3: Elimination Bracket

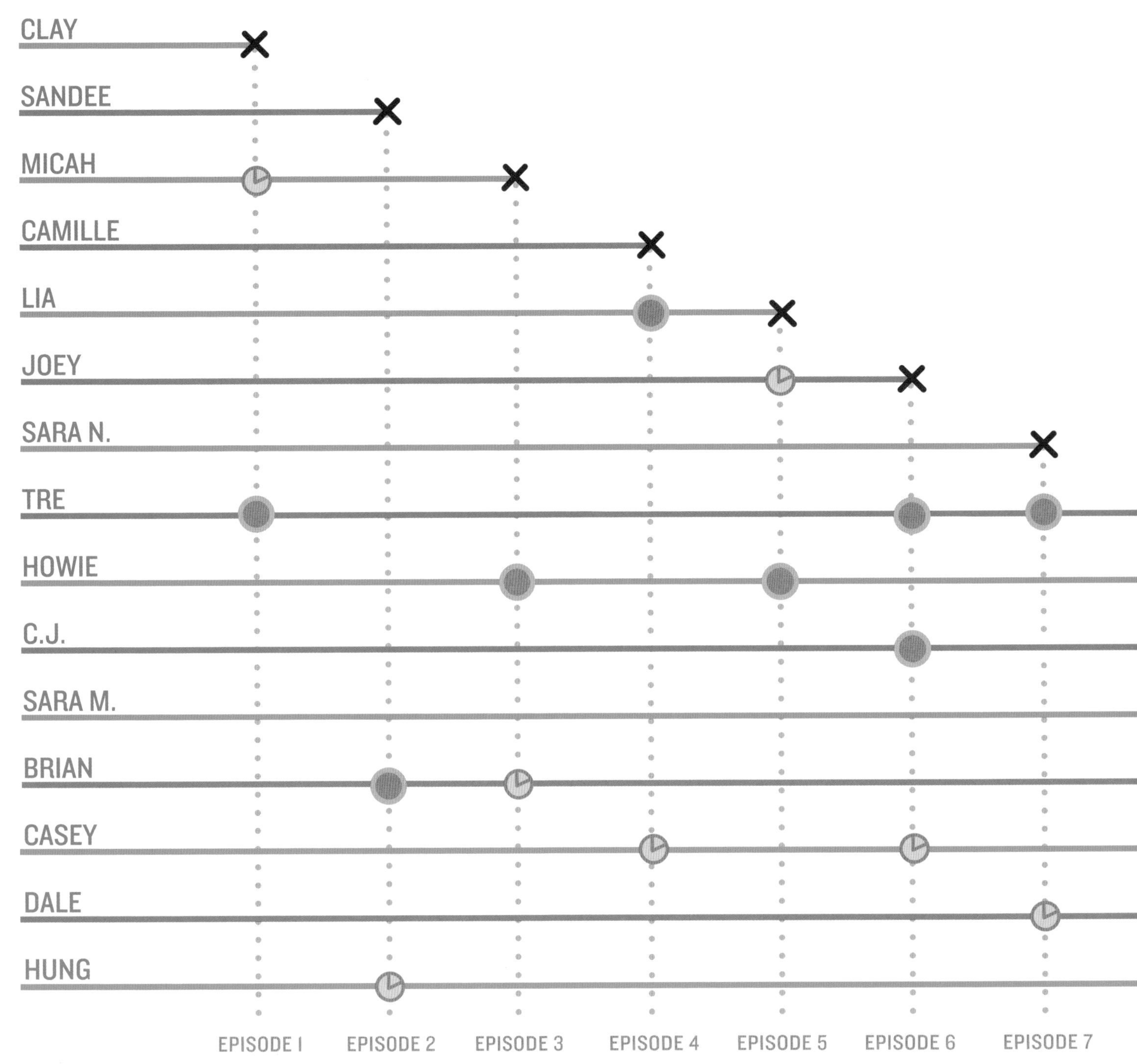

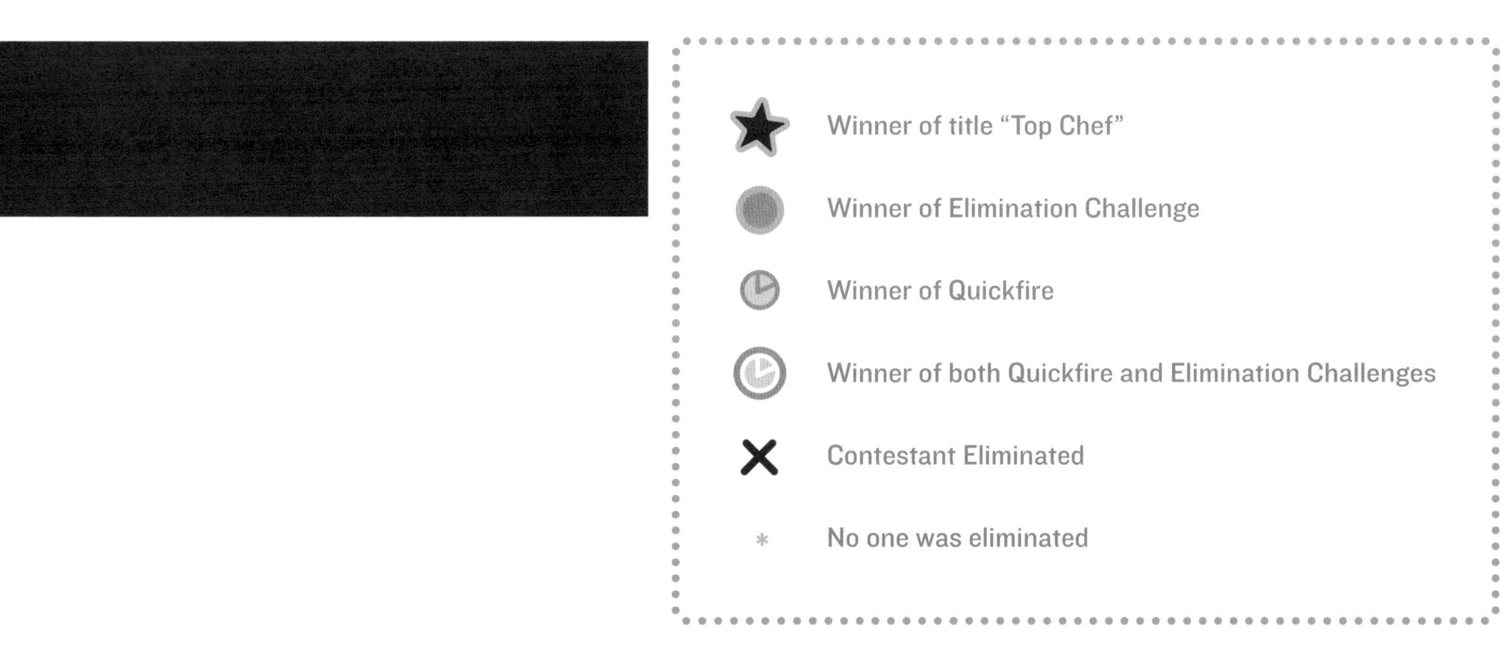
Winner of title "Top Chef"
Winner of Elimination Challenge
Winner of Quickfire
Winner of both Quickfire and Elimination Challenges
Contestant Eliminated
No one was eliminated

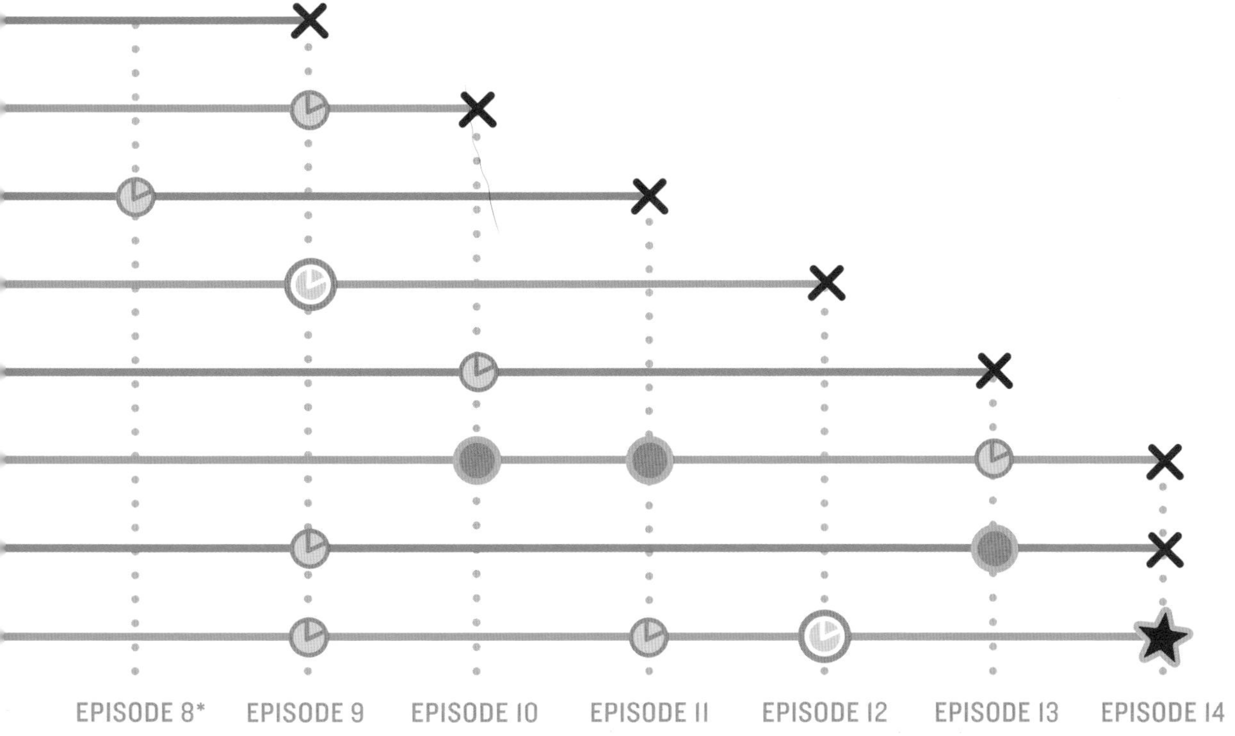
EPISODE 8*
EPISODE 9
EPISODE 10
EPISODE 11
EPISODE 12
EPISODE 13
EPISODE 14

Season 3: Episode Guide

 Episode

 Winner of Title "Top Chef"

 Winner of Elimination Challenge

 Winner of Quickfire

 Guest Judge

Contestant Eliminated

Season 3
Here to Cook

After all the tumult of Season 2 (and the "4-Star All-Star Reunion"), *Top Chef* was probably due for a more peaceful, mature regroup.

Then again, maybe it was just the warmth and beauty of Miami that led to all the sunny vibes. Either way, the pack of chefs who debuted in South Florida was probably the most purely talented so far. Inevitably, in such a batch, there were surprising casualties (Lia, Tre) and contentious personalities (Howie, Hung). Still, the final three competitors—including winner Hung—all but crossed the finish line holding hands.

1 First Impressions

 Create an amuse-bouche using only existing appetizer food and plasticware.

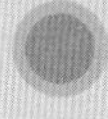 Create a surf-and-turf dish using exotic proteins like buffalo, alligator, geoduck, and eel.

The contestants wield plastic cutlery and brave a safari-style surf and turf. Buddies Hung and Tre wow Bourdain with geoduck and ostrich, while Howie forgets his frog legs and Clay is sent home via Air Cambodia.

 Chef and author Anthony Bourdain

 Micah

Clay

 Tre

2 Sunny Delights

 Create a dish featuring Florida citrus.

 Create an upscale barbecue dish for a summer party.

After a hot day over the grill, Howie and Joey duke it out in the Stew Room. Micah sniffles into her barbecue but it's Sandee who gets burned for "putting lipstick on a pig."

 Chef Norman Van Aken

 Hung

 Sandee

 Brian

3 Family Favorites

 Catch and cook a dish in 30 minutes using whatever shellfish you can catch with one swipe of a fish net.

 Turn traditional family favorites into healthier, more modern dishes for members of an Elks club.

Brian's winning streak makes up for his "dueling snake" debacle in the first episode. At the Elks Lodge, most dishes are dead on arrival, but Micah's meatloaf is inedible even with all the ketchup in America.

 Chef Alfred Portale

 Brian

Micah

 Howie

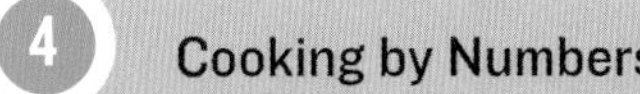

4 Cooking by Numbers

 Create an appetizer to pair with Bombay Sapphire® mixed drinks.

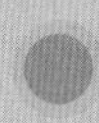 In teams of three, prepare a tasting menu of trios around a central ingredient.

Casey aces the Quickfire with an off-the-cuff French toast and finds herself thrown into the dog pit when she joins Joey and Howie in the Elimination. Camille gets sent home, and for Hung, apparently sweetness doesn't "always" go with creaminess.

 Mixologist Jamie Walker and Chef Barton G. Weiss

 Casey

Camille

 Lia

5 Latin Lunch

 Create a course starting with a premade piecrust.

 Prepare a classical Latin lunch for the cast and crew of the telenovela *Dame Chocolate*.

Joey, revealing he has some pastry experience, takes home the Quickfire, and his new buddy Howie impresses the actors with yet another pork dish. Lia serves up some subpar polenta and the judges say "adios."

 Chef Maria Frumkin

 Joey

 Lia

Howie

6 Freezer Burn

Identify foods by taste or appearance in a culinary quiz.

Pair up and create Bertolli®-inspired Mediterranean entrées that will be frozen overnight.

Casey aces the pop quiz, showing big chops for a self-trained chef. Later, tempers flare as the chefs make frozen dinners. C.J. and Tre freeze everything separately and win, and though Hung has this idea too, Joey, his partner, doesn't get it and is sent home in tears.

 Chef Rocco DiSpirito

 Casey

Joey

 C.J. and Tre

7 Guilty Pleasures

Make a mix-in for Cold Stone Creamery ice cream.

Create a snack for partiers at the Nikki Beach nightclub.

Another ice cream challenge, another round of bizarre flavors. Staying traditional, Dale wins with a fruit cobbler. That night, the chefs get dolled up to go clubbing but serve late-night snacks instead. Tre's shrimp steals the show, while Howie and Sara N. whine their way to the wrong end of the Judges' Table.

 Chef Govind Armstrong

 Dale

Sara N.

Tre

8 Restaurant Wars

Prepare a burger for Red Robin's line of "Adventuresome Burgers."

Divide into two teams and turn an empty space into a restaurant in twenty-four hours.

In the Quickfire, C.J. pulls through with a seafood burger and gets to handpick his team for Restaurant Wars. Though he takes the best of the bunch (Tre, Brian, and Casey), they fail to make a good impression on the judges. Then again, so do their opponents.

 Chef Daniel Boulud

 C.J.

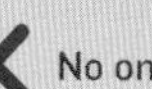 No one

 No one

9 Second Helping

The two teams from the previous episode face off in a kitchen-skills relay.

Each team reopens their restaurant, this time offering at least two options for each course.

It's Restaurant Wars Redux as both teams get a second chance. Tom's secret sommelier (Stephen, of course) may have helped Team Quatre focus on the food, while Team April sends out a few too many dud plates and Tre, April's head chef, gets the axe.

 Chef Geoffrey Zakarian

 Dale, Howie, Hung, and Sara M.

 Tre

 Sara M.

10 Chef Overboard

Create a dish using only what you can find in a particular supermarket aisle.

Work together to cater an ultraexclusive party thrown by Pure nightclub.

Hung lightens up a bit in the Quickfire, turning a couple of boxes of cereal into a psychedelic Smurf village, while Howie strikes out. He gives up in the Aisle Trial and goes 0 for 2 on the boat. Though he tries to quit before he can be eliminated, the judges say "Sorry," then toss him anyway.

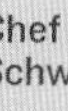 Chef Michael Schwartz

Brian

 Howie

 Casey

11 Snacks on a Plane

Make Padma breakfast using only a blender and a small butane burner.

Devise a delicious entrée for Continental's BusinessFirst service.

Oh, the infamous broccolini. The chefs head to New York City, but before they can even leave the airport, they have to prepare an alternative to that culinary punch line, airplane food. C.J. blows it with his roasted broccolini and is sent packing, but not before weathering some of Bourdain's meanest digs yet.

 Chef and author Anthony Bourdain

 Hung

 C.J.

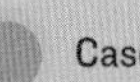 Casey

12 Manhattan Project

Re-create a special dish from New York's famous Le Cirque restaurant.

Turn an onion, a potato, and a chicken into a world-class meal for the chefs at the French Culinary Institute.

After lunch with restaurateur Maccioni, Hung copies the meal without breaking a sweat. Later, faced with the simplest of ingredients, Hung's classical training shines, while Sara M.'s dish leaves the judges unimpressed.

 Restaurateur Sirio Maccioni, French Culinary Institute chefs

 Hung

Sara M.

 Hung

13 Aspen Finale: Part 1

Cook a trout using only a frying pan and a camp stove for seafood expert Eric Ripert.

Prepare elk for hungry rodeo cowboys and cowgirls.

The chefs are whisked into the backcountry, given a fish and a fry pan, and told to impress the king of seafood. Brian flounders, and things only get worse with his mishmash of elk and half the pantry. The rodeo-goers are charmed by his cowpoke act, but the judges send him riding into the sunset.

 Chef Eric Ripert

 Casey

Brian

Dale

14 Aspen Finale: Part 2

Prepare a three-course meal to be served to a table of luminaries from the culinary world.

In the Season 3 finale, the chefs get a little extra help from world-renowned chefs Rocco DiSpirito, Michelle Bernstein, and Todd English. Casey falls short of everyone's expectations, while Dale and Hung, firing on all cylinders, go plate for plate. In the end, Hung's passion finally emerges, winning over the judges, who crown him Top Chef.

 Chefs Michelle Bernstein, Rocco DiSpirito, and Todd English

Hung

Casey and Dale

"A great chef has to be smart, creative, and have a great palate, but he also needs the speed."
HUNG

TOP STATS

Age
30

Hometown
Pittsfield, MA

Currently
Traveling and opening a restaurant in New York City

Favorite piece of equipment
12-inch slicer

Chefs he most admires
My mother, Tran Thuong; Thomas Keller; and Ferran Adrià

Philosophy
"No mercy."

Featured recipes
Steak and Eggs, p. 41
Tuna Tartare, p. 73
Sous-Vide Duck, p. 146
Black Chicken, p. 153
Sautéed Shrimp, p. 171
Chocolate Cakes, p. 230

Hung Huynh

SEASON 3: WINNER
WINS: 2 ELIMINATION CHALLENGES, 4 QUICKFIRES

In the generally sunny and friendly ensemble that made up Season 3's contestants, Hung sometimes seemed like the only chef who remembered that this was a game you were supposed to try to win, not a chance to make new friends.

Perhaps he learned something from watching his old culinary school buddy and fellow Las Vegan, Marcel. Driven by an inspiring immigrant narrative, Hung made it clear from day one that he was in Miami to win—even if that meant annoying some people with his confidence or ignoring a spilled bottle of truffle oil when everybody was running around barefoot. (After watching the episode, Hung now admits the spill was his fault.)

Even Hung's biggest detractors had to be astonished by his technical skills, honed while working at Guy Savoy in Las Vegas. He could bone a chicken in seconds, whip up a killer sous vide, re-create a classic dish at Le Cirque, and even build a trippy Smurflike village out of cereal. As for those who thought that lots of skill meant little heart, well, there were four finale judges who disagreed. And a triumphant Hung doesn't apologize for any of his tactics. "I was there for one thing," he says. "It wasn't winning Fan Favorite."

Sometimes it seemed like you really enjoyed annoying people. Was that your strategy?
I didn't plan it, but it became my strategy once I found out that I annoyed them. If they want to focus on me instead of on their own food, fine. Focus on me and screw up.

So, you came in ready to be a hard ass?
No mercy at all. I purposely separated myself from being close friends with anyone, in case I had to throw them under the bus. If I need to say something bad about someone's dish, I wasn't going to hesitate. There's no friendship involved. It's just skill and food.

What was up with the nutty cereal landscape?
That was the challenge where we had to cook from one aisle of the supermarket. I got coffee and cereal. I thought I'd just have a good time and give everybody a laugh. But the judge didn't really get it.

Was it hard waiting five weeks after the finale to find out who won?
Oh man, I couldn't sleep just thinking about it. But my gut feeling was that I killed it.

Were you frustrated by the idea that your cooking didn't have "soul" just because you were so technically good?
That just doesn't make sense to me. Passion is what drives me. It's why I am what I am. I hope I got that across to America in the end.

TED ALLEN, JUDGE "WHAT I LOVE ABOUT HUNG IS WHEN YOU SEE HIS EYES LIGHT UP WHEN HE HEARS WHAT THE CHALLENGE IS AND KNOWS EXACTLY HOW TO DO IT. HE'S TOTALLY PASSIONATE AND TOTALLY COMMITTED, AND HE'S WORKED HIS ASS OFF. THERE'S A TON OF SOUL IN HIS FOOD. YOU CAN'T MAKE GOOD FOOD WITHOUT LOVING FOOD."

SHARPEN YOUR KNIVES

One of the more impressive moments in *Top Chef* history came during a Season 3 Quickfire when Hung was asked to butcher a tableful of chickens. Hung went to work in a blur of hands and blades, leaving even Tom Colicchio gaping.

Knife skills are essential to any cook, and the first step is choosing the right knife. Hung, being a bit of a maverick, says he uses a long-bladed slicing knife for most all tasks in the kitchen. It's more traditional to employ a 12- or 14-inch classic chef's knife. Whatever you choose, though, it should fit comfortably in your hand. "It has to feel right: solid and not flimsy," Hung says. "You know it when you feel it. Like, 'Oh, yeah. That's right.'"

Also, learn to periodically sharpen your knives with a wet sharpening stone (a magnetic butcher's steel is good for day-to-day maintenance). Remember, Hung says, "It's easier to cut yourself with a dull knife than a sharp one."

"You sit on the couch watching the show like, 'Oh, I can do that.' Well you know what? Ya can't. It's really hard."

DALE

TOP STATS

Age

34

Hometown

Chicago, IL

Currently

Opening Town and Country in Chicago, IL

Favorite piece of equipment

Tongs

Chefs he most admires

Thomas Keller, Daniel Boulud, David Bouley, and Julia Child

Philosophy

"A true chef will extend himself and take risks."

Featured recipes

Seared Scallops, p. 72
Rack of Lamb, p. 91
Seared Elk Loin, p. 104
Meatballs, p. 149

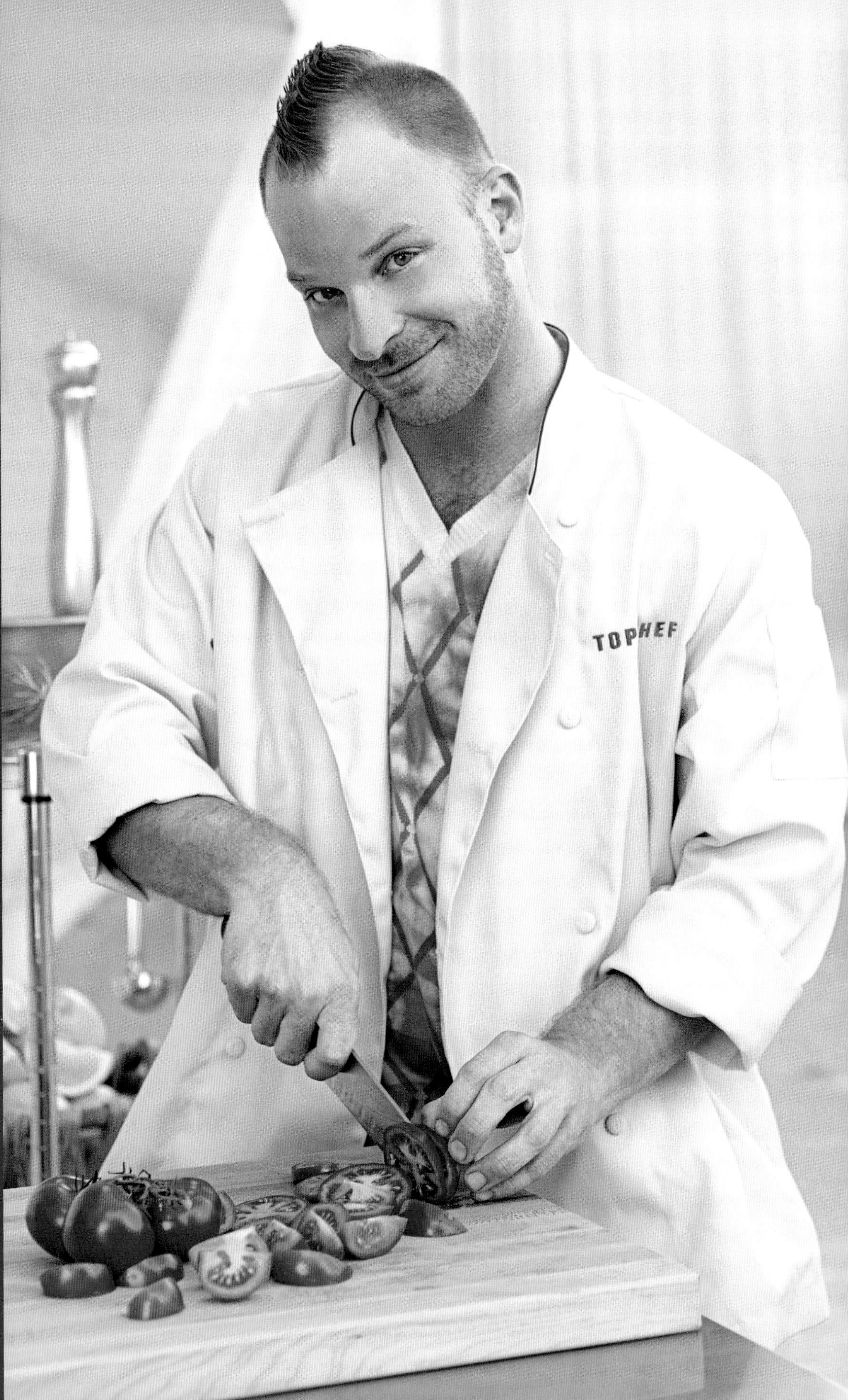

Dale Levitski

SEASON 3
ELIMINATED: EPISODE 14: "ASPEN FINALE: PART 2"
WINS: 1 ELIMINATION CHALLENGE, 2 QUICKFIRES

When we first met Dale, the goofy, self-proclaimed "Big Gay Chef" with the silly mohawk, few would have guessed he'd become one of the more moving stories produced in three years of *Top Chef*.

Burned out and depressed by the closing of the restaurant where he had once been chef, Dale hadn't even cooked professionally for more than a year before the Miami competition began. Over the course of the show, we watched him slowly regain his footing, rediscover what he liked about cooking, and then, surprisingly, become a serious contender for the *Top Chef* crown. Dale was felled by one bad lobster dish but, characteristically, he says the win would have only been icing on the cake; he'd already gotten what he wanted out of the competition. Still, he adds, "I was just hitting my stride. One more week and I would have won the whole thing."

Why were you in such a bad place before the competition?
It was a combination of everything—all four walls of my life crashing in. I had completely lost all focus on what I was doing in life and why.

Is it hard to work your way through something like that while being filmed for national television?
It may have actually been an advantage. The other chefs had all kinds of problems dealing with the isolation and the stress of living in the house. I was battling a pretty severe depression; I wanted to be taken out of my life and put in a little box where cooking is all that would matter. It was like chef rehab for me.

Some fans thought you Season 3 guys liked each other too much.
I'm very proud of our group for doing that. Everybody has rivalries and a sense of competitiveness, but we all agreed from day one not to get into the petty stuff that makes good TV.

Were you bummed out to learn you weren't the only mohawk on the show?
It was hilarious when Sandee showed up that first day. We were both like, "Oh, sure. All the gay people have mohawks."

Have you registered BigGayChef.com yet?
No, but an old friend from high school showed up at my restaurant with a chef's toque that had "Big Gay Chef" embroidered on it. I've gotten a lot of flak for using "the gay angle." The chef I was working for wanted to know why I mentioned it when it doesn't matter. I told her it did matter in the gay community. I felt I had a responsibility to proudly represent who I was.

TED ALLEN, JUDGE "LET'S NOT FORGET, DALE DIDN'T GO TO CULINARY SCHOOL, AND HE MADE IT TO NUMBER TWO BEHIND HUNG. AND JUST BARELY BEHIND HIM. THAT'S A REAL ACHIEVEMENT. DALE ALREADY HAD THE RESPECT OF REALLY STRONG CHEFS IN CHICAGO. NOW HE'S GOT THAT MEASURE OF RESPECT FROM MILLIONS OF OTHER PEOPLE."

"Our season had a better head on its shoulders, and we were really in it for the food."

CASEY

TOP STATS

Age

30

Hometown

Cedar Hill, TX

Currently

Executive chef at Shinsei Restaurant in Dallas, TX

Favorite piece of equipment

A blender

Chefs she most admires

Thomas Keller, Joel Robuchon, Rick Bayless, and Mario Batali

Philosophy

"Cooking technique under pressure is a true gift. If you're practiced and experienced, then it will go easily for you."

Featured recipes

Beef Carpaccio, p. 71

Veal Medallions, p. 114

Coq au Vin, p. 140

Meatballs, p. 149

Casey Thompson

SEASON 3: FAN FAVORITE
ELIMINATED: EPISODE 14, "ASPEN FINALE: PART 2"
WINS: 2 ELIMINATION CHALLENGES, 3 QUICKFIRES

Every season has one: the chef you root for, who's doing great week after week, who looks like she might be going all the way—and then who, inexplicably, without warning, makes some fatal error.

Actually, Season 3 had two such contestants: Tre and, even more heartbreaking, Casey. But the blonde Texan's unfortunate exit at the Aspen finale couldn't erase a truly impressive showing over the first twelve weeks of the competition. With style, verve, and what the judges repeatedly referred to as "soul," Casey was a formidable opponent. And she came to represent the grown-up, friendly side of *Top Chef* that defined Season 3. She seemed to get along with everybody, especially Dale, with whom she still speaks on the phone at least once a day. "She is just the most amazing person in the world," Dale says. "You didn't even get to see how funny and cool she was." Whatever we did see, it was enough to allow Casey to steal the title of Fan Favorite from Dale himself.

What has life been like since the show?
Insane! *Top Chef* has brought many fans into the restaurant. They come right into the kitchen and say, "We wish you would have won." We've actually had to have the staff talk them out of being upset because I can't come out to the table when I'm on the line, cooking their food.

When did you start to get the feeling that you had a shot at winning the competition?
It took me a few weeks to get into the groove. I guess it was the Bombay Sapphire® Quickfire that I really nailed first. Everybody was asking, "How'd you do this?" And I started to think, Hmm, it's pretty cool to win. I kind of want to do this again!

You seemed like you got along with everybody.
Walking in there, it's like the first day of school. You're the new kid and you don't know anybody. In the beginning, I have to say, I didn't like Hung and Howie. I thought they were just big jerks. But then I got to know them and they're really nice guys.

What happened to you in the finale?
I knew right away that it wasn't one of my most successful dishes. I just knew it. But then we went in front of the judges and they always say something good and bad about every dish. I walked away thinking, Well, Casey, you're always your own worst critic. Maybe you still have a shot. So it was kind of cruel to come back, five weeks later, and have to sit there and watch the show live. With my family there, too.

You handled it with a lot of class.
That makes me feel good. Because, believe me, walking out there with a straight face was one of the hardest things I've ever had to do.

GAIL SIMMONS, JUDGE "IN THE END, CASEY REALIZED HER STRENGTH. SHE'S A CHEF WHO NEEDS TO ROLL SOMETHING OVER IN HER BRAIN, TRY IT OUT FIFTEEN DIFFERENT WAYS, REFINE IT, AND THEN SHE'LL NAIL IT."

Brian Malarkey

SEASON 3
ELIMINATED: EPISODE 13, "ASPEN FINALE: PART 1"
WINS: 1 ELIMINATION CHALLENGE, 2 QUICKFIRES

"My strategy was to play it straight and not get into any kind of drama. Just cook good food," Brian says. "It was kind of the Sam approach from Season 2."

Perhaps, but while Sam made it to the final four while generating reams of blog heat, Brian's strategy got him to the same place without, well, anybody really noticing. Friendly and filled with smiles, Brian made it almost to the end without putting his neck too far out on the line. Still, there was no denying that his big flavors and flair for seafood pleased the judges. And who would have guessed that he'd have one of the bawdiest backstage stories of them all?

What surprised you about your time on *Top Chef*?
I'd watched the previous seasons and I'm a competitive guy. I love to compete. But I remember that first day, we were all so happy to meet each other and then Clay got eliminated in that totally brutal way. I mean, they really demoralized him. And, you know, I was in the bottom three too that night. That's when I thought, God, this show is really cutthroat and scary! It kind of makes you lose heart for a while.

What did you do wrong on that challenge?
I cooked snake and eel on that one. I thought I'd come out of the gates really adventurous and try to show everybody that I had it going on. But I ran out of time. I wasn't used to working with the clock. And then Tre won with a real simple risotto. I was like, Damn. They want *less*, not more.

Did the notion that you could only cook seafood bug you?
I enjoyed it. Even after Tom Colicchio told me to branch out, what did I cook? Seafood, seafood, seafood. We were in Miami in the middle of a hot and humid summer, surrounded by the best seafood in the world, and what was Howie cooking? Pork. I used the best ingredients available.

So, why don't you tell me the story of what happened in the bathroom at the French Culinary Institute?
I might as well, because Dale promised he'd tell everybody. I had a very upset stomach—you know, you're on a crazy schedule, stressed out, it happens. I go to the bathroom and my backside is kind of hurting. And I see this spray bottle of baby powder and I think, Great, this will help. So I spray a little on and it burns like hell! I looked at it again and it was baby powder–scented air freshener. I have five minutes until I have to cook my challenge and I'm sitting in the sink, trying to wash off. I told Dale not to tell anybody, but it spread like wildfire. I was just burning up.

"I don't back down. I go for it, put myself out there, and see how it turns out."
BRIAN

TOP STATS

Age
34

Hometown
Bend, OR

Currently
Executive chef at The Oceanaire Seafood Room in San Diego, CA

Chefs he most admires
Bernard Guisse, Alan Gerrard, and Marcus Samuelson

Philosophy
"The less you do with seafood, the better it is."

Featured recipes
Pheasant's Pie, p. 143
Chicken Rigatoni, p. 152
Seafood Sausage, p. 172

C.J. Jacobsen

SEASON 3
ELIMINATED: EPISODE 11, "SNACKS ON A PLANE"
WINS: 1 ELIMINATION CHALLENGE, 1 QUICKFIRE

Go ahead and pick your pun: C.J. towered over his competition during Season 3. He cast a long shadow over the *Top Chef* kitchen. Beating him was a tall order.

You can bet that the six-foot-eight Southern Californian chef has heard all the height jokes you can come up with. But C.J. turned out to be a lot more than just the "tall guy." For one thing, he quickly established himself as a kind of class clown and morale booster in the Miami loft. (His BLTs were legendary, if he says so himself.) Despite his charm, C.J. proved a crafty and talented competitor. Perhaps his most important decision was to cede control of the kitchen during Restaurant Wars to Tre—leaving Tre vulnerable and, ultimately, on his way home. C.J. dodged that bullet, but there was a deadly pile of overcooked broccolini waiting just a few episodes away to do him in.

What was the hardest part of living in the house?
Hung takes exceptionally long showers in the morning—like, thirty-five minutes. And Joey snores so badly we made him sleep, not only out of the room, but on the far side of the living room, as far away as possible.

Any behind-the-scenes romance?
People say to me, "Oh, man. You had all these hot chicks living in the house. How come nobody banged anybody?" Let me tell you, for the first two weeks you're so stressed out you can't do anything. And after twenty-five days or so, all sexuality disappears.

Did you get a lot of hate mail when Tre was eliminated?
People generally liked both of us, I think. In the end, I would have been remiss to name myself head chef. It wasn't the best way for the team to win the competition. Tre had so much more experience. I don't know why I get so much crap for not doing anything when I made four sauces and helped with everything. At the same time, in retrospect, it was kind of an ingenious move, delegating to Tre, because I managed to stick around.

How much is being tall a handicap?
It doesn't help, that's for sure. Everything in a professional kitchen is designed for, like, a five-foot-seven Oaxacan guy. By the end, I thought that the *Top Chef* producers were just trying to get rid of me. They put me on a boat. They put me on a plane. I was like, "OK! Enough! I'll screw up the broccolini already!"

"I came down with cancer. I'm totally in remission . . . I've got a false testicle, and I'm ready to cook."
C.J.

TOP STATS

Age
32

Hometown
El Toro, CA

Currently
Cooking for his own catering company, Redwood Cuisine, in Venice, CA

Chefs he most admires
Mario Batali, Mark Peel, and Nancy Silverton

Philosophy
"Don't freak out, just do your best."

Featured recipes
Crêpes, p. 40
Parmesan Linguine, p. 144
Burger, p. 166

Howie Kleinberg

SEASON 3
ELIMINATED: EPISODE 10, "CHEF OVERBOARD"
WINS: 2 ELIMINATION CHALLENGES, 1 QUICKFIRE

"You son of a bitch!" Those were the words of guest judge Anthony Bourdain in the very first episode of Season 3, when Howie quoted Bourdain to Bourdain as a defense for why he didn't get his Elimination Challenge dish plated in time.

The quick thinking saved Howie that day, but there was still a rough road ahead for the bull-necked, perpetually unhappy-looking Miami native with the Brooklyn accent. His style rubbed plenty of fellow contestants the wrong way, especially when he helped get Sara Nguyen sent home. (To be fair, Howie seemed almost as miserable about the turn of events as Sara did.) By the end of his run, Howie seemed in real danger of implosion. He failed to turn in a Quickfire dish and then attempted to fall on his own chef's knife and pull out of the competition. The judges refused the resignation but sent him packing anyway.

What made you want to go on *Top Chef*?
I've been in this business long enough to know that you can make the best food in the world but it doesn't matter if nobody knows you're there. This was a chance to get known on a national stage. And I was a fanatic for the show. I'd watched every episode of the two other seasons, some of them more than once.

Did that help your performance?
In hindsight, maybe that was a disadvantage for me. I might have overthought things. Like the first day, when I couldn't get my food onto the plate. I was trying to be clever and make sure nothing got cold. But it's very different watching it on TV and being there. You know, chefs are always saying, "Two minutes. I'll get it done in two minutes." But you don't really know what two minutes means until you're on the clock.

What was the most difficult thing for you?
The biggest challenge for me was to not get frustrated and aggravated. That's where it's won and lost in a lot of ways. I kind of felt from the beginning that maybe some people didn't think I should be there. I'm a reactive person. I come in trying to be cordial, but if people don't like me I'm not going to like them. There was one time where Sandee and I were the two who were going to be eliminated. When we walked back into the Stew Room, everybody started clapping because they thought Sandee was staying. Nobody clapped for Howie to stay.

What happened at the very end?
At a certain point you just get tired of standing up there getting ridiculed by these people, even if they're the best chefs in the world. And they had eliminated Tre, who was really my only friend in the house, so I was just tired of it. Plus, I was trying to protect Brian, who was the captain of our team.

Do you think all the attention people paid to your sweating was unfair?
It was just ridiculous. The reality is that if you think you can go into any kitchen, especially in South Florida, and find chefs who aren't sweating, you're crazy.

TOP STATS

Age
31

Hometown
Miami, FL

Currently
Opening Bulldog in Miami, FL

Chefs he most admires
Thomas Keller, Gray Kunz, and Eric Ripert

Cookbooks in his collection
More than 300

Philosophy
"I cook and I cook. I'll make it one way, I'll make it another way, I'll make it ten different ways until I come up with a dish that I like."

Featured recipes
Pork Shoulder, p. 97
Truffle Burger, p. 102
Pork Chops, p. 113

Sara Mair

SEASON 3
ELIMINATED: EPISODE 12, "MANHATTAN PROJECT"
WINS: 1 ELIMINATION CHALLENGE, 1 QUICKFIRE

Season 3 of *Top Chef* was the "Season of the Two Mohawks" (Dale and Sandee) and the "Season of the Two Saras" (M. and N.). Of the two, it was Sara Mair who made the more distinguished mark, lasting through Miami, surviving the Newark Airport challenge, and making it to New York City before finally falling at the French Culinary Institute.

A Jamaican of Portuguese, Scottish, Welsh, and French descent who has worked as a sous-chef to Miami's Michelle Bernstein, Sara is a walking embodiment of how international and cross-cultural fine cooking has become. As if more evidence was needed, she plans to open a cheese dairy on her home island, using European techniques learned on a farm in New Jersey.

How big is *Top Chef* in Jamaica?
It's on in certain areas, but it's not a big deal. In the States, I get recognized. People want autographs and pictures and all that stuff. Down here, people don't care as much. I didn't know anything about the show before I went on.

Do you think that helped or hurt you?
I didn't overanalyze things like some people. I didn't know what to expect, so I just prepared myself to take it day by day and do the best I could. That probably helped.

Well, you made it pretty far for someone who hadn't watched the show.
I did. I think my downfall was that I overdid it. Jamaican food is a mix of so many influences—Chinese, Indian, Jamaican, African, Spanish, English, all of them. It's fusion. I didn't simplify that for my dish, so I don't think it was classic enough for the judges.

What's the funniest thing that happened but didn't appear on-screen?
One night we came home and all the girls decided to have a "spa day." We made masks from oatmeal and avocado and eggs and all this other stuff and then we plastered all the boys' faces with it. We had a camera with us, but something happened to the tape, I think. It was hilarious sitting there with all the boys and their green faces.

TOP STATS

Age
35

Hometown
Kingston, Jamaica

Currently
Working at Island Outpost in Jamaica, developing a Jamaican TV show called *The Local Gourmet*, and doing research for her cheese farm

Favorite comfort food
Chicken fricassee and oxtail

Chefs she admires
Michelle Bernstein and Cindy Hudson

Philosophy
"My cooking is fusion. I rethink classical dishes."

Featured recipes
Eggs in a Hole, p. 42
Halibut, p. 163
Chiles Rellenos, p. 188

Sara Nguyen

SEASON 3
ELIMINATED: EPISODE 7, "GUILTY PLEASURES"
WINS: 0 ELIMINATION CHALLENGES, 0 QUICKFIRES

TOP STATS

Age
26

Hometown
Santa Monica, CA

Currently
Opening Town and Country in Chicago, IL

Chefs she most admires
Eric Ripert, Joel Robuchon, Anita Lo, and Ferran Adrià

Favorite cooking show (besides *Top Chef*)
***Iron Chef*, the Japanese edition**

Philosophy
"I make simple, elegant food that isn't too wishy-washy or highbrow. Food for everybody."

Featured recipe
Chicken Rigatoni, p. 152

Some contestants on *Top Chef* are remembered for a signature dish. Others are remembered for their crazy personalities, or their grit or evolution over the long, thirteen-week season.

Sara N. will always be remembered for one facial expression—the mask of misery and rage she wore upon being told that the gang wasn't going out, as promised, to sample some of Miami's nightlife but instead was going to face an Elimination Challenge involving serving late-night partygoers from a "roach coach." That face reappeared, bathed in tears at Judges' Table, where Howie infamously threw her under the bus. This is a shame, since Sara was actually a mostly lighthearted and talented chef. And she didn't do half-bad for a person who didn't even know what the show was until she was practically on it.

You'd never watched *Top Chef*. So how did you wind up on the show?
One night in New York, my girlfriend and I went out to a club and we happened to meet a bunch of people from Season 2—Sam, Ilan, and Josie. I left early, like three in the morning, but my girlfriend stayed. The next afternoon she came over and said, "Get ready. They're holding auditions right now."

And you went?
Yeah. It supposedly ended at 4:00 and we got there at 3:30. Everybody was squished into the vestibule of the French Culinary Institute, and the producers said that anybody not inside the doors should go home. I thought, Great. I'm hungover and starving. Let's go. But my girlfriend pushed us in through the door, just as they came up and locked it behind us. So, I had no choice!

What happened the night you were eliminated?
When they said there was no challenge, I remember going up to everybody saying, "Is this for real? Are you sure?" We had been working so hard for three weeks and I was really excited to go out. In the limo, I drank half a bottle of wine. I was really fooled.

Do you think it was unfair to the women chefs?
I do, because we dressed to go out. I don't have a problem going out and dressing in a way that gets male attention. But it's the last thing I want in the kitchen.

And what happened with Howie?
In retrospect, I would have done the same thing he did. I should have thrown him under the bus. But I really just couldn't stop crying. I was shaking beneath my clothes. I wish I had been better able to defend myself. But at the reunion, Howie came in and we talked. He said he had been so distressed about seeing me again and felt so bad. I gave him a hug. He's such a great guy. He really is.

Did you and Hung ever bond over your Vietnamese heritage?
I grew up understanding Vietnamese and he's fluent, of course, so he would say things to me behind people's backs. About their food. Like, "Uck, that smells." But then he started to get a little crazy, so I sort of kept my distance.

Tre Wilcox III

SEASON 3
ELIMINATED: EPISODE 9, "SECOND HELPING"
WINS: 3 ELIMINATION CHALLENGES, 0 QUICKFIRES

Right now, somewhere in America, there is a TV fan who is still shocked to have learned that Bennie Junnie "Tre" Wilcox III was eliminated at all—let alone so early—from *Top Chef*. Tre's fate was the strongest evidence that *Top Chef* is indeed a collection of individual competitions, not a cumulative event.

Anybody can fall after an unfortunate night, and that's just what happened to Tre when he took on the task of being his team's head chef during Restaurant Wars. A proud son of Texas, brought down by a lumpy bread pudding. In fact, Tre didn't do too badly for a guy who had barely watched *Top Chef* before actually appearing on it; he only got cable a week before reporting for duty in Miami.

You didn't really know what you were getting yourself into, did you?
Not really. When they called and asked if I wanted to be on the show, it was busy in the kitchen and I said, "I'll have to think about it." The casting woman was like, "There are people who would jump across the Grand Canyon to get on this show." I told her that might be, but I wasn't ready to say yes or no right then. But I love to compete. I'm a competitor.

Did you realize that you'd have to live with all these other people?
I had some idea that the contestants roomed together. That wasn't a big deal to me. I grew up in a military family, and that training kicked in: you've got your bed and your suitcase and you adapt. And you try to be sociable to people, accept them as they are because you can't change them. Howie is a good example; you've got to take Howie as he is. We still keep in touch.

Did you realize that you were a big fan favorite?
I started getting all these emails from aggravated fans: "You were robbed." "I'm not watching anymore." People still come into the restaurant saying that.

So what happened?
It was just a bad day. A very bad day. I definitely stuck my neck out, you know? Maybe I bit off more than I could chew, in terms of knowing that I would either win with what I did or get sent home. I told my team that going into it. I've made a million bread puddings. It's a great dessert. But the clock just ate me up. That's the way it goes.

TOM COLICCHIO, HEAD JUDGE "I GOT A SENSE FROM THE OTHER CONTESTANTS THAT HE WAS CLEARLY ONE OF THE GUYS TO BEAT. I KNEW GETTING RID OF HIM WAS GOING TO BE TOUGH, BUT IT WAS THE RIGHT DECISION THAT NIGHT. WE CAN'T MAKE DECISIONS BASED ON WHETHER OR NOT THE BLOGGERS ARE GOING TO BEAT US UP."

TOP STATS

Age
30

Hometown
Duncanville, TX

Currently
Working as a private chef in Dallas, TX

Favorite piece of equipment
A passionate staff

Chefs he most admires
Christopher Lee, Thomas Keller, and Andrew Carmellini

Philosophy
"Make it nice or make it twice."

Featured recipes
Shrimp, p. 93
Linguine, p. 144
Ostrich Fillet, p. 150

Clay Bowen

"Hell, I'm from Mississippi. Pick it up and eat that son of a bitch!"

BIO BITE

Packed his knives

Episode I, "First Impressions"

This good ol' boy from Mississippi wasn't nuts like Ken, or a newbie like Suyai, he was just . . . in a little over his head. With his **aw-shucks charm**, you couldn't help but feel a little bad for the guy, even though his leathery wild boar must have been tough to stomach.

Sandee Birdsong

"This is totally 'Chef Camp.' In two nights I've learned more than I've learned in a year."

BIO BITE

Packed her knives

Episode 2, "Sunny Delights"

A Southern **soul food kinda gal** with no formal training, Sandee was a Season 3 wild card. It's a shame she left over some bad barbecue, but maybe the house was only big enough for one mohawk.

Micah Edelstein

"There are some people here that probably will do anything to win, and I'm not like that."

BIO BITE

Packed her knives

Episode 3, "Family Favorites"

Micah started out with guns blazing, taking home the very first Quickfire and just missing a win at the barbecue party. But her whining in the kitchen seemed excessive (at least to Hung), and the judges weren't happy with all her **kvetching about ketchup**.

Camille Becerra

"I learned a lot and I had fun doing it. That's what cooking's all about."

BIO BITE

Packed her knives

Episode 4, "Cooking by Numbers"

Camille flew under the radar for most of Season 3, but that's not to say she didn't know how to whip up a top quality meal. Her food, though, was **a little *too* soft-spoken**—flavoring with tea is a neat idea, but Chef Alfred Portale wasn't amused.

Lia Bardeen

"I guess I didn't really understand how complex franks and beans are."

BIO BITE

Packed her knives

Episode 5, "Latin Lunch"

A sweet-faced sous chef from New York's Jean-Georges, Lia left the kitchen much too soon. Her early elimination over a plate of bad polenta was almost as shocking as Tre's four episodes later. Everyone, including Padma, thought she'd go much farther—Padma says Lia's elimination was one of the hardest to take.

Featured recipe

Poached Shrimp, p. 86

Joey Paulino

"With me, to get a point across, you gotta get a little aggressive."

BIO BITE

Packed his knives

Episode 6, "Freezer Burn"

Joey was a study in contrasts. The judges brought this **sensitive tart-maker** to tears, but then again, he was one of the only other chefs to stand up to Howie's bullying. Joey had a big heart, but that doesn't help when you're trying to reheat bad pasta.

Featured recipe

Trio of Tarts, p. 226

Top Chef Finales

After all the trickery and plot twists and creative challenges *Top Chef* contestants endure, there can be nothing more relieving, and more nerve-wracking, than these words: "Make us the best meal of your life." Welcome to the *Top Chef* finale.

1

Harold's Winning Menu

1ST COURSE

Seared Diver Scallop with Blood Orange and Fennel Salad

2ND COURSE

Olive-Oil Poached Bass

3RD COURSE

Pan-Roasted Quail with Herb Spaetzle, Cherries, and Foie Gras

4TH COURSE

Duo of Beef with Kobe Strip Loin and Braised Kobe Short Ribs with White Polenta

5TH COURSE

Fig Tart with Cheeses

2

Ilan's Winning Menu

1ST COURSE

Pincho of Pan Con Tomate with Angulas, Oestra Caviar and Tomatillos

2ND COURSE

Macadamia Nut Gazpacho with Pan-Roasted Moi

3RD COURSE

Seared Squab with Foie Gras, Shrimp, Braised Leeks, and Lobster Sauce

4TH COURSE

Braised and Grilled Beef Short Rib with Mushrooms and Romesco Sauce

5TH COURSE

Tangelo Soup with Hawaiian Fruit, Surinam Cherry Sorbet, and Bay Leaf Fritter

3

Hung's Winning Menu

1ST COURSE

"Fish & Chips" Hamachi, Potatoes, Olive Oil, and Tomato Vinaigrette

2ND COURSE

Shrimp with Palm Sugar, Cucumber Salad, and Coconut Foam

3RD COURSE

Sous-Vide Duck with Truffle-Scented Broth

4TH COURSE

Molten Chocolate Cakes with Vanilla Crème Fraîche, Raspberry Coulis, and Nougatine Tuiles

Season 1 Finale

There was no question that two deeply worthy chefs made it to the final round of the first finale, held in Las Vegas.

Both Tiffani and Harold were insanely talented, no-nonsense cooks, ready to wow the judges' panel. In order to taste both contestants' food, the judges had to start early: "We woke up at 6:30 a.m. and ate our first five-course meal starting at 9 a.m.," Gail Simmons remembers. "Then we had a break and ate another at 2 p.m." If *Top Chef* is always divided between the chefs' performance in the kitchen and their relationships with other contestants outside of it, this was the first time that the connection between the two became clear. Tiffani had sowed ill will throughout the competition and she reaped her biggest detractor, Dave Martin, as a finale assistant. Dave and Stephen showed up hungover and less than motivated to help their captain steal the prize. In spite of this, Tiffani opted to cook two dishes per course—a huge gamble considering what was at stake. Meanwhile, Harold, ably supported by Miguel and Lee Anne, turned out a Kobe beef dish that Simmons still describes as among the best she's had on the show.

1. Finalists Harold and Tiffani are joined by the their finale sous-chefs and former rivals, Lee Anne, Miguel, Stephen, and Dave.
2. Season 1 finale judges: Chef Hubert Keller, host Katie Lee Joel, Head Judge Tom Colicchio, and Judge Gail Simmons.
3. Tension in the kitchen.
4. Tiffani concedes the *Top Chef* title.

Season 2 Finale

1. The four finalists arrive in Hawaii. 2. The judges enjoy a traditional Hawaiian feast. 3. Ilan and his finale sous-chefs, Elia and Betty, plan the winning meal. 4. Marcel and his finale sous-chefs, Sam and Michael, check out the local produce.

It is a reality-television cliché to say, "You couldn't have scripted this!" But it's hard not to think just that about *Top Chef*'s Season 2 finale.

Here, after twelve competitions, were the cast's two most bitter rivals—personally, stylistically, and gastronomically. It would be Foam vs. Fideos. Mousse-do vs. Faux-hawk. Outcast vs. Popular Guy. Marcel vs. Ilan. Part one of the finale in Hawaii was hardly less dramatic, ending with the dismissal of Sam Talbot and Elia Aboumrad. Eventually, Marcel learned that if you live by molecular gastronomy, you can die by molecular gastronomy. The Hawaiian humidity doomed his vinaigrette "droplets" and left him with a boring salad as a second course. Meanwhile, Ilan's macadamia nut gazpacho was a triumph and it was he who got the final smirk.

Season 3 Finale

Season 3 featured a trio of finalists: Dale, Hung, and Casey.

Also a first, the three gathered atop a wooded Aspen, Colorado mountain to serve their dishes head to head—appetizer vs. appetizer, meat vs. meat, and so on. Each of the chefs was paired with a celebrity "sous-chef" who was allowed to help with prep but not give any advice. The first shocker was Casey's big fizzle. Despite her partner Michelle Bernstein's most aggressive eye-rolls, she chose to braise pork belly—a stretch anywhere, given the allotted time, but culinary suicide in the thin air of Colorado. "I was surprised she didn't get the hint. I have a very expressive face," Bernstein says. The other surprise (though maybe it shouldn't have been by that point) was Dale. His scallop dish and lamb with eggplant earned the highest praise Tom Colicchio may have ever given: "These are dishes you should carry with you for the rest of your life." Sadly for Dale, Hung got similarly lavish praise for his sous-vide duck. With the contestants tied at two courses each, it came down to a classic *Top Chef* battle between ambition and execution: Dale's fanciful but failed lobster vs. Hung's excellent but safe chocolate cake. In the end, the start-to-finish excellence of Hung's meal won the day.

1. Finalists Hung, Casey, and Dale pick their ingredients. 2. Judge Padma Lakshmi gets in the spirit. 3. Chef Eric Ripert and Head Judge Tom Colicchio taste the offerings. 4. Culinary producer and former contestant Lee Anne Wong sets out the finale ingredients.

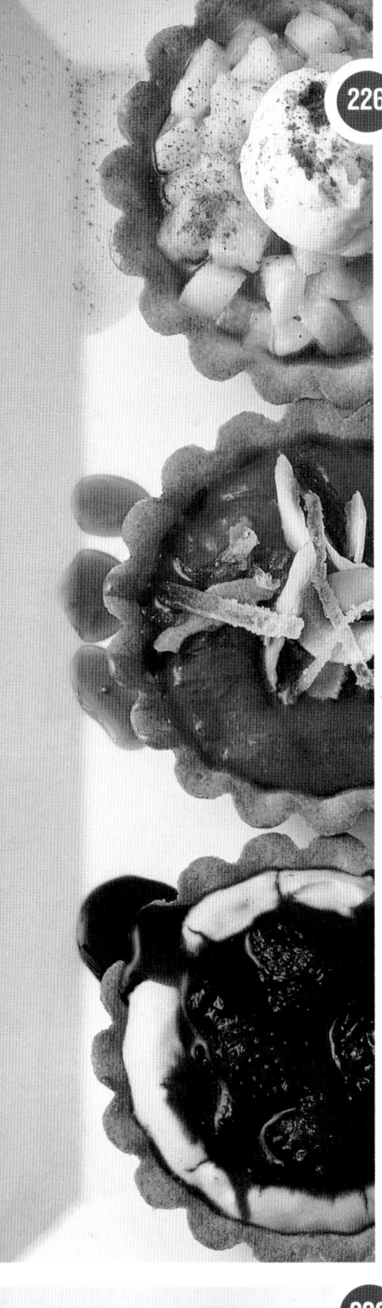

Dessert

233

236

240

Trio of Tarts

Berry Cream, Roasted Mango Puree, and Warm Apple Compote

CHEF: Joey
SEASON 3, EPISODE 5
QUICKFIRE CHALLENGE: Create a course starting with a premade piecrust.

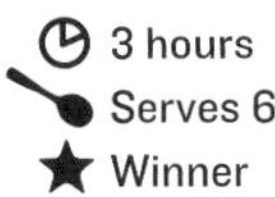

3 hours
Serves 6
Winner

"What nobody knows is, I have some pastry experience."
JOEY

Tart Shells:
Two 9-inch frozen pie shells
All-purpose flour for rolling

Berry Mini Tarts:
½ cup balsamic vinegar
3 tablespoons granulated sugar
½ cup seedless raspberries
½ cup seedless blackberries
½ cup chopped strawberries
½ cup blueberries
3 tablespoons light brown sugar
2 teaspoons Grand Marnier®
2 tablespoons sour cream
2 tablespoons cream cheese, softened

Mango Mini Tarts:
½ cup port
10 tablespoons packed light brown sugar
1 ounce crystallized ginger, diced (about ¼ cup)
2 cups diced mango (from about 2 medium mangoes)
½ teaspoon mild curry powder
1 tablespoon dark rum
2 tablespoons toasted shredded sweetened coconut

Apple Mini Tarts:
½ cup white port
3 tablespoons packed light brown sugar
¼ teaspoon ground cardamom
2 tablespoons unsalted butter
2 Red Delicious apples, peeled, cored, and chopped
1 Bartlett pear, peeled, cored, and chopped
1 teaspoon cornstarch
2 teaspoons fresh lime juice
¼ teaspoon Maldon sea salt
¼ teaspoon ground cinnamon
3 tablespoons heavy cream
1 teaspoon brandy
Pinch of sugar

For the Tart Shells:

1. Preheat the oven to 400°F.
2. Thaw the pie shells until they are pliable and roll out on a lightly floured surface to flatten and even them out to a thickness of slightly less than ⅛ inch. (If the pastry gets too warm, refrigerate briefly, then reroll the dough on a lightly floured surface with a lightly floured rolling pin.) Cut out circles big enough to hang over the rims of six 4-inch tart shells with removable bottoms. Carefully press the pastry into the bottom and sides of the shells. Using a kitchen fork, randomly prick the bottom of the pastry. Cut a piece of parchment paper large enough to cover the bottom of each shell and come up the sides, and fit one into each shell. Fill the bottom of the shells with pastry weights or dried beans.
3. Bake until lightly browned, about 15 minutes. Remove from the oven and place on a wire rack to cool completely. Remove the shells from the tins.

For the Berry Mini Tarts:

1. In a medium saucepan, combine the vinegar and granulated sugar and place over medium heat. Cook, stirring to dissolve the sugar, until reduced to a syrup, 5 to 7 minutes.

2. Reserve 4 raspberries and 4 blackberries for the topping. Place all the remaining berries in a small saucepan. Add the brown sugar and place over medium heat. Cook until the fruit has broken down and the mixture is thick and caramelized. Add the Grand Marnier® and cook, stirring to release any bits stuck to the pan, until the alcohol has evaporated. Remove from the heat, transfer to a container, and chill until ready to serve.
3. In a medium bowl, combine the sour cream and cream cheese and stir well with a fork to combine. Add 1 teaspoon of the fruit compote and stir to incorporate.
4. Divide the sour cream mixture between two of the tart shells, making a well in the center. Add the fruit compote to the well and top with the remaining raspberries and blackberries. Drizzle with the balsamic syrup.

For the Mango Mini Tarts:

1. In a blender, combine the port, 2 tablespoons of the brown sugar, and the crystallized ginger and blend until smooth. Transfer to a medium saucepan and bring to a simmer over medium heat. Simmer until reduced to a syrup, 5 to 7 minutes. Strain and set aside.
2. While you're making the syrup, in a medium saucepan, combine the mango, curry powder, and remaining ½ cup brown sugar. Place over medium heat and cook until the mango has broken down and starts to caramelize. Add the rum and cook, stirring to release any bits stuck to the pan, until the alcohol has evaporated. Transfer to a blender and blend until smooth. Remove from the heat, transfer to a container, and chill until ready to serve.
3. Divide the mango filling between two of the remaining tart shells. Drizzle with the port syrup and top with the toasted coconut.

For the Apple Mini Tarts:

1. In a small saucepan, combine the port, 2 tablespoons of the brown sugar, and the cardamom and place over medium heat. Cook, stirring to dissolve the sugar, until reduced to a syrup, 5 to 7 minutes.
2. While you're making the syrup, in a medium saucepan, heat the butter over medium heat. Add the apples, pear, and remaining 1 tablespoon brown sugar and cook, covered, until the fruit is soft and just beginning to break down. Combine the cornstarch with 2 teaspoons cold water and stir to dissolve. Add to the apple mixture and cook for 2 minutes to thicken. Add the lime juice. Remove from the heat, transfer to a container, and chill until ready to serve.
3. In a small bowl, toss the salt with the cinnamon. Strain the mixture through a fine-mesh sieve, discarding the cinnamon and keeping the cinnamon-covered salt.
4. In a chilled bowl with chilled beaters, whip the cream for 1 minute. Add the brandy and sugar and whip until soft peaks form.
5. Divide the fruit mixture between the remaining two tart shells, drizzle with the port syrup, top with the whipped cream, and sprinkle with the cinnamon salt.

"Very nice. You have a future in tarts."

CHEF MARIA FRUMKIN, GUEST JUDGE

Potato Cannoli
with Coffee Whipped Cream and Chocolate Mousse

CHEF: Marcel
SEASON 2, EPISODE 11
QUICKFIRE CHALLENGE: Create a dish using Nestlé Chocolatier products.

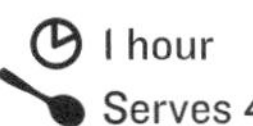
1 hour
Serves 4

HOW TO:
Have Fun with Salt

Salt has long been the unsung hero of the pastry kitchen, allowing the flavors of everything from lemon to chocolate to shine while taking none of the credit. Many pastry chefs in recent years, however, have been using salt and pepper on their own terms, to draw a bright or spicy contrast with the sweet elements in a dessert. Caramels are salted, apple compotes are topped with crunchy sea salt (see the apple tart on page 226), and pears are poached in peppercorn-infused wine. Marcel says he wanted to add pepper to his chocolate- and coffee-filled potato cannoli but thought that was beyond the pale for most diners. Maybe in a few years.

1 cup vanilla wafers
1 to 2 russet potatoes
Nonstick vegetable oil spray (optional)
Vegetable oil for frying
Salt
8 ounces bittersweet chocolate, chopped
4 cups heavy cream
Superfine sugar
5 dried guajillo chiles, stemmed and seeded
1 teaspoon instant espresso powder, or 1 tablespoon very finely ground espresso beans
4 small scoops vanilla ice cream

1. In a food processor, grind the vanilla wafers to a fine powder and set aside.
2. Peel the potatoes and use a mandoline to cut them into long, paper-thin slices. Trim off the rounded ends and roll each slice into a tube about 1 inch in diameter; wrap a length of kitchen string around the center and tie to help the roll keep its shape. Make 10 to 12 tubes, allowing 2 per serving plus some for breakage. (Alternatively, spray cannoli molds with cooking spray, wrap the potato slices around the molds, then wrap each tube in parchment paper, tying it closed with kitchen string.)
3. In a large, heavy pot, heat 2 to 3 inches of oil to 325°F. Working in batches, add the potato tubes and fry, turning with tongs or a slotted spoon, until lightly browned, 3 to 4 minutes. Transfer to paper towels to drain. (Immediately remove the paper, if using, and slide the tubes off the molds.) Increase the oil temperature to 375°F and return the potato tubes to the oil to cook until well browned and crisp, about 2 minutes. Transfer to paper towels to drain. Season lightly with salt and set aside. When cool, remove the strings.
4. In the top of a double boiler over simmering water, melt the chocolate, stirring until smooth. Combine half of the chocolate with ¼ cup of the cream and superfine sugar to taste to make a sauce. Set the sauce and the remaining chocolate aside.
5. In a skillet, toast the chiles over high heat, pressing down with a spatula, until fragrant and lightly browned in spots, about 3 minutes. Put the chiles in a food processor or a spice mill and process until finely ground. In a small saucepan, bring 1 cup of the cream to a simmer and add the chiles. Simmer for 10 minutes, then remove from the heat, cover, and let steep for 10 minutes. Transfer the cream and chiles to a blender and blend until smooth. Pour the cream through a fine-mesh sieve set over a bowl. Sweeten to taste with superfine sugar.
6. In a chilled bowl using chilled beaters, whip the remaining 2 ¾ cups cream until medium-stiff peaks form. Put half of the whipped cream in a separate bowl and gently fold in the espresso. Fold the reserved melted chocolate into the other half of the whipped cream. Put the coffee and chocolate whipped cream mixtures into separate piping bags (or use zip-top bags with one corner cut off).
7. On each of 4 serving plates, spoon a bit of the chocolate sauce, then some of the chile-infused cream. For each serving, fill 2 potato cannoli, piping coffee cream into one end and chocolate cream into the other, and place on the plate. Place a small scoop of ice cream next to the cannoli and garnish the plate with the confectioners' vanilla wafers. Serve immediately.

Blini with Kona Coffee "Caviar"
and Hawaiian Chocolate Mousse

CHEF: Marcel
SEASON 2, EPISODE 13
ELIMINATION CHALLENGE: Cook the best meal of your life.

- 8 ounces Hawaiian semisweet chocolate, chopped
- 2 cups heavy cream
- 1 cup freshly brewed Kona coffee, cooled to lukewarm
- 1 teaspoon sodium alginate
- 2 tablespoons sugar
- 1 teaspoon calcium chloride
- 4 blinis (homemade or store-bought)

45 minutes, plus chilling overnight
Serves 4

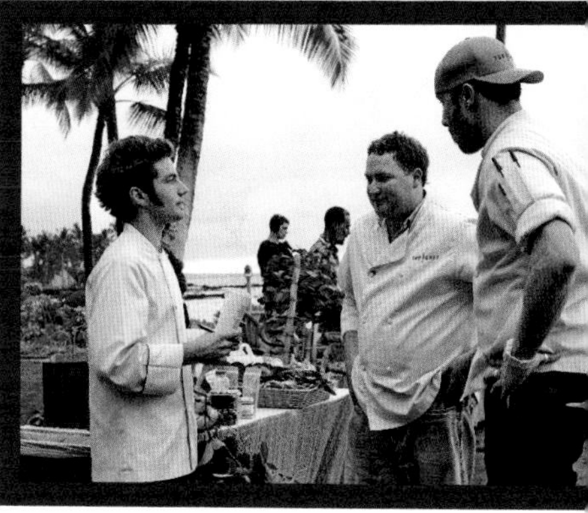

1. In a heat-proof bowl, combine the chocolate and 1 cup of the cream. Set the bowl over a saucepan of simmering water. Stir occasionally until the chocolate is almost melted. Remove from the heat and stir until smooth. Let cool slightly.
2. In a chilled bowl with chilled beaters, whip the remaining 1 cup cream until soft peaks form.
3. Using a large rubber spatula, stir one-third of the whipped cream into the chocolate mixture to lighten it, then gently fold the rest of the whipped cream into the chocolate mixture until just combined. Cover and refrigerate the mousse overnight.
4. In a small saucepan, combine the coffee, sodium alginate, and sugar. Using an immersion blender or a whisk, mix until smooth. Place over high heat and cook until the temperature reaches 205°F. Remove from the heat and pour through a fine-mesh sieve into a bowl. Refrigerate until cold.
5. When ready to serve, combine 2 cups water and the calcium chloride in a medium bowl. Whisk together to dissolve the calcium chloride.
6. Fill another medium bowl with cold water and set aside.
7. Fill a plastic syringe with the chilled coffee and alginate mixture, taking care not to draw any of the surface foam into the syringe. Drop the coffee mixture one drop at a time into the calcium chloride solution. Allow the drops to rest in the bath for 5 minutes; do not let them soak longer, or the center of each ball will continue to solidify. Using a small fine-mesh sieve, gently lift the "caviar" out of the solution and transfer it to the cold water to rinse.
8. Place 1 blini on each of 4 serving plates. Spoon chilled chocolate mousse on top of the blinis. Drain the rinsed "caviar" in the sieve, then place a few on top of each serving of mousse. Serve immediately.

"How smart! A blini with 'caviar.' That's great—I love that."

CHEF AND RESTAURATEUR WYLIE DUFRESNE, GUEST JUDGE

CHEF AND RESTAURATEUR HUBERT KELLER, GUEST JUDGE "TOTALLY EXCITING, A CONVERSATION PIECE. VERY UNIQUE."

Molten Chocolate Cakes

with Vanilla Crème Fraîche, Raspberry Coulis, and Nougatine Tuiles

CHEF: Hung
SEASON 3, EPISODE 14
ELIMINATION CHALLENGE: Cook the best meal of your life.

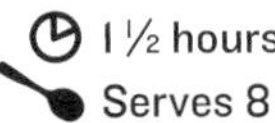

1 ½ hours
Serves 8

Raspberry Coulis:

- 1 pint fresh raspberries
- 2 tablespoons granulated sugar, or to taste
- 1 tablespoon fresh lemon juice, or to taste

Vanilla Crème Fraîche:

- 1 cup heavy cream
- 3 tablespoons crème fraîche
- 1 teaspoon vanilla extract
- ½ teaspoon almond extract
- 1 tablespoon granulated sugar

Molten Chocolate Cakes:

- 9 ounces bittersweet chocolate, coarsely chopped
- 1 cup (2 sticks) unsalted butter, plus more for the baking cups
- 4 large eggs plus 4 large egg yolks
- ½ cup granulated sugar
- 2 tablespoons all-purpose flour

To Serve:

- 1 cup fresh raspberries
- Fresh mint leaves

Nougatine Tuiles (see left)

For the Raspberry Coulis:

Put all the ingredients in a food processor and puree. Strain through a fine-mesh sieve, pushing down on the solids. Discard the seeds. Taste and add more sugar or lemon juice if needed. Cover and refrigerate until ready to serve.

For the Vanilla Crème Fraîche:

1. Put the cream in a large bowl and beat with an electric mixer until soft peaks form. Add the crème fraîche, vanilla, almond extract, and granulated sugar and beat until medium peaks form.
2. Refrigerate while you make the chocolate cakes.

For the Molten Chocolate Cakes:

1. Preheat the oven to 400°F. Butter eight 4- to 6-ounce ramekins or individual muffin cups.
2. In the top of a double boiler, combine the chocolate and butter and place over barely simmering water. Stir until melted. Remove from the heat and let cool slightly.
3. In a large bowl, beat the eggs and yolks until frothy. Add the sugar and continue beating until doubled in volume. Beat in the chocolate mixture, then beat in the flour. Divide the batter among the ramekins. Bake until the sides are set but the center remains soft, 11 to 14 minutes.

To Serve:

Run a small knife around the cakes to loosen, and turn the cakes out onto plates. Spoon raspberry coulis around the cakes and top with a dollop of crème fraîche. Garnish with raspberries and mint. Pass the tuiles around the table.

ON THE SIDE:

Nougatine Tuiles

- 2 tablespoons unsalted butter, cut into pieces
- 2 tablespoons light corn syrup
- ¼ cup confectioners' sugar
- ¼ cup slivered almonds

1. Preheat the oven to 350°F and line 2 baking sheets with Silpats™ (silicone mats).
2. In a medium saucepan, combine the butter, corn syrup, and confectioners' sugar. Place over medium heat and bring to a simmer, whisking, and simmer for 1 minute. Stir in the almonds and remove from the heat. Drop teaspoons of the mixture onto the baking sheets about 3 inches apart. Spread out thinly with the back of a spoon. Bake until golden brown, 12 to 15 minutes. Remove from the oven and let cool slightly on the baking sheets.
3. Pat the tuiles with paper towels to remove excess butter, carefully remove from the baking sheet with a metal spatula, and place on a plate alongside the chocolate cakes.

Fig Tart with Cheeses

CHEF: Harold
SEASON 1, EPISODE 12
ELIMINATION CHALLENGE: Cook the best meal of your life.

- ⅔ cup pine nuts
- 1 cup all-purpose flour
- 1 tablespoon sugar
- Pinch of salt
- 5 tablespoons unsalted butter, at room temperature
- 1 large egg yolk
- 4 ounces dried Black Mission figs
- ½ cup sugar
- 1 vanilla bean, split lengthwise, seeds scraped and reserved
- 1 cup heavy cream
- 4 large eggs
- 1 ounce fig jam
- 4 fresh figs, halved, for garnish
- 8 ounces Pecorino tartufo cheese
- 8 ounces Gorgonzola dolce cheese
- 8 ounces Taleggio cheese
- 1 tablespoon honey
- 8 slices sourdough baguette, toasted

45 minutes
Serves 8

1. Preheat the oven to 325°F.
2. Put the pine nuts in a food processor and pulse to roughly chop. Add the flour, sugar, and salt and pulse until the nuts are finely ground. Transfer the mixture to a medium bowl.
3. Add the butter, egg yolk, and 2 tablespoons water and use a pastry cutter or your fingertips to combine until the mixture resembles coarse meal. Form the dough into a flat disk, wrap in plastic wrap, and refrigerate for at least 30 minutes.
4. Meanwhile, in a medium saucepan, cook the dried figs, sugar, ¾ cup water, and the vanilla bean and seeds for 15 to 20 minutes, until the figs are very soft.
5. Transfer the mixture to a blender, add the cream, and blend to combine; add the eggs and blend briefly to combine. Set aside.
6. Remove the dough from the refrigerator and remove the plastic. Pat the dough evenly into a 9-inch tart pan with a removable bottom. Fit a piece of aluminum foil into the tart shell to help it keep its shape; bake for 10 minutes, then remove the foil and bake for another 6 to 8 minutes, until golden brown.
7. Fill the tart shell with the fig mixture and bake for 24 to 28 minutes, or until the filling is just set in the center. Transfer to a wire rack to cool to room temperature.
8. Cut into 8 wedges. Place each wedge on a serving plate and top with fig jam. Arrange a fresh fig half alongside.
9. Cut the cheeses into 1-ounce pieces and place them alongside the tart wedges. Drizzle the Taleggio with the honey. Serve with the toasted bread.

WHAT IS . . .

The Cheese Course?

The cheese course is served after the main course and before dessert, and at its simplest is a selection of no more than three cheeses, with plain bread—preferably a baguette—on the side.

For your cheese selection, you can choose different styles made from one type of milk, or you can choose cheeses made from different milks. In either case, be sure that each cheese is sufficiently different in texture, flavor, and color to make the selection interesting.

Arrange the cheeses on the plate from mildest to strongest, with plenty of space between them. Fresh fruit like grapes and pears are good palate cleansers, and figs and apricots go nicely with many cheeses. Also try a little honey, a spoonful of mild compote (such as black cherry), an onion or shallot marmalade or confit, or even spices and nuts.

RESTAURATEUR DREW NIEPORENT, GUEST JUDGE "THE CHEESES WERE VERY SMARTLY CHOSEN."

Marshmallow and Cookie Ice Cream

CHEF: Cliff
SEASON 2, EPISODE 3
QUICKFIRE CHALLENGE: Serve an original ice cream to crowds at the Redondo Beach Seaside Lagoon.

45 minutes, plus chilling at least 3 hours
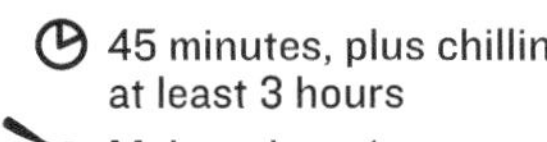
Makes about 1 quart

2 cups heavy cream
1 cup milk
½ cup sugar
Pinch of salt
6 large egg yolks
½ cup chocolate cookie crumbs
½ cup mini marshmallows
¼ cup graham cracker crumbs
¼ cup toasted slivered almonds

"The avenue I took was what I like in ice cream. I want something crunchy, I want something soft, and cookies, because I like cookies."
CLIFF

1. In a large, heavy saucepan, combine the cream, milk, sugar, and salt. Place over medium heat and bring just to a boil, stirring occasionally.
2. Whisk the egg yolks in a large heat-proof bowl. Add the hot cream mixture in a slow, steady stream, whisking constantly, then pour the mixture back into the pan and cook, stirring, over medium-low heat until the custard is thick enough to coat the back of a spoon and reaches a temperature of 170°F. Do not let the custard boil.
3. Pour the custard through a fine-mesh sieve into a clean heat-proof bowl. Cool to room temperature, stirring occasionally, then transfer to a container and refrigerate until cold, at least 3 hours (or make the custard the day before and refrigerate overnight).
4. Transfer the custard to an electric ice cream maker and prepare according to the manufacturer's directions. At the last minute, add the cookie crumbs, marshmallows, graham cracker crumbs, and toasted almonds and mix to incorporate. Transfer to an airtight container and freeze to firm up.

Banana Scallops, Banana Guacamole and Chocolate Ice Cream

CHEF: Richard
SEASON 4, EPISODE 7
QUICKFIRE CHALLENGE: Create an amazing dessert.

Chocolate Ice Cream:

8 ounces 72% bittersweet chocolate, cut into pieces

2 cups heavy cream

1 cup milk

¾ cup sugar

6 large egg yolks

Banana Scallops:

4 ripe bananas, cut into 1-inch pieces (to resemble scallops)

½ cup demerara sugar

Banana Guacamole (see right)

1 hour, plus overnight freezing

Serves 8

Winner

For the Chocolate Ice Cream:

1. In a medium heat-proof bowl set over a pan of barely simmering water, melt the chocolate, stirring occasionally, until smooth. Set aside to cool.
2. In a large, heavy saucepan, combine the cream, milk, and ½ cup of the sugar. Place over medium heat and bring just to a boil, stirring occasionally.
3. Whisk the egg yolks in a large heat-proof bowl with the remaining ¼ cup sugar until combined and light yellow. Add the melted chocolate and whisk until fully incorporated. Add the hot cream mixture, whisking constantly, then pour the mixture back into the pan and cook, stirring, over medium-low heat until the custard is thick enough to coat the back of a spoon and reaches a temperature of 170°F.
4. Pour the custard through a fine-mesh sieve into a clean heat-proof bowl. Cool to room temperature, stirring occasionally, then transfer to a container and refrigerate until cold, at least 3 hours (or make the custard the day before and refrigerate overnight). Transfer the custard to an electric ice cream maker and prepare according to the manufacturer's directions. Transfer to an airtight container and freeze.

For the Banana Scallops:

Just before you're ready to serve, heat a small nonstick skillet over medium-high heat. Spread the sugar over a plate and press the top and bottom ends of the banana scallops into the sugar to coat. Place the banana scallops in the skillet a few at a time and sear until softened and the sugar coating has caramelized, about 1 minute each side.

To Serve:

Spoon the guacamole onto serving plates. Top with the banana scallops and garnish with the herbs. Drizzle with the remaining lime-ginger syrup. Place a scoop of chocolate ice cream alongside.

Note:

To make a small amount of ginger juice, finely grate fresh ginger, then squeeze in the palm of your hand to extract the juice.

ON THE SIDE:

Banana Guacamole

½ cup fresh lime juice

4 teaspoons fresh ginger juice (see note)

½ cup sugar

¼ to ½ teaspoon red pepper flakes, to taste

4 ripe bananas

¼ cup chopped fresh cilantro, plus more for garnish

¼ cup chopped fresh basil, plus more for garnish

2 tablespoons chopped fresh tarragon, plus more for garnish

1. In a medium saucepan, combine the lime juice, ginger juice, sugar, and red pepper flakes. Place over medium heat, bring to a simmer, and simmer for 10 minutes or until slightly syrupy, stirring constantly and checking that the mixture doesn't boil over.

2. Place the bananas in a medium bowl and mash them with a potato masher or fork. Stir in the lime-ginger syrup, reserving about ¼ cup for garnish. Stir in the cilantro, basil, and tarragon.

Strawberry Apple Crisp
with Hazelnut Whipped Cream

CHEF: Brian H.
SEASON I, EPISODE 2
ELIMINATION CHALLENGE: Make a sexy dessert for a fetish party.

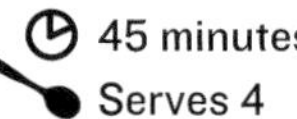

45 minutes
Serves 4

> "The crisp was very nice. I really liked the rough edges and the cream on top. That was very sensual."
> GAIL SIMMONS, JUDGE

Hazelnut Crisp:

4 tablespoons unsalted butter, at room temperature, plus more for the pan
½ cup all-purpose flour, plus more for the pan
¾ cup cake flour
2 cups confectioners' sugar
6 large egg whites
1 tablespoon vanilla extract
¼ cup finely chopped hazelnuts

Apples:

¼ cup sugar
2 large Fuji apples, peeled, cored, and cut into ⅛-inch-thick slices
2 tablespoons fresh orange juice
Pinch of ground cinnamon
Pinch of freshly grated nutmeg
4 tablespoons salted butter

Hazelnut Whipped Cream:

1 pint heavy cream
¼ cup sugar
¼ cup Frangelico® liqueur

To Serve:

2 cups strawberries, quartered, at room temperature

For the Hazelnut Crisp:

1. Preheat the oven to 375°F. Butter and flour 2 large, rimless baking sheets.
2. Sift the flours and the confectioners' sugar together into the bowl of an electric mixer. Add the butter, egg whites, and vanilla and beat until thoroughly incorporated.
3. Using an offset spatula, spread the paste evenly onto the prepared baking sheets, spreading it as thinly as possible. Sprinkle the hazelnuts evenly over the paste.
4. Bake for 15 to 17 minutes, until golden brown (the crisp will be darker at the edges; do not let it burn). Transfer the crisp to a wire rack to cool to room temperature, then break it into roughly shaped pieces. Set aside.

For the Apples:

1. Sprinkle the sugar into a large sauté pan or skillet. Arrange the apples in a single layer over the sugar and place the pan over medium-high heat.
2. Sprinkle the orange juice over the apples and sprinkle with the cinnamon and nutmeg. Dot the butter over the top. Simmer for 10 to 15 minutes, until the apples are soft. Set aside.

For the Hazelnut Whipped Cream:

In a chilled bowl with chilled beaters, whip the cream for about 1 minute, then add the sugar and liqueur and whip until soft peaks form. Refrigerate, covered, until ready to serve.

To Serve:

Divide the apples among 4 dessert dishes. Top with a layer of strawberries and a dollop of whipped cream. Stick a hazelnut crisp into the top and serve immediately.

The Total Orgasm

Lemon Pastry Puffs, Tapioca Pillows, and Cold Hot-Chocolate Shots

CHEF: Miguel
SEASON 1, EPISODE 2
ELIMINATION CHALLENGE: Make a sexy dessert for a fetish party.

More than 3 hours, plus chilling overnight
Serves 12 to 18
Winner

> "The bottom line is, if you don't bring sex to the table, you're going to go home."
> MIGUEL

Cold Hot Chocolate:

- 8 ounces milk chocolate, chopped
- 1 pint heavy cream
- 1 cup milk
- 1 cinnamon stick

Pastry Puffs:

- 9 tablespoons unsalted butter, plus more for the baking sheets
- 1 cup plus 2 ¼ teaspoons granulated sugar
- ½ teaspoon salt
- 1 cup all-purpose flour
- 7 large eggs
- ½ cup fresh lemon juice
- 3 large egg yolks
- 4 fresh thyme sprigs

Tapioca Pillows:

- ½ cup small pearl tapioca, soaked overnight, if necessary, according to the package instructions
- One 13 ½-ounce can unsweetened coconut milk
- 1 cup milk
- 1 cup granulated sugar
- 1 teaspoon salt
- 2 large eggs, beaten
- 1 teaspoon ground cinnamon
- ½ teaspoon ground ginger
- ½ teaspoon vanilla extract
- 1 tablespoon minced fresh cilantro
- 4 ripe mangoes
- 12 to 18 fresh chives
- 2 cups passionfruit juice
- 2 tablespoons cornstarch

Spicy Whipped Cream:

- 1 ½ cups heavy cream
- 3 tablespoons confectioners' sugar
- 1 teaspoon ground cayenne, or more to taste
- 1 teaspoon ground cinnamon

To Decorate and Serve:

- 8 ounces white chocolate
- Red food coloring
- 4 ounces bittersweet chocolate
- 1 pint fresh strawberries, hulled and cut into ¼-inch dice
- ¼ cup pepitas (hulled pumpkin seeds)

For the Cold Hot Chocolate:

In a small saucepan, heat the chocolate, cream, milk, and cinnamon stick over medium-high heat, stirring constantly. Bring to a simmer, then remove from the heat and let cool. Remove and discard the cinnamon stick. Cover with a piece of plastic wrap directly on the surface of the chocolate and refrigerate overnight.

For the Pastry Puffs:

1. Preheat the oven to 375°F. Butter 2 baking sheets.
2. In a medium saucepan, combine 1 cup water, 6 tablespoons of the butter, the 2 ¼ teaspoons sugar, and the salt. Cook over medium heat until the butter is melted, then raise the heat to high and bring to a rapid boil. Remove from the heat and add the flour; beat with a wooden spoon until the mixture comes away from the sides of the pan. Add 4 of the eggs, one at a time, beating well after each addition.
3. Put the dough in a piping bag with a 1-inch plain round tip (or in a heavy-duty zip-top bag with one corner cut off) and pipe 1 ¼-inch balls onto the prepared baking sheets. Dip your fingertips in water and smooth the tops of the balls.
4. Bake for 20 minutes, then lower the oven temperature to 300°F and bake for 10 to

15 minutes longer, until golden brown. Turn off the oven. Remove the baking sheets from the oven and use a small, sharp knife to make a small hole in the side of each puff to allow steam to escape. Return the puffs to the baking sheets and put them in the turned-off oven for 10 minutes to dry. Set aside to cool completely.

5. In a heat-proof bowl set over a saucepan of simmering water, combine the lemon juice, 1 cup sugar, the remaining 3 eggs, egg yolks, and thyme. Whisk for 8 to 10 minutes until thickened. Remove from the heat, add the remaining 3 tablespoons butter, and whisk until smooth. Let cool, then cover and refrigerate until chilled. Discard the thyme sprigs. Put the filling in a piping bag fitted with a small plain tip and set aside.

For the Tapioca Pillows:

1. In a small saucepan, combine the tapioca, coconut milk, milk, ½ cup of the sugar, salt, eggs, cinnamon, and ginger. Cook, stirring constantly, over medium heat for 15 to 25 minutes, until the tapioca is soft and translucent. Stir in the vanilla and cilantro. Let cool to room temperature, then cover and refrigerate until chilled.
2. Peel the mangoes and use a mandoline or sharp knife to cut them into 12 to 18 large, paper-thin slices. Trim the remaining flesh off the pits and set the trimmings aside.
3. Lay the mango slices flat on a work surface and put about 1 tablespoon of the tapioca on one end of each slice. Roll the slices up like an egg roll, folding in one or both sides to contain the pudding, and tie each roll closed with a chive.
4. In a small saucepan, combine the passionfruit juice and remaining ½ cup sugar and cook over high heat for about 5 minutes, until the sugar is dissolved. In a cup, combine the cornstarch and 2 tablespoons water, stirring until smooth. Add to the juice mixture and bring to a boil. Boil for 2 minutes, or until thickened. Let cool.

For the Spicy Whipped Cream:

In a large chilled bowl using chilled beaters, whip the cream, confectioners' sugar, cayenne, and cinnamon until soft peaks form. Set aside.

To Decorate and Serve:

1. In a heat-proof bowl set over a saucepan of simmering water, melt the white chocolate. Put about ¼ cup of the chocolate in a cup and add food coloring to tint it pink. In a separate bowl over simmering water, melt 2 ounces of the bittersweet chocolate. Dip the top of each cream puff in white chocolate and set aside until the chocolate is set. Dab a bit of pink chocolate in the center of the white chocolate, then use a toothpick to make a dot of bittersweet chocolate in the center of the pink. To fill the puffs, poke a small hole in the bottom of each puff and pipe in the lemon filling.
2. In a blender or food processor, puree the mango trimmings. Divide the puree among 12 to 18 tall shot glasses. Put ½ teaspoon of the strawberries on top of the puree in each glass. Fill the glasses with the cold hot chocolate and top with a dollop of the whipped cream. Shave some of the remaining bittersweet chocolate over the whipped cream. (Save the rest for another use.)
3. Spoon a bit of the passionfruit gelée into each of 12 to 18 Chinese soupspoons. Place the tapioca pillows on top of the gelée and garnish with the pepitas.
4. Serve the chocolate shots, pastry puffs, and tapioca pillows on a large platter.

"Although there's nothing sexy about Miguel, his dish was fantastic."

MADAME S., OWNER OF MR. S SEX SHOP, GUEST JUDGE

Low-Fat Berry Cheesecake

CHEF: Elia
SEASON 2, EPISODE 4
ELIMINATION CHALLENGE: Create a meal under 500 calories.

30 minutes, plus chilling overnight
Serves 8 to 10

WHAT ARE . . . Flaxseeds?

Smooth and shiny, golden or brown, flaxseeds are rich in omega-3 fats, which promote bone health, help lower blood pressure, and lower the risk of heart attack and stroke. Furthermore, these little wonders—also good sources of dietary fiber and crucial trace elements like manganese—have been shown to lower cholesterol and help prevent cancer.

- 1 cup organic plain granola (no fruits or nuts)
- 1 cup flax cereal (flakes; no fruits or nuts)
- 2 large egg whites
- 1 tablespoon unflavored gelatin (measured from 2 envelopes)
- 1 ½ cups low-fat strawberry yogurt
- Two 8-ounce packages low-fat cream cheese
- 2 teaspoons vanilla extract
- 2 cups fresh blackberries
- 1 cup halved fresh strawberries
- Mint leaves for garnish

1. Preheat the oven to 375°F.
2. Put the granola and flax cereal into a large, heavy-duty zip-top bag. Gently crush with a rolling pin to form coarse crumbs.
3. In a medium bowl, lightly beat the egg whites. Add the cereal mixture and stir to combine. Transfer the mixture to an 8-inch springform pan and spread evenly over the bottom of the pan and a little up the sides, patting it down so it all stays together.
4. Bake for 15 minutes, or until lightly browned and crisp. Remove from the oven and let cool completely.
5. Pour ⅓ cup water into a small saucepan and sprinkle the gelatin over the water. Let stand for 10 minutes. Place over very low heat and stir until the gelatin dissolves.
6. In a food processor, combine the yogurt, cream cheese, and vanilla and blend until smooth. With the motor running, slowly add the warm gelatin mixture in a thin stream through the hole in the lid.
7. Pour the filling over the crust. Cover with plastic and chill overnight to set. Run a dull knife around the sides of the pan to loosen the cake, then release the pan sides and transfer to a serving platter.
8. Scatter the top with the berries and garnish with the mint leaves. Cut into wedges and serve.

Blogging Top Chef

"We've always strived to build strong relationships between our characters and our fans," says Bravo Media president Lauren Zalaznick. "If you can get people to care so much that one hour of television isn't enough, well, that's an amazing feat."

Those for whom one hour *isn't* enough, who jones for a little *Top Chef* fix between episodes, know where to look: BravoTV.com. There, in an ever-expanding list of *Top Chef* blogs, the judges expand on and explain their decisions. Former contestants, including Carlos Fernandez and Harold Dieterle, handicap the current season. Viewers chime in with their thoughts and conspiracy theories. And self-described "*Top Chef* nerds" like Anthony Bourdain and Rocco DiSpirito contribute running, often breathless, journals of what it's like to be both a chef and a fan.

The king of *Top Chef* interactivity is unquestionably Bravo SVP and executive producer Andy Cohen, who not only contributes a daily written blog on all things Bravo but also hosts "Watch What Happens," which airs on the website just after each episode. On the live video segments, Cohen debriefs the eliminated chef, interviews judges, takes viewer calls and questions, and offers behind-the-scenes insight. He also winds up in some pretty awkward situations, as when he was preparing to broadcast after the Season 2 finale.

"I had to watch the finale live in a room with Marcel and Ilan, who spent the entire episode on-screen ruthlessly griping at each other. Then we had to go on the air and talk about it," Cohen remembers. "It was just one of the most uncomfortable situations I've ever been in."

To read more, go to BravoTV.com.

Bourdain's Blog

8/8/07 Season 3, Episode 7

Low Spark and High Heels . . . In the Roach Coach

Who EVER finds themselves yearning suddenly for cauliflower in their ice cream sundae? Who has ever—in recorded history—thought to themselves: "Gee . . . this ice cream would be so much better if only there were tempura flakes on it"? Or yearned, while spooning vanilla ice cream into their face, for FOAM?

8/22/07 Season 3, Episode 9

Train in Vain

A thrilling episode this week, with a surprising and sad ending. In many ways, the last few episodes have (in their own pain-inducing way) better illustrated the skill set you REALLY need to succeed as a Top Chef than straight, head-to-head cook-offs ever could—how to do things you might not be particularly good at while under pressure. How to get knocked out of your comfort zone—without warning—and still soldier through. How to deal with things going wrong all around you—without losing your cool. How to step up and above your normal responsibilities—and manage to pull it off.

As most who've spent any time as professional chefs know all too well, the phrases "It's not my job" and "It's unfair" have no real meaning when you're in charge of a kitchen.

9/5/07 Season 3, Episode 10

Sympathy for the Devil

There was rejoicing in TV-land last night, as designated bad guy Howie whiffed on three pitches and was sent home for good. For many who have posted on this site, offended by his petulance, his obstinacy, the veritable Niagara of sweat that flowed freely from his brow, it was none too soon. But . . . but . . . what do we do now? With no bad guy?

And was Howie all that bad?

Tom's Blog

11/15/06 Season 2, Episode 5

I'm Getting Grumpy

I don't have patience for over-the-top food descriptions, mostly because they seem to say, "look at how fancy this dish is!" and I'm not a big fan of fancy food. I'm OK with food that requires a high level of skill to prepare. And I don't have a problem with fine dining—provided I'm in the mood for it. But the word "fancy" speaks to me of pretension, embellishment, the need to impress. About presentation over substance.

9/20/07 Season 3, Episode 12

The Final Four

This week's episode just may be one of my favorites yet. Why? Because it was all about the food. It provided two very straightforward challenges, without gimmicks, that gave both the judges and the viewers a great way to analyze the cooking skills of our five remaining chefs.

Harold's Blog

11/22/06 Season 2, Episode 6

Half Pirate, Half Hippie

I was thoroughly surprised to see Betty's horns shoot out of her head like that. I guess everyone else saw it, but I really didn't. She's fiery, man. Fiery. It just makes you wonder how real that smile is all the time. I had suspicions when I saw her and Marcel go at it the first time, but this time she got the bus driver's uniform, she put it on, she got behind the wheel of the bus and started driving over people.

6/29/07 Season 3, Episode 3

Sweet Vindication

You know, there was a teeny outrage during our wedding challenge when we used wedding cake mix in Season 1, and the cakes were fine. There were no complaints about the cake. And now, again, other people used premade ingredients and it's like, "Oh, smart idea." I thought that was kind of funny. Vindicating a little.

Rocco's Blog

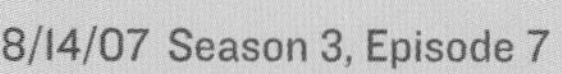

8/14/07 Season 3, Episode 7

Suck It Up Time

There and then I learned, whatever reason you cook, you have to know one thing—your job is to feed people and make them happy. If that means slopping blue cheese on a bad burger for a bunch of margarita-swilling Parisians, then so be it. And by the way, it's a conscious decision. Every *Top Chef* Elimination Challenge is ostensibly about cooking, but it's also so much more.

8/23/07 Season 3, Episode 9

Tre Sara, Sara

WHAT A NIGHT! It's OK—I have been wrong before. In one of the best surprise endings of the season, my judgment about Sara's unholy self-appointment as head chef was premature. She WON! The underdog prevailed. In a series of unexpected twists and turns, true to the nature of the restaurant business, the outcome of this week's episode of *Top Chef* couldn't have been predicted. Holy Parisian Gnocchi, Batman!

Andy's Blog

5/2/06 Season 1, Episode 10

Top Chef Reunion

Like President Bush, I am a "decider"—and, like our Brainiac-in-Chief, I made a very big decision at the *Top Chef* reunion taping. I decided to indulge in everything the craft service table had to offer in a significant way. Of course, the decision was made against my own will because I am powerless next to a craft service table, which is replenished constantly with snacky foods, healthy treats, and main courses.

2/1/07 Season 2, Episode 13

Watch What Happens: Awkward Moments Edition!

As for Marcel, his hair in person is something to behold; I saw no gel, foam, gelée, or mousse propping it up, it is just an outstanding concoction of molecular follicology.

Reunions

Bravo Media president Lauren Zalaznick says that the number-one question she gets from people about *Top Chef* is, "What are the contestants really like?"

"Then, when people actually meet, say, Stephen Asprinio or Harold Dieterle at one of our events, they always nudge me: 'They're just like they are on the show.' And I say, 'Yeah, I know. They're not actors. That's who they are!'" This desire from fans to see how their beloved contestants act outside the usual reality-show frame helps explain why reunion shows have become such an anticipated part of the *Top Chef* experience. "I think people have become so fanatical about the series that they want to see the chefs, and the judges, in a relaxed atmosphere, looking back on the season," says Andy Cohen, who hosts the reunions.

Each reunion has been an entertaining mix of high-concept montages, Stew Room outtakes, Judges' Table bloopers, and candid admissions—not to mention the presentation of the $10,000 award for "Fan Favorite." And for every sweet moment of reconciliation, there's another that makes you squirm with guilty pleasure. As Cohen says of the Season 1 reunion, "It was like Jerry Springer: totally disturbing, but totally compelling."

SAM

CASEY

Fan Favorites

Don't have what it takes to snag the title of Top Chef? There is one safety net in place to insure that not everybody but the winner goes home empty-handed.

The race for Fan Favorite and its $10,000 prize—voted on by viewers via BravoTV.com and text message—has become one of the more exciting *Top Chef* subplots. In perhaps the least surprising development ever, charmer Sam Talbot won in Season 2, while Season 3 featured a much closer race between Casey Thompson and Dale Levitski. In the end it went to Casey, giving her some consolation for her flubbed finale.

1 Season 1 Reunion

Most uncomfortable moment:
Tiffani Faison leaves the stage in tears.

Happiest moments:
Stephen Asprinio makes a surprisingly tender apology to Candice Kumai; Miguel "Chunk le Funk" Morales farts, and the editors, for once, leave it in.

2 Watch What Happens Special

Most uncomfortable moments:
Padma Lakshmi claims to have gotten "heavy" during Season 2; Cliff Crooks has to explain the "hair-shaving" incident.

Happiest moments:
Viewing a tape of the immortal Jacques Pépin showing Ilan Hall the real meaning of "Top Chef"; Michael Midgley in a tux.

3 Season 3 Reunion

Most uncomfortable moments:
The look on Casey Thompson's face when C.J. Jacobsen offers to make out with her; Howie Kleinberg sheds a tear.

Happiest moment:
Cohen says to Hung Huynh, "So, a lot of people watching the show thought you were kind of an @$!hole."

watch
what
happens

"It Is What It Is"
A Top Chef Glossary

Maybe you missed the food words day in French class, or found yourself scratching your head while watching chefs and judges babble on about *sous-vide* this and *amuse* that.

High-level cooking has its own special language of precise terms (and strange pronunciations) that might seem mysterious—until now. That macaroni's not burnt, it's brûléed!

aioli ("ay-OH-lee" or "i-OH-lee")
A thick, cold, mayonnaise-like sauce that originated in Provence, in southern France, often served with simply cooked or steamed vegetables and fish.

al dente ("al-DEN-tay")
Literally "to the tooth" in Italian, "al dente" describes food—most commonly pasta or rice—that is cooked through but still firm, offering slight resistance when chewed, and not soft or mushy at all. When cooking pasta, be sure to start tasting pieces well before the recommended cooking time is up: as soon as it loses its raw taste and the center is no longer bright white, it's done.

amuse-bouche ("ah-MOOZE boosh")
Literally "mouth amuser" in French. A small, one- or two-bite-sized dish served just before the main part of a meal.

antipasto ("ahn-tee-PAHS-toe")
Literally "before the meal" in Italian. A selection of hors d'oeuvres usually featuring cured meats, cheeses, simply grilled or marinated vegetables at room temperature, and olives.

back/front of the house
"Back of the house" is a phrase used in the restaurant business to describe the kitchen area, presided over by the executive chef; the "front of the house" is the dining room and customer waiting area, presided over by the maître d' or host.

beignet ("ben-YAY")
Refers to a doughnut popular in southern Louisiana—a deep-fried, yeast-raised rectangle (no hole), dusted liberally with confectioners' sugar.

blanch
To cook, usually very briefly, in boiling water. Vegetables are often blanched to loosen their skins for peeling or to soften them before cooking them further by another method.

braise ("BRAYZ")
To brown in fat, then cook slowly in liquid at low heat.

brûlée ("broo-LAY")
In informal use, to caramelize the surface of a food (as in crème brûlée) with a kitchen torch, salamander grill, or oven broiler.

caramelize
To heat until the sugars in a food liquefy and turn brown.

carpaccio ("car-PAH-chi-oh")
Thinly sliced (and sometimes pounded) food served raw and simply garnished. The classic Italian carpaccio is beef or another land-based protein, but restaurateurs now use "carpaccio" to refer to seafood, vegetables, or fruit prepared in the same manner.

ceviche ("seh-VEE-chay")
A South American dish of raw fish or other seafood tossed with citrus juice and fresh herbs and vegetables such as hot chiles, tomatoes, scallions, and cilantro.

charcuterie ("shar-COOT-eh-ree")
A selection of cured meats served as an appetizer or first course, often accompanied by cornichons or other pickled vegetables and occasionally a wedge of cheese and bread.

chiffonade ("shiff-on-AHD")
To cut leafy greens or herbs into very thin ribbons. To chiffonade basil, for example, stack the leaves, roll them into a tight cigarlike roll, and cut across the roll into thin strips.

clarify
To remove impurities or sediment from a liquid.

confit ("con-FEE")
Food cooked slowly in deep fat. Traditionally, "confit" refers to duck-leg quarters cooked in duck or goose fat.

consommé ("kon-suh-MAY")
A crystal-clear meat, fish, or vegetable broth. To clarify the broth, egg whites are added and the broth is brought to a boil; the egg whites form a "raft" on the surface of the liquid that attracts impurities that can then be discarded.

daikon ("DIE-con")
A large, white-fleshed Asian radish with white or black skin.

deglaze
To add a liquid (often wine) to a hot pan in which food is being or has been sautéed, stirring to scrape up any of the browned bits of food in the bottom of the pan, which add flavor and body to the dish or sauce.

demi-glace ("DEH-mee-glahs")
Brown sauce (also known as "sauce espagnole") that has been combined with a splash of sherry or Madeira and reduced until thick.

flambé ("flahm-BAY")
To ignite the alcohol in a mixture using a long lighter or kitchen match.

fold
To very gently incorporate one ingredient or mixture into another.

gelée ("jeh-LAY")
Loosely used, a jelled or jellylike sauce.

jicama ("HEE-kah-mah")
A round root vegetable with creamy white, crisp flesh and light brown skin. Jicama can be eaten raw or cooked and is common in Latin American dishes.

julienne ("joo-lee-EHN")
To cut into long, thin strips.

Kobe ("KOH-bee")
An extremely expensive, high-grade type of beef from cattle raised to exacting standards in Kobe, Japan. The animals are fed a special diet that includes beers, and are massaged regularly with sake.

the line
Where the food for each restaurant order is cooked, staffed by line cooks and usually the sous-chef. The line is made up of several stations, such as sauté, fryer, grill, and salad.

mandoline
A manual slicing tool used in professional kitchens. Its adjustable blades make quick work of slicing fruits or vegetables paper thin, cutting them into perfectly uniform julienne strips or matchsticks, or making waffle cuts.

mignonette ("meen-yon-EHT")
Traditionally made with red wine vinegar, minced shallots, cracked black pepper, salt, and sometimes parsley, mignonette sauce is a classic accompaniment to raw oysters and other shellfish.

mince
To cut into very small pieces—as small as possible without pureeing. To mince garlic or fresh herbs, first chop roughly with a chef's knife, then hold the tip of the knife on the cutting board with your palm while you rock the blade over the food, moving it back and forth, always keeping the knife in contact with the board.

mise en place ("MEEZ-on-plahs")
Literally "set in place" in French. "Mise en place" refers to the organized chef's practice of preparing in advance all the ingredients and tools that will be needed to make a dish or a meal and arranging them in a logical way in the kitchen.

moi ("MOY")
A fish indigenous to Hawaii that is also known as Pacific threadfish. Moi is similar to sea bass in texture and flavor.

mojo ("MO-ho")
In Cuban cooking, "mojo" refers to a sauce of olive oil, citrus (such as sour orange) juice, and garlic. Other Caribbean cultures use the term to describe various hot sauces containing chiles.

morcilla ("more-SEE-yah")
Spanish blood sausage commonly made of pork meat and fat, pig's blood, and rice or onions.

offal ("OFF-uhl")
Also known as "variety meats," the organs, glands, tail, feet, snout, tongue, and other parts of the animal that are today relatively uncommon in Western kitchens.

pan roast
To roast in a pan. A meat or vegetable can be seared in an ovenproof pan on the stovetop, then transferred to the oven to finish cooking. Informally, "pan roasting" can refer to meat or vegetables that are cooked (in very little fat) on the stovetop over high heat.

poach
To cook food (usually meat or fish) in barely simmering water or another liquid.

poi ("POY")
A staple of the Hawaiian diet, poi is cooked and mashed taro. Eaten fresh, it is mild tasting with a pasty texture; after a few days, poi starts to ferment and become desirably sour.

poke ("PO-keh")
A Hawaiian appetizer of cubed raw seafood (commonly ahi tuna) tossed with seaweed, roasted and ground kukui nuts (candlenuts), tomato, green onion, shoyu (a Japanese soy sauce), or other ingredients.

puree
To chop or mash a food until it achieves a smooth, uniform consistency.

reduce
To cook a liquid at a brisk simmer or boil in order to evaporate it, thickening and concentrating its flavor.

roulade ("roo-LAUD")
Thin slices of meat (such as beef) rolled around a filling, then cooked and sliced.

saffron
The dried stigmas of the saffron flower, used as a spice. Saffron has a strong flavor and lends a distinctive yellow color to dishes such as paella, risotto, and bouillabaisse.

sauté
To cook food in a small amount of fat in a shallow pan or skillet on the stovetop, stirring frequently.

sear
To cook over high heat in order to quickly brown the exterior of a piece of food (usually meat or fish).

semifreddo (seh-mee-FRAY-doh)
Literally "half cold" in Italian. A dessert that is partially frozen custard, fruit or other gelatos, coffee, and so on.

sommelier ("suh-mel-YAY")
A trained and experienced wine specialist. Working at a restaurant, the sommelier is responsible for buying and storing wines for the restaurant's cellar, and will work with the chef to pair wines (and sometimes beers and spirits) with dishes on the menu.

sous-chef ("SOO-shef")
In a restaurant kitchen, the executive chef's second in command. The sous-chef oversees the line cooks and does much of the actual cooking, planning, scheduling, and ordering for the kitchen.

sous vide ("soo-VEED")
Literally "under vacuum" in French. A method of cooking food in vacuum-sealed plastic bags submerged in a bath of water at a carefully maintained temperature.

succo ("SOOK-oh")
An Italian word for "juice," usually applied to vegetable or fruit juices (as opposed to meat juices, or *sugo*).

sweetbreads
The thymus glands of a calf or lamb.

tartare ("tar-TAR")
Diced beef or fish served raw, with various toppings and seasonings.

thermal immersion circulator
A machine in which vacuum-sealed food is cooked in a water bath that is circulating at a precisely defined temperature.

truffle
A variety of underground mushroom of the genus *Tuber*. "Truffle" can also refer to a confection made of chocolate ganache formed into balls and either left plain, dusted with cocoa, or encased in a chocolate shell.

truss
To tie a whole chicken or other fowl with butcher's twine or kitchen string so that its shape remains compact and cooks evenly.

tuile ("TWEEL")
A crisp, thin cookie. As soon as the cookies come out of the oven, they are often removed from the baking sheet and draped over a curved surface (such as a rolling pin), where they cool and harden into a rounded shape.

Index

L

M

N

O

T

V

W

Y

Z

Table of Equivalents

The exact equivalents in the following tables have been rounded for convenience.

Liquid/Dry Measurements

U.S.	Metric
¼ teaspoon	1.25 milliliters
½ teaspoon	2.5 milliliters
1 teaspoon	5 milliliters
1 tablespoon (3 teaspoons)	15 milliliters
1 fluid ounce (2 tablespoons)	30 milliliters
¼ cup	60 milliliters
⅓ cup	80 milliliters
½ cup	120 milliliters
1 cup	240 milliliters
1 pint (2 cups)	480 milliliters
1 quart (4 cups, 32 ounces)	960 milliliters
1 gallon (4 quarts)	3.84 liters
1 ounce (by weight)	28 grams
1 pound	448 grams
2.2 pounds	1 kilogram

Lengths

U.S.	Metric
⅛ inch	3 millimeters
¼ inch	6 millimeters
½ inch	12 millimeters
1 inch	2.5 centimeters

Oven Temperature

Fahrenheit	Celsius	Gas
250°	120°	½
275°	140°	1
300°	150°	2
325°	160°	3
350°	180°	4
375°	190°	5
400°	200°	6
425°	220°	7
450°	230°	8
475°	240°	9
500°	260°	10

Acknowledgments and Credits

This book was produced by

Melcher Media, Inc.
124 West 13th Street
New York, NY 10011
www.melcher.com

Publisher Charles Melcher
Associate Publisher Bonnie Eldon
Editor in Chief Duncan Bock

Executive Editor Lia Ronnen
Associate Editor Lauren Nathan
Editorial Assistant Daniel Del Valle
Contributing Editor William Bostwick

Production Director Kurt Andrews

Designer Jessi Rymill

Food Stylist Roscoe Betsill
Prop Stylist Deborah Williams

In association with

BRAVO's success is built on creativity. We believe that there is creativity in the everyday passions that surround food, fashion, beauty, design, and pop culture—in other words, life as we and our viewers live it. It's our job to find ways to represent creative energy in exceptionally engaging ways. *Top Chef* is just one example of our viewers' and on-line users' constant craving for more—in this case more recipes, more stories about food, what it takes to be a chef and the behind-the-scenes intensity that surround food and those who make it. Together we have made *Top Chef* the smashing achievement that it is, inside what has got to be the most fun, challenging, truly creative environment anyone could want on the job.

—Lauren Zalaznick, President BRAVO Media

Acknowledgments

Thanks to Jeff Zucker, Jeff Gaspin, and so many others at NBC Universal for their consistent support of BRAVO Media's wish to come off the television screen, onto the web, and now into your kitchen. Who knows where you'll find us next!

Thanks to Ted Allen, Tom Colicchio, Padma Lakshmi, and Gail Simmons.

Thanks to the team at BRAVO: Frances Berwick, Cameron Blanchard, Melissa Bloom, Victoria Brody, Andrew Cohen, Johanna Fuentes, Neysa Gordon, Jason Klarman, Susan Malfa, Lauren McCollester, Lauren Miller, Kim Niemi, Jane Olson, Kate Pappa, Judith Randsell, Dave Serwatka, and Ellen Stone.

Thanks to the team at Magical Elves: Doneen Arquines, Rich Buhrman, Liz Cook, Dan Cutforth, Bill Egle, Gayle Gawlowski, Jane Lipsitz, Shauna Minoprio, Molly O'Rourke, Erin Rott, Nan Strait, Andrew Wallace, and Webb Weiman.

Thanks to the contestants who participated in this book: Elia Aboumrad, Stephen Asprinio, Cliff Crooks, Harold Dieterle, Tiffani Faison, Carlos Fernandez, Betty Fraser, Ilan Hall, Hung Huynh, C.J. Jacobsen, Howie Kleinberg, Dale Levitski, Sara Mair, Brian Malarkey, Dave Martin, Miguel Morales, Sara Nguyen, Sam Talbot, Casey Thompson, Marcel Vigneron, Tre Wilcox III, and Lee Anne Wong.

Thanks also to Cynthia Arntzen, Anthony Bourdain, Jennifer Daniel, Max Dickstein, Alissa Faden, Sheila Feren, Liam Flanagan, Pozelet Fleischman, Bill LeBlond, Lisa Maione, Mark Miller, Robert Swanson, Alex Tart, Amy Treadwell, Rebecca Wiener, and Carl Williamson.

Thanks to all our sponsors, without whom *Top Chef* would not be possible.

Photography and Illustration Credits

Carin Baer/BRAVO: p. 12; p. 24, top two images; p. 29, middle left; p. 31, top right; p. 32, bottom; p. 39; p. 45; p. 49; p. 80; p. 83; p. 127; p. 129; p. 131, top, bottom; p. 133, top; p. 167; p. 168; p. 181, Cliff, Ilan, Frank, Elia, Betty; p. 222; p. 229; p. 243, Harold; p. 244, Sam; Matthias Clamor/BRAVO: p. 214; p. 217; p. 218; Courtesy of Andy Cohen: p. 9, right; p. 11, bottom; p. 13, top left, top right, bottom right; p. 15; p. 24, bottom two images; Jennifer Daniel: p. 66–67; p. 200–201; Chuck Hodes/BRAVO: p. 1; p. 18–19; p. 20–21; p. 21–22; David Moir/BRAVO: p. 9, left; p. 11, top; p. 33; p. 55; p. 57; p. 59; p. 61; p. 108; p. 111; p. 160; p. 180, Dave, Tiffani; p. 181, Stephen, Candice; p. 185; p. 221; p. 239; Barbara Nitke/BRAVO: p. 26; p. 27, bottom right; p. 29, top right; p. 31, bottom left; p. 32, second image from top; p. 207; p. 223; p. 243, Tom, Rocco; Rafael Pichardo/BRAVO: p. 92; Giovanni Rufino/BRAVO: p. 243, Andy; p. 245; Scott Schafer/BRAVO: p. 124; p. 126; p. 128; p. 130; p. 132; p. 134; p. 135; p.136; p. 137; Courtesy of Dave Serwatka: p. 11, middle; p. 13, middle left; Virginia Sherwood/BRAVO: p. 54; p. 56; p. 58; p. 60; p. 62–63; p. 64–65; p. 206; p. 208; p. 210; p. 212; p. 213; p. 215; p. 216; p. 219; Isabella Vosmikova/BRAVO: p. 25; p. 27, top right; p. 29, bottom left; p. 32, top; p. 125; p. 131; p. 133, bottom; p. 181, Marcel; Glenn Watson/BRAVO: p. 13; p. 27, top middle, bottom left; p. 29, top left, bottom right; p. 30; p. 31, top left, bottom right; p. 32, third and fourth images from top; p. 40; p. 41; p. 42; p. 71; p. 86; p. 93; p. 102; p. 118; p. 145; p. 150; p. 153; p. 171; p. 173; p. 180, Joey, Howie; p. 209; p. 211; p. 242; p. 244, Casey; Michael Yarish/BRAVO: p. 27, top left; p. 28; p. 31, middle left; p. 133, middle; p. 240